The Principles of Cartesian Philosophy

BARUCH SPINOZA

The Principles of Cartesian Philosophy

and

Metaphysical Thoughts

Followed by
Lodewijk Meyer

Inaugural Dissertation on Matter (1660)

Translated by
SAMUEL SHIRLEY

With Introduction and Notes by
STEVEN BARBONE
and
LEE RICE

Hackett Publishing Company, Inc.
Indianapolis/Cambridge

04 03 02 01 00 99 98   1 3 4 5 6

Cover design by Listenberger & Design Associates
Interior design by Dan Kirklin

Library of Congress Cataloging-in-Publication Data

Spinoza, Benedictus de, 1632–1677.
    [Renati des Cartes Principia philosophiae. English]
    The principles of Cartesian philosophy; and, Metaphysical
thoughts/Baruch Spinoza. Followed by Inaugural dissertation on
matter/Lodewijk Meyer; translated by Samuel Shirley;
introduction and notes by Steven Barbone and Lee Rice.
        p.   cm.
    Includes bibliographical references.
    ISBN 0-87220-401-4 (cloth)   ISBN 0-97220-400-6 (paperback)
    1. Descartes, René, 1596–1650.   Principia philosophiae.
2. Philosophy—Early works to 1800.   3. Metaphysics—Early works to
1800.   4. Methodology—Early works to 1800.   5. Prime matter
(Philosophy)—Early works to 1800.   I. Barbone, Steven, 1960–.   II. Rice,
Lee, 1941–   .   III. Spinoza, Benedictus de, 1632–1677.   Cogitata
metaphysica.   English.   IV. Meijer, Lodewijk, 1629–1681.   Disputatio
philosophica inauguralis de materia, ejusque affectionibus motu et
quiete.   English.   V. Title.   VI. Title: Metaphysical thoughts.
VII. Title: Inaugural dissertation on matter.
B1863.E53S487—1998
199'.492—dc21   97-51491
                                                                    CIP

CONTENTS

Contents

Metaphysical Thoughts

ABBREVIATONS

The following standard abbreviations are used in the introduction and notes following:

Works of Spinoza:

CM	*Metaphysical Thoughts* (CM1/2 is Part 1, Chapter 2)
E	*Ethics* (followed by arabic numeral for part and internal references)
Ep	Letter (followed by arabic numeral)
KV	*Short Treatise (Korte Verhandeling)* (KV1/2/3 is Part 1, Chapter 2, Paragraph 3)
PPC	*Principles of Cartesian Philosophy* (followed by arabic numeral for part and internal references)
TIE	*Treatise on the Emendation of the Intellect* (followed by arabic numeral for paragraph)
TP	*Political Treatise* (TP1/2 is Chapter 1, Paragraph 2)
TTP	*Politico-Theological Treatise* (followed by chapter and page numbers)

Works of Descartes:

Med	*Meditations* (followed by arabic number)
PPH	*Principles of Philosophy*
Rep	*Replies to Objections*

Internal References (for the *Ethics*, *PPC*, and *PPH*):

A	Article
App	Appendix
Ax	Axiom
Cor	Corollary
Def	Definition
Dem	Demonstration
Exp	Explanation
GenSchol	General Scholium
Lem	Lemma

P   Proposition
Post   Postulate
Pref   Preface
Prol   Prologue
Schol   Scholium

Page numbers, where given, are to the Shirley translations of the Letters,[1] *Ethics* and TIE,[2] and TTP.[3] Page numbers, where given for Descartess *Meditations*, are taken from the Cress translation,[4] and other translations of Descartes are those of the editor; page numbers, where given, are to the Adam-Tannery edition (AT).[5]

1. Baruch Spinoza, *The Letters*, tr. Samuel Shirley, with introduction and notes by Steven Barbone, Lee Rice, and Jacob Adler (Indianapolis/Cambridge: Hackett, 1995). Page references without Ep references are to our introduction and/or notes.
2. Baruch Spinoza, *Ethics, Treatise on the Emendation of the Intellect, and Selected* Letters, 2nd ed., tr. Samuel Shirley, introduction by Seymour Feldman (Indianapolis/Cambridge: Hackett, 1992).
3. Baruch Spinoza, *Theological-Political Treatise*, tr. Samuel Shirley, introduction by Seymour Feldman (Indianapolis/Cambridge: Hackett, 1998).
4. René Descartes, *Meditations on First Philosophy*, 3rd ed., tr. Donald Cress (Indianapolis/Cambridge, Hackett, 1993).
5. René Descartes, *Oeuvres de Descartes*, 11 vols., rev. edition, ed. Charles Adam and Paul Tannery (Paris: Vrin, 196476: reprinted 1996).

Introduction

Steven Barbone
and
Lee Rice

The PPC is the earliest work published by Spinoza and the sole work published in his lifetime to bear his name. It was originally published in Latin in 1663 with a preface by his friend, Lodewijk Meyer,[6] who was also one of those who oversaw the publication of the posthumous writings following Spinoza's death in 1677.[7] Because its publication was under Spinoza's own direction, it is one of his few works that does not present difficulties of a textual nature.

In a letter[8] to Henry Oldenburg, the Secretary of the Royal Society of London,[9] Spinoza fully explains the circumstances leading to the publication. He had previously dictated to Johannes Caesarius, a pupil living in the same house as Spinoza in Rijnsburg,[10] a summary in geometrical order of the second part of Descartes's *Principles of Philosophy* (PPH) together with his *Metaphysical Thoughts* (CM). Friends in Amsterdam asked him to prepare a similar geometrical version of the first part of PPH, which he subsequently completed in less than two weeks. Spinoza stipulated that his friends should edit his Latin manuscript for style, and that they should also add a brief preface explaining that he did not accept all of Descartes's views and had written in it many things contrary to his own views. Meyer then prepared the preface for Spinoza's approval.

Spinoza himself reviewed and emended his friend's preface prior to publication, and it is worthwhile to quote his letter[11] in its entirety:

---

6. On Meyer, see *Letters*, 14–16.
7. See *Letters*, 1–2.
8. Ep13, written in July 1663.
9. On Oldenburg, see *Letters*, 8–12.
10. See Ep8–9, for information on Caesarius. It has also been conjectured that the student in question was not Caesarius but Alfred Burgh (see *Letters*, 43–344, for information on Burgh).
11. Ep15, written in August of 1663. This letter was first discovered and published by Victor Cousin in 1847.

My dear friend,

The Preface which you sent me through our friend de Vries I now return to you through him. As you will see for yourself, I have made a few notes in the margin; but there still remain a few things that I have thought it better to let you have by letter.

First, where on page 4 you inform the reader of the occasion of my composing the First Part, I should like you also at the same time to point out, either there or wherever you please, that I composed it within two weeks. Thus forewarned, no one will imagine that what I present is so clear that it could not have been expounded more clearly, and so they will not be put out by a mere word or two, which in some places they may find obscure.

Second, I should like you to mention that many of my demonstrations are arranged in a way different from that of Descartes, not to correct Descartes, but only the better to preserve my order of exposition and thus to avoid increasing the number of axioms. And it is also for the same reason that I have had to prove many things that Descartes merely asserts without proof, and to add other things that Descartes omitted.

Finally, my very dear friend, I beg you most earnestly to leave out what you wrote at the end against that petty man, and to delete it entirely. And although I have many reasons for making this request of you, I shall mention only one. I should like everyone to be able readily to accept that this publication is meant for the benefit of all men, and that in publishing this book you are motivated only by a wish to spread the truth, and so you are chiefly concerned to make this little work welcome to all, that you are inviting men in a spirit of goodwill to take up the study of the true philosophy, and your aim is the good of all. This everyone will readily believe when he sees that no one is attacked, and that nothing is advanced that might be offensive to some person. If, however, in due course that person or some other chooses to display his malicious disposition, then you can portray his life and character, and not without approval. I therefore beg you to be good enough to wait until then, and to allow yourself to be persuaded, and to believe me to be your devoted and zealous friend,

  B. de Spinoza.

Although it is clear that Spinoza's main purpose in preparing the PPC was expository, he makes it no less clear that he is not simply repeating Descartes's arguments, but attempting to reorder them in a more satisfactory manner and to clarify their meaning. We cannot determine the passage whose deletion Spinoza requests, since it was apparently deleted as requested. Who is that petty man (*illum homunculum*) of whom Spinoza writes? Perhaps Caesarius, but a recent article suggests it may have been the contemporary Christian and orthodox Cartesian Florentius Schuyl who had published his Latin translation of Descartes's *Traité de l'homme* (*De homine*) six months after Spinoza's PPC appeared. Some have also suggested that it was the poet, Joost den Vondel.[12]

A Dutch edition of the same work, prepared by Spinoza's friend Peter Balling,[13] appeared a year later in 1664. It contains some changes and a number of new passages; and, although less than the augmented and revised second edition for which Meyer raises hopes in his preface, it is more than a translation. There is little reason to doubt that these changes were made either by Spinoza or by Balling under Spinoza's direction, and the Gebhardt edition of the PPC and the CM, the basis of Shirley's translation, was the first edition to take them into account.

In his "Reply to the Second Set of Objections," Descartes distinguished two methods within the geometrical style or mode of writing (*mos geometricus*). Both depend upon an order of demonstration in which the known is placed before the unknown so that deductions are constructed from those truths that are known intuitively and directly.[14] But the method of demonstration is further divided into analytic and synthetic, both compatible with mathematical or geometrical order in general. In analysis (or the analytic method), "one demonstrates the true means by which the matter was methodically discovered, as it were from effect to cause, if the reader wishes to follow the method and to attend sufficiently to its details."[15] Analysis thus represents the process of discovery, and the basis for following a particular order of demonstration: by developing the ideas in the order of their genesis, the author almost biographically reveals how the ideas came to be and invites the reader to reconstruct the process and to rediscover the same truths in the same way. The method of synthesis proceeds in the opposite direction, from cause to effect. Beginning with a set of definitions, postulates, and axioms, theorems or propositions are

---

12. See Th. de Valk, "Spinoza en Vondel," *De Beiaard* 6 (1921), 440–458. For additional information on the passage, see Wim Klever, "Qui était l'Homunculus?" *Bulletin de l'association des amis de Spinoza* 29 (1993b), 24–27.
13. See *Letters*, 15–17 and Ep17 for more information on Balling.
14. AT7, 155–157.
15. AT7, 155.

derived in such a way that the reader is compelled to assent to them if he has granted the axioms and definitions.[16] Synthesis comes closest to our modern notion of the order of justification (contrasted to that of discovery), but it is important to note that, just as many contemporary philosophers question the demarcation between discovery and justification or its logical status, so the explanations given by Descartes are not wholly clear.

Descartes himself preferred the method of analysis as the best method of teaching but conceded that formal synthesis was a useful means of drawing attention to the distinct components of arguments, increasing precision, and detecting hidden assumptions. Indeed, in the "Reply to the Second Set of Objections," he provides a short set of definitions, postulates, axioms, and theorems (propositions) demonstrated from these to summarize the proofs given for the existence of God and the real distinction between mind and body in the *Meditations*.[17] Spinoza and his circle believed that many professed Cartesians had simply committed Descartes's conclusions to memory without genuine understanding of their meaning or justification—perhaps substituting the authority of Descartes for that of Aristotle. So they concluded that a precise synthetic exposition of this thought was necessary. Indeed, in his preface Meyer hopes that a revised edition will offer the entire third part of Descartes's PPH rather than just the few brief pages before the manuscript comes to an abrupt end.

Curley has argued[18] that Spinoza's method in the PPC is paradoxical. Under Curley's reading of PPH the work was *already* in synthetic form, and Spinoza's reorderings and interpolations would thus show that he misunderstood Descartes's distinction between analysis and synthesis. Curley's analysis depends in part upon a special interpretation of another of Descartes's works, *Conversation with Burman*, to which Spinoza may not have had access; and the analysis itself has had its critics.[19] As noted previously, however, any lack of clarity that Spinoza had may have been a result of Descartes's own rather elliptical presentation, and comparable distinctions are still hotly debated by contemporary philosophers.

Both Descartes and Spinoza concede that it is difficult to make sharp

16. AT7, 156–157.
17. AT7, 160–170.
18. Edwin Curley, "Spinoza as an Expositor of Descartes," in S. Hessing, ed. *Speculum Spinozanum* (London: Routledge & Kegan Paul, 1977), 133–142.
19. See, for example, D. Garber and L. Cohen, "A Point of Order: Analysis, Synthesis, and Descartes's *Principles*," *Archiv für Geschichte der Philosophie* 64 (1982), 136–147.

distinctions among axioms, postulates, and even propositions. Descartes notes in his "Reply to the Second Set of Objections" that several axioms would have been better explained "and should have been proposed as theorems rather than axioms, if I had wished to be more exact."[20] Meyer also explains in his preface that some axioms formulated by Spinoza can also be demonstrated as theorems. Spinoza himself suggests[21] that there is no real difference between a definition of the essence of a thing's existing outside the mind and a proposition or axiom, except that the axiom is often wider than the first two and may extend to eternal truths. Axioms or postulates are, in practice if not always in theory, simply propositions that an author considers self-evident and not necessary to prove *for the purposes at hand*; and we know that, in his own revisions of his *Ethics*, Spinoza frequently changed the status of a claim among these categories.

Whatever may be the final verdict on the degree to which Spinoza's reaxiomatization of Descartes corresponds to Descartes's own intentions or to his sense of the analysis-synthesis distinction, we can say that the published work consisted of three parts of rather different origins and probably from different periods of Spinoza's own development. The CM (probably dating from no later than 1660) is the earliest of these and is written in what Spinoza would consider to be the analytic method. Its structure and placement as an appendix to the PPC indicates that the concepts that it discusses are introduced as lexical clarifications for the preceding work; many of these concepts are introduced in the PPC only as brief definitions or as components of axioms. We know from Spinoza's letter to Oldenburg that the second part (and probably the few pages of the third) were likely written for Caesarius as an introduction to Cartesian physics. The most recently composed was the first part, dealing primarily with Descartes's analysis of God and of the thinking self.

Even though the PPC and the CM are free of most of the textual problems that plague Spinoza's other writings, their dual role as both interpretations of Descartes and developments of Spinoza's own thought do raise a variety of problems. It is to some of these that we now turn.

Spinoza as Expositor of Descartes

In the PPC, as Meyer notes in his preface, Spinoza frequently offers

---

20. AT7, 164.
21. In Ep9 to Simon de Vries.

demonstrations different from those of Descartes, offers them where Descartes had made only assertions without proof, and also rearranges the order of axioms, postulates, and propositions to better conform to the method of synthesis. Spinoza also makes extensive use of other works by Descartes: the *Correspondence*, *Dioptrics*, *Meditations*, and the "Replies to Objections." This has led some earlier interpreters to conclude that the PPC is not a relevant guide to Spinoza's own philosophy or method.[22] This viewpoint is no longer shared by the majority of scholars. Even in the effort to rearrange Descartes's ideas in proper order, Spinoza often had to change the mode of argument and also draw inferences, which are lacking in Descartes (and some of which Descartes probably would not have accepted in any case). Nor could Spinoza avoid some criticism in exposing the principal conclusions, which Descartes had sought to draw from the axioms. The acknowledged points of difference are clearly those mentioned by Meyer in his preface. Spinoza denies the distinction between intellect and will (freedom of will), the claim that mind is a distinct substance, and he rejects the frequent appeals by Descartes to the realm of "mystery" (that some things surpass human understanding). Additionally, one finds a considerable number of thinly veiled criticisms of Descartes.[23] The CM is also largely independent of Descartes, as we shall see later. Finally, Spinoza frequently goes well beyond the sketchy remarks of Descartes in developing a theme, such as his discussion of Zeno's paradoxes at PPC2P6Schol.

In the lengthy prolegomenon, which Spinoza provides for PPC1, he takes up the structure of Descartes's methodological doubt (Med1 and Med2) and the frequent criticism that, because all things are uncertain as long as we are ignorant of our origin, and since the existence of God is not known through itself, we can never be certain of anything (including the proposition that God exists). This is the standard "vicious circle" argument: Descartes first posits clarity and distinctness as a criterion of truth, from which he derives the existence of God as a guarantor of the truth of clear and distinct ideas.

Spinoza's first interpretation of Descartes relies heavily on remarks that Descartes makes in PPH1A13. Under this reading, we cannot doubt our clear and distinct ideas but only our *memory* of demonstrations and deduc-

22. For example, see H. A. Wolfson, *The Philosophy of Spinoza* (Cambridge, Mass.: Harvard University Press, 1934), I, 32–33. And indeed Spinoza's idea of Descartes may tell us more about Spinoza than about Descartes. Cf. E2P37Schol.
23. See, for example, PPC1P8Def, PPC1P9Schol, PPC1P15Schol, and PPC2P2CorSchol.

tions in which they figure. Even though divine veracity is required as a guarantor of the demonstrations, it is not required for the truth of the clear and distinct first principles, which are apprehended directly and without demonstration. God's existence, accordingly, follows from clear and distinct ideas whose truth we cannot doubt even though it is not an a priori truth directly known through itself. It is not clear that Spinoza's interpretation is a sound one because in the same section Descartes also suggests the possibility that the mind may have been created with a nature that inclines it to being deceived, and hence it could have no certain knowledge without prior acquaintance with its creator.

Apparently recognizing the unsatisfactory nature of his first attempted resolution, Spinoza provides an alternative reply. Here he grants that we can be certain of nothing beyond our own existence as thinking things so long as we have no clear and distinct idea of God, but he suggests that we may possess such an idea regardless of whether we conclude from it that God exists. The clarity and distinctness of the idea of God is thus separated (psychologically, though not logically) from the knowledge that God exists, and the existential knowledge is not necessary to guarantee the truth of clear and distinct ideas such as those of mathematics.

In his first reading, Spinoza maintains the autonomy and validity of clear and distinct ideas and introduces the idea of God only to guarantee memory in demonstration rather than the validity of our direct intuitions. In the second reading, the idea of divine veracity is necessary to establish the truth of clear and distinct ideas, but the proof of God's existence is not. In providing alternative interpretations, Spinoza in fact does indicate how Descartes *might have avoided* the vicious circle. Descartes himself, however, tended to waver and to move between the two poles which these interpretations illustrate. When immersed in his mathematical studies, he tended to affirm the autonomy of clear and distinct ideas; and, when attending to the methodological doubt as a remedy for scepticism, he tended to deny the validity of these ideas if they were unsupported by at least the veracity (if not the existence) of God. So the ambiguity of a dual interpretation lies not in Spinoza's failure to grasp Descartes, but rather in Descartes's own indecisions. Gilson has suggested that modern readers of Descartes may well profit from Spinoza's suggestive interpretations on this and other points in the PPC.[24]

---

24. E. Gilson, "Spinoza interprète de Descartes." *Chronicon Spinozanum* 3 (1923), 68–87.

It has also been claimed that Spinoza's reinterpretation of the doubt alters considerably the foundations on which Descartes had hoped to construct both his system and his method.[25] Much the same point can be made for the Cartesian *cogito*. Spinoza's treatment of the *cogito* in the prolegomenon to PPC1 is extremely cursory, and even though it is developed to a greater extent in what follows (PPC1P1–P4), some commentators have suggested that Spinoza has entirely missed its uniqueness in establishing the nature of the rational soul in Descartes's psychology.[26] Once again, however, one may claim that Spinoza's reading reflects one legitimate interpretation and that it is the very ambiguities and indecisions in Descartes's own thought that underlie any perceived inadequacies. Contemporary Descartes scholarship offers a bewildering array of readings, which adequately supports such a claim.

Spinoza does not, however, always attempt to make Descartes consistent with himself. In the PPC, he takes over, with only slight modifications, the ten definitions offered by Descartes in the appendix to his "Reply to the Second Set of Objections" without making any effort to reconcile the definition of substance with that given in PPH1A51. In the Reply, substance is the subject of properties or attributes, and although there are two kinds of substance (extended and thinking), there can be as many substances as there are minds and individual bodies. But the definition in PPH characterizes substance rather as that which needs no other thing in order to exist, adding that ". . . in fact only one single substance can be understood, . . . , namely God."[27] Spinoza was later to combine both of Descartes's definitions into a single definition, which supported his own monism,[28] but here in the PPC he continues to follow Descartes in applying the term to both created and infinite substances without trying to reconcile the two definitions.

In the examples of the geometrical mode that Descartes appends to the "Reply to the Second Set of Objections," he provides three proofs for the existence of God. The first[29] is the ontological argument, which Spinoza

25. See, for example, Charles Appuhn's introduction to his translation of the PPC (225–226) for a more critical view of both of Spinoza's interpretations. Edwin Curley also treats the doubt differently from Spinoza: see his *Descartes Against the Skeptics* (Cambridge: Harvard University Press, 1978).
26. See Martial Gueroult, *Etudes sur Descartes, Spinoza, Malebranche et Leibniz* (Hildesheim: Georg Olms Verlag, 1970), 64–78.
27. PPH1A51; AT8, 24.
28. See E1Def3; E1P14.
29. AT7, 166–167.

accepts and expands.[30] The second proof[31] is an a posteriori argument from effect to cause based on the claim that we possess an idea of God. This is the argument elaborated also in Med3, and it is also accepted and expanded by Spinoza (PPC1P6). Descartes's third proof[32] is based on two axioms (eight and nine), which state respectively that whatever can produce a greater or 'more difficult' effect can accomplish a lesser, and that it is greater to create or to conserve substance than to create or to conserve its attributes or properties. Spinoza found both of these axioms unintelligible and does not include them among the ten axioms that open PPC1. Descartes's third proof is presented in PPC1P7, and following a lengthy scholium, it is rejected. Then Spinoza introduces a series of new lemmas and corollaries; they provide the deductive basis for a new demonstration that terminates the proposition.

Even though Spinoza's reconstructions of the first two proofs are more highly elaborated than in Descartes, his reconstruction of the third makes use of a number of claims to which Descartes would probably not have assented. He assumes that existence and perfection vary proportionately, that degrees of perfection or existence range from zero (the impossible) through infinity (the necessary), and that existence and power (*potentia*)[33] are coextensive.

These examples illustrate Spinoza's reworking of Descartes, and we have provided notes throughout the PPC to various propositions, axioms, and definitions where Spinoza either expands or supplements Descartes. We have also supplied a set of cross-references for the PPC, primarily to the PPH but also to the "Replies to Objections," all of which Spinoza had access to and some of which he himself refers to in his own elaboration and reworking of Descartes in the PPC itself. There is far more in the PPC or the CM than a simple summary of Cartesian philosophy, and these works are of considerable value for understanding Spinoza's own development.

30. PPC1P5. See also E1P11Dem1.
31. AT7, 167168.
32. AT7, 168169.
33. The development of Spinoza's own account of power is dealt with by two excellent studies: Charles Ramond, *Quantité et qualité dans la philosophie de Spinoza* (Paris: Presses Universitaires de France, 1995), and Eugenio Fernández Garcia, "*Potentia* et *potestas* dans les premiers écrits de B. Spinoza," *Studia Spinozana* 4 (1988), 195–223. Ramond deals primarily with Spinoza's metaphysics and physics, with parallels to both Descartes and Leibniz, whereas Fernández provides an extended discussion of the role of these concepts in Spinoza's political thought.

The examples provided, as well as others noted later, make it clear that Spinoza is not always faithful to Descartes. Even where one may rightly claim, however, that his interpretations fall short of the mark, his errors are likely to be both interesting and instructive with respect to his own reflections on Descartes; and surely those reflections provide a significant part of the wellspring from which Spinoza developed his own mature philosophy in the *Ethics* and the political tractates.

Spinoza and Cartesian Physics

In 1663, the same year that the PPC was published, Spinoza moved from Rijnsburg to Voorburg, where he became a neighbor of Christian Huygens. We must presume that, beginning at about this time, he began to receive information from Huygens concerning his work on the laws of impact and his development and critique of Cartesian physics.[34] The influence of Huygens in Spinoza's correspondence after that date is quite marked and reflects both his growing dissatisfaction with Cartesian physics and his efforts to develop a new basis for the analysis of matter and motion.[35] Despite a growing dissatisfaction with Cartesian physics, Spinoza writes to Oldenburg in November of 1665 that he finds all the Cartesian laws of impact except one acceptable.[36] Eleven years later, in May of 1676, he writes to Walther von Tschirnhaus that all Descartes's laws of motion are of no service and wrong.[37] During this period Spinoza has developed at least the basic outline (probably without the details) of an alternative physical theory, the basic structure of which is offered in Part II of the *Ethics* following Proposition 13, and which contains a new dynamic account of the individuation of bodies. Spinoza's dissatisfaction with the Cartesian treatment of extension as neither active nor figuring in the divine essence had already been expressed in PPC1P9Schol.

Despite Spinoza's growing dissatisfaction with Descartess physics,

---

34. See André Lécrivain, "Spinoza et la physique cartésienne," *Cahiers Spinoza* 1 (1977), 235–266; *Cahiers Spinoza* 2 (1978), 93–206. Cf. especially 1/239–241. Lécrivain's study, which arose from a two-year seminar (1971–1973) given at the Ecole Normale Supérieure de Fontenay-St. Cloud, the most ambitious and detailed study to date of PPC2 and Spinoza's development of Cartesian physics. Much of the detail of our presentation here is drawn from his analysis.
35. See Ep26; Ep29; Ep30A; Ep32; Ep33; Ep38; Ep40; Ep70; and Ep72.
36. Ep32, 195. The law rejected is the sixth (PPH2A51).
37. Ep81.

PPC2 appears to reproduce faithfully the general structure of that physics. This structure is as follows:

1. Postulate, definitions, axioms, and lemmas: Spinoza adds definitions for a number of terms used but not defined by Descartes in PPH2.

2. A deduction of the essence of extension and motion, roughly corresponding to PPH2A4–35. The analysis of extension is given in PPC2P1–6, motion, in P7–12.

3. Deduction of the causes of motion and the laws of communication of motion. This section contains all the principles, laws, and rules that Descartes offers in PPH2. It has four principal parts: deduction of the general cause of motion (P12–17), the principles of the communication of motion (P18–23), the laws of impact (P24–31), and the role played by ambient bodies (P32–37).

Even though the logical interrelations among these sections remain faithful to Descartes, many details of demonstration and definition are added, consistent with Spinoza's intent to develop the physical basis synthetically. Details of the differences and developments are specified in the notes to PPC2 itself.

An interesting example of Spinoza's development and enhancement of Cartesian theory is found in the lengthy scholium to P6, which deals with Zeno's paradoxes of motion. One of Spinoza's objectives in this scholium is the explication of the fundamental principles of a science of motion, which would also be a science of understanding.[38] Such a project would be possible only if extension and motion are intelligible, and Zeno's arguments are a challenge, not just to their intelligibility, but also to the mathematization of physics (and, therefore, for Spinoza, of metaphysics and psychology) in general. The paradoxes also constitute a special challenge to Cartesian physics because of two specific difficulties in his physics:

1. The relationship between Descartes's insistence that the instants of which time is composed are not divisible and his acceptance of the infinite divisibility of the physical continuum.

---

38. This is what Bennett calls "the primacy of the physical model" in Spinoza. See Jonathan Bennett, *A Study of Spinoza's Ethics* (Indianapolis/Cambridge: Hackett, 1984), 126. We refer to (and defend) it later as a form of logical *physicalism*.

2. The compatibility of infinite divisibility in principle with an effective
   infinite division (mentioned by Spinoza in PPC2Def7), which threatens
   to go beyond the structure of Euclidean mathematics.

While the first part of the scholium reaffirms the claim that motion is
always relative to place (in conformity with Galileo and in opposition to the
Aristotelian and scholastic dynamics), the lengthy second part is devoted to
the refutation of two of the paradoxes. Spinoza notes that empirical refutation would be insufficient because Zeno's arguments are targeted at the
rational and mathematical understanding of motion. The first paradox is
that of the rotating wheel, which Spinoza correctly notes is an argument,
not against motion itself, but rather against instantaneous velocity—perhaps he has in mind here Descartes's claim that the transmission of light is
instantaneous.[39] Spinoza rejects both the claim that infinite velocities exist
and the parallel claim that there is a lower limit to the metric of time, which
takes him to the second paradox which he considers, usually interpreted as
that of the moving arrow. In resolving this paradox, Spinoza goes beyond
Descartes in denying that there exists any unit of time that is so small that
a smaller cannot be conceived. His reply can be interpreted[40] as a conscious
effort to resolve the difficulties inherent in the Cartesian concept of time:
one must in fact consider time in such a way that no assignable limit can be
given to the divisibility of an instant (i.e., under the form of a differential).
Although this interpretation in fact contradicts the account of the metric
time given by Descartes in the PPH, it is quite similar to the resolution of
the Achilles paradox that Descartes offered elsewhere,[41] which is also a
mathematically impeccable solution.[42]

It lies outside the scope of this introduction to resolve the various inter-
pretive problems encountered in PPC2. Lécrivain has outlined to a considerable degree the extent to which Spinoza's exposition and development of
Cartesian physics goes beyond Descartes. Descartes's reflections on physics, however, developed and changed throughout his own life: sorting the
complex developments of PPC2 into categories of development or enhancement versus transgression is not, and could not be, our intent. This part of

39. *Dioptrics*, First Discourse, AT6, 84.
40. See Lécrivain (1978), 138–141 for a more detailed account of this point.
41. In his letter to Clerselier, 1646, AT4, 442–447.
42. See Lécrivain (1978), 140–141; and also Renée Bouveresse, "Note sur la physique de Spinoza," in *Spinoza et Leibniz: L'idée d'animisme universel* (Paris: Vrin,
1992), 313–319.

the PPC attests not only to Spinoza's continued meditation on the foundations of physical theory but also to the general vitality and ongoing development of Cartesian physics.

One such development is included here as an appendix: the inaugural dissertation of Spinoza's friend Meyer. Meyer received his doctorate in Amsterdam on 19 March 1660. His dissertation, "Matter, its Affections, and Motion and Rest," was first printed in 1922.[43] This printing suffered from some typographical errors and textual problems, and an edited version of the Latin text with French translation was prepared by Renée Bouveresse and Dominique Descotes.[44] The dissertation exemplifies a much greater dependence upon Descartes but shows signs of the same sorts of amplifications and developments that are more dominant in PPC2. It thus stands somewhere between the original physical theory developed by Descartes and the emended and reworked theory that Spinoza offers his readers. So far as we know, it appears here in its first English translation.

We have devoted most of the prior discussion to the issue of Spinoza's own understanding of and relation to the physics of Descartes, but something must also be said concerning Spinoza's own attitude toward physics and the various problems that he raises and attempts to resolve in Descartes's theory. The existing literature displays two extreme positions on this question. According to one, Spinoza's understanding of, and interest in, the new physics was minimal and short-lived.[45] Such a position would explain both the fact that Spinoza made no real contribution to the growth and development of the new physics, as well as his hesitations in the PPC concerning the resolution of some of the difficulties in Descartes's own theory. But it does little to explain the large number of Spinoza's letters devoted to questions of chemistry, optics, astronomy, and physics, let alone his familiarity with current works in these areas that is displayed in those

43. In the *Chronicon Spinozanum* 2 (1922), 183–195.
44. See Renée Bouveresse, *Spinoza et Leibniz: L'idée d'animisme universel* (Paris: Vrin, 1992), 295–304 (French) and 305–312 (Latin). For information on Meyer, see *Letters*, 13–21; the introduction to Louis Meyer, *La philosophie interprète de l'Ecriture sainte*, translation, introduction and notes by Jacqueline Lagrée and Pierre-François Moreau (Paris: Intertextes Editeur, 1988), 1–19; and K.O. Meinsma, *Spinoza et son cercle*, translated by S. Roosenburg and J.-P. Osier with appendices and notes by Henry Méchoulan and Pierre-François Moreau (Paris: Vrin, 1983), 194–198, 255–259, and 486–488.
45. This is, for example, the interpretation of Nancy Maull, "Spinoza in the Century of Science," in *Spinoza and the Sciences*, ed. Marjorie Grene and Debra Nails (Dordrecht: Reidel, 1986), 3–13.

and other letters.[46] It is certainly true that, toward the end of his life, occupied with the urgent task of completing the TP and making final revisions in the *Ethics*, his own reflections on physics were less frequent.[47] Others have argued that Spinoza's philosophy is fundamentally an ethical system and has little relationship to his speculations in physics.[48]

Opposing these positions is, for example, Wim Klever, who argues that Spinoza's reflections on physics were both profound and integral to his philosophical theories.[49] In an extensive number of studies on the background of Spinoza's historical development, Klever and others have pointed convincingly to Spinoza's continued work and experimentation, to the growth of his dissatisfaction with Cartesian physics, and to the introduction of a new dynamic physical theory as a model for his account of mind in the second part of the *Ethics* (following E2P13).[50]

The question of the interest (and even competence) of Spinoza in physical theory and of the relation of this theory as he conceived it to his own philosophical theory is a complex one, and here we can indicate only the direction in which we believe the answer lies. The position that Spinoza

46. See, for example, Ep6; Ep9; Ep10; Ep13; Ep30; Ep30A; Ep32; Ep39; Ep40; Ep41; Ep45; Ep46; Ep81; and Ep83.
47. In Ep81 (1676) he writes to Tschirnhaus, "I have not hesitated on a previous occasion to affirm that Descartes' principles of natural things are of no service, not to say quite wrong" (352). When Tschirnhaus writes to enquire further on these principles, Spinoza replies (Ep83, 1676), ". . . I shall sometime discuss this with you more clearly; for as yet I have not had the opportunity to arrange in due order anything on this subject" (355).
48. See, for example, Pierre-François Moreau, *Spinoza: l'expérience et l'éternité* (Paris: Presses Universitaires de France, 1994b), esp. 282–296.
49. See, for example, Klever's "Anti-falsificationism: Spinoza's Theory of Experience and Experiments," in *Spinoza: New Issues and Directions*, ed. E. Curley and P.-F. Moreau (Leiden: Brill, 1990); "Moles in Motu: Principles of Spinoza's Physics," *Studia Spinozana* 4 (1988), 165–194; "The Motion of the Projectile—Eucidation of Spinoza's Physics," *Studia Spinozana* 9 (1995), 335–340; "Spinoza's Life and Works," in *The Cambridge Companion to Spinoza*, ed. D. Garrett (Cambridge: Cambridge University Press, 1996).
50. Spinoza's correspondence with the Royal Society in London, as well as his dissatisfaction with some of Boyle's experimental findings, are also supportive of this claim. See Ep6; Richard McKeon, *The Philosophy of Spinoza* (New York: Longmans, Green, & Co., 1928), chapter 4, "Spinoza and Experimental Science" (130–159); and Heine Siebrand, "Spinoza and the Rise of Modern Science in the Netherlands," in *Spinoza and the Sciences*, eds. M. Grene and D. Nails (Dordrecht: Reidel, 1986), 61–91. The studies by McKeon and Siebrand are the most well-balanced studies of the questions we have encountered in English.

was solely or even chiefly a working and reflective experimental scientist is simply wrong and not borne out by the historical evidence. The position of those who, like Moreau, see no logical connection between Spinoza's physical theory and his metaphysics is equally wrong. Bennett[51] is probably correct in insisting that Spinoza's physicalistic model of the universe pervades his entire system and in fact was transformed both into his model for psychology and his paradigm for political theory. The others fail to distinguish physicalism as a logical category for a metaphysical theory from physics as the development of an empirically grounded and conceptually adequate account of nature. Spinoza, like Descartes, was not a physicist: their interest was directed at foundational questions in physics because they believed, quite correctly, that these foundations are sufficient for the establishment of the entire system of human knowledge (what the logical empiricists were much later to call "unified science"). Spinoza, unlike Descartes and as a result of his dissatisfaction with Cartesian physics, made a prolonged effort to establish a new and better basis for physical theory (a dynamic theory of physical individuation). He was never able to develop fully such an account as a physical theory,[52] but it remains integral to his metaphysical development. Accordingly, apart from its worth as an exposition, development, and enhancement of the Cartesian physics, PPC2 (and the brief fragment of PPC3) represents a precious store of information on the development of Spinoza's own mature thoughts in metaphysics, ethics, and psychology.

The Metaphysical Thoughts

Even though the PPC has attracted more attention from those interested in the development of Descartes's thought and little from those studying the evolution of Spinoza's, the CM has attracted little attention from either group. In terms of the former, the explanation certainly lies in the fact that much if not most of the discussions in the CM are simply independent of Descartes. Meyer notes in his preface that it was Spinoza's intention in the PPC to propound Descartes's positions and demonstrations, not only as they are found in his writings, but also ". . . to prove many things which

---

51. See Jonathan Bennett, *A Study of Spinoza's Ethics* (Indianapolis and Cambridge: Hackett, 1984), esp. 35–40, 81–110, and 125–134.
52. This is the sense of Bennett's argument (*A Study of Spinoza's Ethics*, 106–110) that many of the dynamic concepts Spinoza introduces in the *Ethics* are "placeholders" for concepts of physics not yet developed.

Descartes propounded without proof, and to add others which he completely omitted." He goes on to add that" . . . in all these writings, in Parts I and II and the fragment of Part III of the *Principia* and also in the *Cogitata Metaphysica*, our author has simply given Descartes's opinions and their demonstrations just as they are found in his writings, or such as should validly be deduced from the foundations laid by him." We have already seen that this is somewhat misleading because much in the PPC goes beyond Descartes's corresponding reflections, which are often at best sketchy. And, if Meyer's remarks on the PPC can be misleading, they are even more apt to do so for the CM.

The CM opens with the definition of being and its division into beings whose essence does and does not involve existence (substance and modes). This is followed by a discussion of various types of putative beings that do not qualify as real beings under the initial definitions. Its second part deals primarily with the nature of God as infinite substance and closes with a brief discussion of finite substance and human mind. If, as seems probable, the CM is in fact earlier than the PPC, the logic of its presentation becomes more evident: it is less an exposition or development of Descartes than an introduction to modern philosophy from a broadly Cartesian perspective. This Cartesian philosophy coexisted with earlier scholastic traditions, particularly that of Suarez, throughout the seventeenth century.[53] In some cases, Cartesian elements were actually combined with the older scholastic tradition in the teaching at Leiden. Freudenthal[54] has identified two now obscure Dutch teachers, Burgersdijk and Heereboord, both of whom represent this mixed tradition. Burgersdijk taught at Leiden from 1620 to 1635 and wrote several students' manuals professing fidelity to the spirit of Aristotle but displaying the influence of Descartes. His student, Adriaan Heereboord,[55] was professor of logic and ethics at Leiden from 1641 to 1661 and appears to have attempted a synthesis of Aristotle and Descartes. He was in fact one cause for the University's becoming later known as a center of Dutch Cartesianism. Although we have no positive evidence,

53. See C. L. Thijssen-Schoute, *Lodewijk Meyer en diens verhouding tot Descartes en Spinoza* (Leiden: Brill, 1954).
54. See J. Freudenthal, *Spinoza und die Scholastik* (Leipzig: Verlag von Veit, 1899).
55. On Heereboord see also K. O. Meinsma, *Spinoza et son cercle*, translated by S. Roosenburg and J.-P. Osier with appendices and notes by Henry Méchoulan and Pierre-François Moreau (Paris: Vrin, 1983), 113 and 128.

some have speculated that Spinoza may have studied with him at Leiden following Spinoza's excommunication from the Amsterdam synagogue.

The CM offers not only a compendium of philosophical terminology but also in some cases the first discussions of Spinoza of such terms as necessity, impossibility, and contingency—concepts that later became fundamental in his own development of the *Ethics*. The concept of eternity applied to uncreated or infinite substance is here also carefully distinguished from duration as a mode of thought that applies to finite individual things. The discussion of the attributes of God in Part Two of the CM combines elements of Descartes's thought with that of earlier thinkers such as Suarez, and it reveals at least some of the sources from which Spinoza was later to draw his own account of infinite attributes, which is quite different from that of Descartes.

In the CM, Spinoza also quite intentionally breaks with the Cartesian definition of will as he himself was later to develop it in the PPC.[56] For Descartes, the faculty of will is inherently active, while that of understanding is passive. In CM2/12 Spinoza defines will as the affirming that such-and-such is good or not good, and he then goes on to identify it with the mind's essential function of judgment (affirmation and denial). From this it follows that the mind is essentially free when it is wholly self-determined. Even though Spinoza continues to maintain that the will acts freely (a claim that he denies in the *Ethics*), he shifts the meaning of both freedom and willing in the direction of the analysis that he later offers in the *Ethics*. The problem that continues to plague him, both in the PPC and in the CM, is that of reconciling divine omnipotence and omniscience with such a freedom. In CM1/3 he confesses ignorance of their compatibility, even though the problem is resolved in the *Ethics* by denying the possibility of this freedom, even in the form in which he recasts it in the CM.

Just as Spinoza's reflections in the years 1661–63 led him to a dissatisfaction with Cartesian physics, the CM illustrates a similar set of dissatisfactions with Descartes's account of God, human behavior, and appetition at an even earlier period. Both works represent the beginnings of his own development of a new philosophical system that would resolve the inconsistencies that he found in Descartes. The development of this system was to take place at the level of both political theory (in the TTP and the TP) and

---

56. See PPC1P15Schol.

a monistic metaphysics, which contained a new theory of human behavior (in the *Ethics*). Even though his death cut short the prospect of such a systematic development of a new physical theory, the outlines of that theory are clearly adumbrated in the *Ethics* as well. In these early works, accordingly, we have an eloquent testimonial not only to the fecundity of Descartes's own thought in the development of modern philosophy but also of the early reflections which led Spinoza out of Cartesianism to a new philosophical system.

Parts I and II[1] of
René Descartes's
THE PRINCIPLES
OF PHILOSOPHY

demonstrated in the geometric manner

by

Benedict de Spinoza
of Amsterdam.

To which are added his
Metaphysical Thoughts,

in which are briefly explained the more
difficult problems that arise in both the
general and the special part of Metaphysics.

Amsterdam.
Published by Johannes Rieuwertsz,
in the quarter commonly called
The Dirk van Assen-Steeg,
under the sign Martyrologium. 1663.

---

1. The frontispiece announces only Parts I and II of the PPC; Part III is not mentioned here.

PREFACE.

To the honest reader,
Lodewijk Meyer gives greetings.

It is the unanimous opinion of all who seek wisdom beyond the common lot that the best and surest way to discover and to teach truth is the method used by mathematicians in their study and exposition of the sciences, namely, that whereby conclusions are demonstrated from definitions, postulates, and axioms. And indeed rightly so. Because all sure and sound knowledge of what is unknown can be elicited and derived only from what is already known with certainty, this latter must first be built up from the ground as a solid foundation on which thereafter to construct the entire edifice of human knowledge, if that is not to collapse of its own accord or give way at the slightest blow. That the things familiar to mathematicians under the title of definitions, postulates, and axioms are of this kind cannot be doubted by anyone who has even the slightest acquaintance with that noble discipline. For definitions are merely the perspicuous explanations of the terms and names by which matters under discussion are designated, whereas postulates and axioms—that is, the common notions of the mind—are statements so clear and lucid that no one who has simply understood the words aright can possibly refuse assent.

But although this is so, you will find that with the exception of mathematics hardly any branch of learning is treated by this method. Instead, a totally different method is adopted, whereby the entire work is executed by means of definitions and logical divisions interlinked in a chain, with problems and explanations interspersed here and there. For almost all who have applied themselves to establishing and setting out the sciences have believed, and many still do believe, that the mathematical method is peculiar to mathematics and is to be rejected as inapplicable to all other branches of learning.

In consequence, nothing of what they produce is demonstrated with conclusive reasoning. They try to advance arguments that depend merely on likelihood and probability, and in this way they thrust before the public a great medley of great books in which you may look in vain for solidity and certainty. Disputes and strife abound, and what one somehow establishes with trivial arguments of no real weight is soon refuted by another, demolished and shattered with the same weapons. So where the mind, eager for unshakable truth, had thought to find for its labors a placid stretch of water that it could navigate with safety and success, thereafter attaining the haven

1

of knowledge for which it yearned, it finds itself tossed on a stormy sea of opinion, beset on all sides with tempests of dispute, hurled about and carried away on waves of uncertainty, endlessly, with no hope of ever emerging therefrom.

Yet there have not been lacking some who have thought differently and, taking pity on the wretched plight of Philosophy, have distanced themselves from this universally adopted and habitual way of treating the sciences and have entered upon a new and indeed an arduous path bristling with difficulties, so as to leave to posterity the other parts of Philosophy, besides mathematics, demonstrated with mathematical method and with mathematical certainty. Of these, some have arranged in mathematical order and passed on to the world of letters a philosophy already accepted and customarily taught in the schools, whereas others have thus treated a new philosophy, discovered by their own exertions. For a long time, the many who undertook this task met with no success, but at last there arose that brightest star of our age, René Descartes. After bringing forth by a new method from darkness to light whatever had been inaccessible to the ancients, and in addition whatever could be wanting in his own age, he laid the unshakable foundations of philosophy on which numerous truths could be built with mathematical order and certainty, as he himself effectively proved, and as is clearer than the midday sun to all who have paid careful attention to his writings, for which no praise is too great.

Although the philosophical writings of this most noble and incomparable man exhibit the mathematical manner and order of demonstration, yet they are not composed in the style commonly used in Euclid's *Elements* and other geometrical works, the style wherein Definitions, Postulates, and Axioms are first enunciated, followed by Propositions and their demonstrations. They are arranged in a very different way, which he calls the true and best way of teaching, the Analytic way. For at the end of his "Reply to Second Objections,"[2] he acknowledges two modes of conclusive proof. One is by analysis, "which shows the true way by which a thing is discovered methodically and, as it were, a priori"; the other is by synthesis, "which employs a long series of definitions, postulates, axioms, theorems and problems, so that if any of the conclusions be denied, it can be shown immediately that this is involved in what has preceded, and thus the reader, however reluctant and obstinate, is forced to agree."

However, although both kinds of demonstration afford a certainty that

2. See AT7, 155–156; cf. the slight variation in the French version at AT9, 121–122.

lies beyond any risk of doubt, not everyone finds them equally useful and convenient. There are many who, being quite unacquainted with the mathematical sciences and therefore completely ignorant of the synthetic method in which they are arranged and of the analytic method by which they were discovered, are neither able themselves to understand nor to expound to others the things that are discussed and logically demonstrated in these books. Consequently, many who, either carried away by blind enthusiasm or influenced by the authority of others, have become followers of Descartes have done no more than commit to memory his opinions and doctrines. When the subject arises in conversation, they can only prate and chatter without offering any proof, as was once and still is the case with the followers of the Peripatetic philosophy. Therefore, to provide them with some assistance, I have often wished that someone, skilled both in the analytic and synthetic arrangement and thoroughly versed in Descartes's writings and expert in his philosophy, should set his hand to this task, and undertake to arrange in synthetic order what Descartes wrote in analytic order, demonstrating it in the way familiar to geometricians. Indeed, though fully conscious of my incompetence and unfitness for such a task, I have frequently thought of undertaking it myself and have even made a start. But other distractions, which so often claim my attention, have prevented its completion.

I was therefore delighted to hear from our Author that, while teaching Descartes's philosophy to a certain pupil of his, he had dictated to him the whole of Part II of the *Principia* and some of Part III, demonstrated in that geometric style, and also the principal and more difficult questions that arise in metaphysics and remain unresolved by Descartes, and that, at the urgent entreaties and pleadings of his friends, he has permitted these to be published as a single work, corrected and amplified by himself. So I also commended this same project, at the same time gladly offering my services, if needed, to get this published. Furthermore I urged him—indeed, besought him—to set out Part I of the *Principia* as well in like order to precede the rest, so that the work, as thus arranged from its very beginning, might be better understood and give greater satisfaction. When he saw how reasonable was this proposal, he could not refuse the pleas of a friend and likewise the good of the reader. He further entrusted to my care the entire business both of printing and of publishing because he lives in the country far from the city and so cannot give it his personal attention.[3]

---

3. It appears from Ep12, however, that Spinoza was able to make corrections to the page proofs.

Such then, honest reader, are the contents of this little book, namely, Parts I and II of Descartes's *Principia Philosophiae* together with a fragment of Part III, to which we have added, as an appendix, our Author's *Cogitata Metaphysica*. But when we here say Part I of the *Principia*, and the book's title so announces, we do not intend it to be understood that everything Descartes says there is here set forth as demonstrated in geometric order. The title derives only from its main contents, and so the chief metaphysical themes that were treated by Descartes in his *Meditations* are taken from that book (omitting all other matters that concern Logic and are related and reviewed only in a historical way). To do this more effectively, the Author has transposed word for word almost the entire passage at the end of the "Reply to the Second Set of Objections," which Descartes arranged in geometric order.[4] He first sets out all Descartes's definitions and inserts Descartes's propositions among his own, but he does not place the axioms immediately after the definitions; he brings them in only after Proposition 4, changing their order so as to make it easier to prove them, and omitting some that he did not require.

Although our Author is well aware that these axioms (as Descartes himself says in Postulate 7) can be proved as theorems and can even more neatly be classed as propositions, and although we also asked him to do this, being engaged in more important affairs he had only the space of two weeks to complete this work, and that is why he could not satisfy his own wishes and ours. He does at any rate add a brief explanation that can serve as a demonstration, postponing for another occasion a lengthier proof, complete in all respects, with view to a new edition to follow this hurried one. To augment this, we shall also try to persuade him to complete Part III in its entirety, "Concerning the Visible World" (of which we give here only a fragment, since the Author ended his instruction at this point and we did not wish to deprive the reader of it, little as it is). For this to be properly executed, some propositions concerning the nature and property of Fluids will need to be inserted at various places in Part II, and I shall then do my best to persuade the Author to do this at the time.[5]

It is not only in setting forth and explaining the Axioms that our Author frequently diverges from Descartes but also in proving the Propositions themselves and the other conclusions, and he employs a logical proof far

---

4. AT7, 160–170.
5. For evidence that Spinoza was developing his own theory of fluids, see Ep6, 78–81.

different from that of Descartes. But let no one take this to mean that he intended to correct the illustrious Descartes in these matters, but that our Author's sole purpose in so doing is to enable him the better to retain his already established order and to avoid increasing unduly the number of Axioms. For the same reason, he has also been compelled to prove many things that Descartes propounded without proof, and to add others that he completely omitted.

However, I should like it to be particularly noted that in all these writings, in Parts I and II and the fragment of Part III of the *Principia* and also in the *Cogitata Metaphysica*, our Author has simply given Descartes's opinions and their demonstrations just as they are found in his writings, or such as should validly be deduced from the foundations laid by him. For having undertaken to teach his pupil Descartes's philosophy, his scruples forbade him to depart in the slightest degree from Descartes's views or to dictate anything that did not correspond with, or was contrary to, his doctrines. Therefore no one should conclude that he here teaches either his own views or only those of which he approves. For although he holds some of the doctrines to be true, and admits that some are his own additions, there are many he rejects as false, holding a very different opinion.[6]

Of this sort, to single out one of many, are statements concerning the Will in the Scholium to Proposition 15 of Part I of the *Principia* and in Chapter 12, Part II of the Appendix, although they appear to be laboriously and meticulously proved. For he does not consider the Will to be distinct from the Intellect, far less endowed with freedom of that kind. Indeed, in making these assertions, as is clear from Part 4 of the *Discourse on Method*, the "Second Meditation," and other passages, Descartes merely assumes, and does not prove, that the human mind is an absolutely thinking substance. Although our Author does indeed admit that there is in Nature a thinking substance, he denies that this constitutes the essence of the human mind.[7] He maintains that, just as Extension is not determined by any limits, so Thought, too, is not determined by any limits. And therefore, just as the human body is not Extension absolutely, but only as determined in a particular way in accordance with the laws of extended Nature through motion and rest, so too the human mind or soul is not Thought absolutely,

---

6. Meyer notes three main differences: the substantiality of the human soul, the distinction between the will and intellect, and the freedom to suspend judgment. Spinoza notes his differences with Descartes; see Ep2, 62–63; Ep21, 154–158.

7. Cf. E2P11.

but only as determined in a particular way in accordance with the laws of thinking Nature through ideas, and one concludes that this must come into existence when the human body begins to exist. From this definition, he thinks it is not difficult to prove that Will is not distinct from Intellect, far less is it endowed with the freedom that Descartes ascribes to it.[8] Indeed, he holds that a faculty of affirming and denying is quite fictitious, that affirming and denying are nothing but ideas, and that other faculties such as Intellect, Desire, etc., must be accounted as figments, or at least among those notions that men have formed through conceiving things in an abstract way, such as humanity, stoniness, and other things of that kind.[9]

Here, too, we must not omit to mention that assertions found in some passages, that this or that surpasses human understanding, must be taken in the same sense (i.e., as giving only Descartes's opinion). This must not be regarded as expressing our Author's own view. All such things, he holds, and many others even more sublime and subtle, can not only be conceived by us clearly and distinctly but can also be explained quite satisfactorily, provided that the human intellect can be guided to the search for truth and the knowledge of things along a path different from that which was opened up and leveled by Descartes. And so he holds that the foundations of the sciences laid by Descartes and the superstructure that he built thereon do not suffice to elucidate and resolve all the most difficult problems that arise in metaphysics. Other foundations are required if we seek to raise our intellect to that pinnacle of knowledge.

Finally, to bring my preface to a close, we should like our readers to realize that all that is here treated is given to the public for the sole purpose of searching out and disseminating truth and to urge men to the pursuit of a true and genuine philosophy. And so in order that all may reap therefrom as rich a profit as we sincerely desire for them, before they begin reading we earnestly beg them to insert omitted passages in their proper place and carefully to correct printing errors that have crept in. Some of these are such as may be an obstacle in the way of perceiving the force of the demonstration and the Author's meaning, as anyone will readily gather from looking at them.

8. Cf. E2P48; E2P49Cor and Schol.
9. On Spinoza's nominalism, see E2P40Schol1; Lee Rice, "Tanquam Naturae Humanae Exemplar: Spinoza on Human Nature," *The Modern Schoolman* 68 (1991), 291–303; Lee Rice, "Le nominalisme de Spinoza," *Canadian Journal of Philosophy* 24/1 (1994), 19–32.

THE PRINCIPLES OF PHILOSOPHY

demonstrated in the geometric manner.

Part 1.

Prolegomenon.

Before coming to the Propositions and their Demonstrations, I have thought it helpful to give a concise account as to why Descartes doubted everything, the way in which he laid the solid foundations of the sciences, and finally the means by which he freed himself from all doubts. I should indeed have arranged all this in mathematical order had I not considered that the prolixity involved in this form of presentation would be an obstacle to the proper understanding of all those things that ought to be beheld at a single glance, as in the case of a picture.

Descartes, then, so as to proceed with the greatest caution in his enquiry, attempted,

1. to put aside all prejudice,

2. to discover the foundations on which everything should be built,

3. to uncover the cause of error,

4. to understand everything clearly and distinctly.

To achieve his first, second, and third aims, he proceeded to call everything into doubt, not indeed like a Sceptic whose sole aim is to doubt, but to free his mind from all prejudice so that he might finally discover the firm and unshakable foundations of the sciences, which, if they existed, could thus not escape him. For the true principles of the sciences ought to be so clear and certain that they need no proof, are placed beyond all hazard of doubt, and without them nothing can be demonstrated. These principles, after a lengthy period of doubting, he discovered. Now when he had found them, it was not difficult for him to distinguish true from false, to uncover the cause of error, and so to take precautions against assuming as true and certain what was false and doubtful.

To achieve his fourth and final aim, that of understanding everything

7

clearly and distinctly, his chief rule was to enumerate the simple ideas out of which all others are compounded and to scrutinize each one separately. For when he could perceive simple ideas clearly and distinctly, he would doubtless understand with the same clarity and distinctness all the other ideas compounded from those simple ideas. Having thus outlined my program, I shall briefly explain in what manner he called everything into doubt, discovered the true principles of the sciences, and extricated himself from the difficulties of doubt.

Doubt concerning all things.

First, then, he reviewed all those things he had gathered from his senses—the sky, the earth, and the like, and even his own body—all of which he had hitherto regarded as belonging to reality. And he doubted their certainty because he had found that the senses occasionally deceived him, and in dreams he had often been convinced that many things truly existed externally to himself, discovering afterwards that he had been deluded. And finally there was the fact that he had heard others, even when awake, declare that they felt pain in limbs they had lost long before.[10] Therefore he was able to doubt, not without reason, even the existence of his own body. From all these considerations he could truly conclude that the senses are not a very strong foundation on which to build all science, for they can be called into doubt; certainty depends on other principles of which we can be more sure. Continuing his enquiry, in the second place he turned to the consideration of all universals, such as corporeal nature in general, its extension, likewise its figure, quantity, etc., and also all mathematical truths. Although these seemed to him more certain than any of the things he had gathered from his senses, yet he discovered a reason for doubting them.[11] For others had erred even concerning these. And there was a particularly strong reason, an ancient belief, fixed in his mind, that there was an all-powerful God who had created him as he was, and so may have caused him to be deceived even regarding those things that seemed very clear to him.[12] This, then, is the manner in which he called everything into doubt.

---

10. The first two arguments are given in Med1, 13–15; (AT7, 18–20) and PPH1A4, whereas the third is not given until Med6, 50 (AT7, 76–77).
11. Med1, 15 (AT7, 20).
12. Med1, 15–16 (AT7, 21–22).

The discovery of the foundation of all science.

Now in order to discover the true principles of the sciences, he proceeded to enquire whether he had called into doubt everything that could come within the scope of his thought; thus he might find out whether there was not perchance still something left that he had not yet doubted. For if in the course of thus doubting he should find something that could not be called into doubt either for any of the previous reasons or for any other reason, he quite rightly considered that this must be established as a foundation on which he could build all his knowledge.[13] And although he had already, as it seemed, doubted everything—for he had doubted not only what he had gathered from his senses but also what he had perceived by intellect alone—yet there was still something left to be examined, namely, himself who was doing the doubting, not insofar as he consisted of head, hands, and other bodily parts (since he had doubted these) but only insofar as he was doubting, thinking, etc. Examining this carefully, he realized that he could not doubt it for any of the foregoing reasons. For whether he is dreaming or awake as he thinks, nevertheless he thinks, and is.[14] And although others, or even he himself, had erred with regard to other matters; nevertheless, because they were erring, they were. He could imagine no author of his being so cunning as to deceive him on that score; for it must be granted that he himself exists as long as it is supposed that he is being deceived. In short, whatever other reason for doubting be devised, there could be adduced none of such a kind as not at the same time to make him most certain of his existence. Indeed, the more reasons are adduced for doubting, the more arguments are simultaneously adduced to convince him of his own existence. So, in whatever direction he turns in order to doubt, he is nevertheless compelled to utter these words: "I doubt, I think, therefore I am."[15]

Thus, in laying bare this truth, at the same time he also discovered the foundation of all the sciences, and also the measure and rule for all other truths—that whatever is perceived as clearly and distinctly as this, is true.[16]

It is abundantly clear from the preceding that there can be no other foundation for the sciences than this; everything else can quite easily be called into doubt, but this can by no means be doubted. However, with

---

13. Med2, 17 (AT7, 24).
14. Med2, 17–18 (AT7, 24–25).
15. Med2, 18 (AT7, 25); *Discourse on Method* 4 (AT6, 32–33).
16. Spinoza follows the *Discourse on Method*, rather than the *Meditations* or PPH, in deriving this principle directly from the *cogito*.

regard to this foundation, it should be particularly noted that the statement, "I doubt, I think, therefore I am," is not a syllogism with the major premise omitted. If it were a syllogism, the premises should be clearer and better known than the conclusion 'Therefore I am', and so 'I am' would not be the prime basis of all knowledge. Furthermore, it would not be a certain conclusion, for its truth would depend on universal premises which the Author had already called into doubt. So 'I think, therefore I am' is a single independent proposition, equivalent to the following—'I am, while thinking'.

To avoid confusion in what follows (for this is a matter that must be perceived clearly and distinctly), we must next know what we are. For when this has been clearly and distinctly understood, we shall not confuse our essence with others. In order to deduce this from what has gone before, our Author proceeds as follows.

He recalls to mind all thoughts that he once had about himself, that his soul is something tenuous like the wind or fire or the ether, infused among the denser parts of his body; that his body is better known to him than his soul; and that he perceives the former more clearly and distinctly.[17] And he realizes that all this is clearly inconsistent with what he has so far understood. For he was able to doubt his body, but not his own essence insofar as he was thinking. Furthermore, he perceived these things neither clearly nor distinctly, and so, in accordance with the requirements of his method, he ought to reject them as false. Therefore, understanding that such things could not pertain to him insofar as he was as yet known to himself, he went on to ask what was that, pertaining peculiarly to his essence, which he had not been able to call into doubt and which had compelled him to conclude his own existence. Of this kind there were— that he wanted to take precautions against being deceived, that he desired to understand many things, that he doubted everything that he could not understand, that up to this point he affirmed one thing only and everything else he denied and rejected as false, that he imagined many things even against his will, and, finally, that he was conscious of many things as proceeding from his senses. Because he could infer his existence with equal certainty from each of these points and could list none of them as belonging to the things that he had called into doubt, and finally, because all these things can be conceived under the same attribute, it follows that all these things are true and pertain to his nature. And so whenever he said, "I think," all the following modes of thinking

17. Med2, 18 (AT7, 25–26).

were understood—doubting, understanding, affirming, denying, willing, nonwilling, imagining, and sensing.[18]

Here it is important to note the following points, which will prove to be very useful later on when the distinction between mind and body is discussed. First, these modes of thinking are clearly and distinctly understood independently of other matters that are still in doubt. Second, the clear and distinct conception we have of them would be rendered obscure and confused if we were to intermingle with them any of the matters of which we are still in doubt.

Liberation from all doubts.

Finally, to achieve certainty about what he had called into doubt and to remove all doubt, he proceeds to enquire into the nature of the most perfect Being, and whether such exists. For when he realizes that there exists a most perfect Being by whose power all things are produced and preserved and to whose nature it is contrary that he should be a deceiver, then this will remove the reason for doubting that resulted from his not knowing the cause of himself. For he will know that the faculty of distinguishing true from false was not given to him by a supremely good and truthful God in order that he might be deceived. And so mathematical truths, or all things that seem to him most evident, cannot be in the least suspect.[19] Then, to remove the other causes for doubting, he goes on to enquire how it comes about that we sometimes err. When he discovered that this arises from our using our free will to assent even to what we have perceived only confusedly, he was immediately able to conclude that he can guard against error in the future provided that he gives assent only to what he clearly and distinctly perceives. This is something that each individual can easily obtain of himself because he has the power to control the will and thereby bring it about that it is restrained within the limits of the intellect.[20] But since in our earliest days we have been imbued with many prejudices from which we are not easily freed, in order that we may be freed from them and accept nothing but what we clearly and distinctly perceive, he goes on to enumerate all the simple notions and ideas from which all our thoughts are compounded and to examine them one by one, so that he can observe in each of

---

18. This enumeration is taken from Med2, 20 (AT7, 28).
19. Med3, 34–35 (AT7, 51–52); Med5, 46–47 (AT7, 70–71).
20. Med4, 35–42 (AT7, 52–62).

them what is clear and what is obscure. For thus he will easily be able to distinguish the clear from the obscure and to form clear and distinct thoughts. So he will easily discover the real distinction between soul and body, and what is clear and what is obscure in the deliverance of our senses, and lastly wherein dreaming differs from waking.[21] Thereafter he could no longer doubt that he was awake nor could he be deceived by his senses. Thus he freed himself from all doubts listed previously.

However, before I here make an end, I think I ought to satisfy those who argue as follows: "Because the existence of God is not self-evident to us, it seems that we can never be certain of anything, nor can it ever be known to us that God exists. For from premises that are uncertain (and we have said that, as long as we do not know our own origin), nothing certain can be concluded."

To remove this difficulty, Descartes replies in the following manner. From the fact that we do not as yet know whether the author of our origin may have created us such as to be deceived even in those matters that appear to us most certain, it by no means follows that we can doubt those things that we understand clearly and distinctly through themselves or through a process of reasoning, that is, as long as we are paying attention to it. We can doubt only those things previously demonstrated to be true, which we may remember when we are no longer attending to the reasoning from which we deduced them, and which we have thus forgotten. Therefore, although the existence of God can be known not through itself but only through something else, we can nevertheless attain certain knowledge of God's existence provided that we carefully attend to all the premises from which we conclude it. See *Principia* Part I Article 13, and "Reply to Second Objections," No. 3, and at the end of the "Fifth Meditation."

However, because some do not find this reply satisfactory, I shall give another.[22] When we were speaking previously of the certainty and sureness of our existence, we saw that we concluded it from the fact that, in whatever direction we turned the mind's eye, we did not find any reason for doubting that did not by that very fact convince us of our existence. This was so whether we were considering our own nature, whether we were imagining the author of our nature to be a cunning deceiver—in short, whatever reason for doubting we invoked, external to ourselves. Hitherto we had not

---

21. Med6, 47–59 (AT7, 71–90).
22. See our introduction for a discussion of the status of this alternative reply to the charge of circularity.

found this to be so in the case of any other matter. For example, while attending to the nature of a triangle, although we are compelled to conclude that its three angles are equal to two right angles, we cannot reach this same conclusion if we suppose that we may be deceived by the author of our nature. Yet this very supposition assured us of our existence with the utmost certainty. So it is not the case that, wherever we turn the mind's eye, we are compelled to conclude that the three angles of a triangle are equal to two right angles; on the contrary, we find a reason for doubting it in that we do not possess an idea of God such as to render it impossible for us to think that God is a deceiver. For one who does not possess the true idea of God—which at the moment we suppose we do not possess—may quite as easily think that his author is a deceiver as think that he is not a deceiver, just as one who does not have the idea of a triangle may indifferently think its angles are equal or not equal to two right angles.

Therefore we concede that, except for our existence, we cannot be absolutely certain of anything, however earnestly we attend to its demonstration, as long as we do not have the clear and distinct conception of God that makes us affirm that God is supremely truthful, just as the idea we have of a triangle makes us conclude that its three angles are equal to two right angles. But we deny that, for this reason, we cannot attain knowledge of anything. For, as is evident from all that has already been said, the whole matter hinges on this alone, that we are able to form such a conception of God as so disposes us that it is not as easy for us to think that God is a deceiver as to think that he is not a deceiver, a conception that compels us to affirm that he is supremely truthful. When we have formed such an idea, the reason for doubting mathematical truths will be removed. For in whatever direction we now turn the mind's eye with the purpose of doubting one of these truths, we shall not find anything that itself does not make us conclude that this truth is most certain, just as was the case with regard to our existence.

For example, if after discovering the idea of God we attend to the nature of a triangle, its idea will compel us to affirm that its three angles are equal to two right angles, whereas if we attend to the idea of God, this too will compel us to affirm that he is supremely truthful, the author and continuous preserver of our nature, and therefore that he is not deceiving us with regard to this truth. And attending to the idea of God (which we now suppose we have discovered), it will be just as impossible for us to think that he is a deceiver as to think, when attending to the idea of a triangle, that its three angles are not equal to two right angles. And just as we can form such an idea of a triangle in spite of not knowing whether the author of our nature is deceiving us, so too we can achieve a clear idea of God and set it before us even though also doubting whether the author of our nature is deceiving us in all things. And provided we possess this idea, in whatever way we may have acquired it, it will be enough to remove all doubts, as has just now been shown.

So having made these points, I reply as follows to the difficulty that has been raised. It is not as long as we do not know of God's existence (for I have not spoken of that) but as long as we do not have a clear and distinct idea of God, that we cannot be certain of anything.[23] Therefore, if anyone wishes to argue against me, his argument will have to be as follows: "We cannot be certain of anything until we have a clear and distinct idea of God. But we cannot have a clear and distinct idea of God as long as we do not know whether the author of our nature is deceiving us. Therefore, we cannot be certain of anything as long as we do not know whether the author of our nature is deceiving us, etc." To this I reply by conceding the major premise and denying the minor. For we do have a clear and distinct idea of a triangle, although we do not know whether the author of our nature is deceiving us; and granted that we have such an idea of God, as I have just shown at some length, we cannot doubt his existence or any mathematical truth.[24]

With this as preface, I now enter upon the work itself.

Definitions.

1. Under the word *Thought,* I include all that is in us and of which we are immediately conscious. Thus all operations of the will, intellect, imagination, and senses are thoughts. But I have added 'immediately' so as to exclude those things that are their consequences. For example, voluntary motion has thought for its starting-point, but in itself it is still not thought.

2. By the word *Ideas,* I understand the specific form (*forma*) of a thought, through the immediate perception of which I am conscious of that same thought.[25]

So whenever I express something in words while understanding what I

23. To be clear, the opposition, as some have claimed, is not between the existence of God and an idea of God, but between having and not having a clear and distinct idea of God.
24. Cf. TIE 79; TTP6note6, 000.
25. Cf. Med3, 25 (AT7, 37) where Descartes notes that ideas are "like images of things." Cf. Spinoza's own definition: E2Defs.3–4; Ep60, 290.

am saying, this very fact makes it certain that there is in me the idea of that which is meant by those words. And so I do not apply the term 'ideas' simply to images depicted in the fantasy; indeed I do not here term these 'ideas' at all, insofar as they are depicted in the corporeal fantasy (i.e., in some part of the brain) but only insofar as they communicate their form to the mind itself when this is directed toward that part of the brain.[26]

3. By the *objective reality of an idea*, I understand the being of that which is presented through the idea, insofar as it is in the idea.[27]

In the same way one can speak of 'objective perfection' or 'objective art', etc. For whatever we perceive as being in the objects of ideas is objectively in the ideas themselves.

4. When things are, in themselves, such as we perceive them to be, they are said to be *formally* in the objects of ideas, and *eminently* when they are not just such in themselves as we perceive them to be but are more than sufficient to account fully for our perception.[28]

Note that when I say that the cause contains eminently the perfections of its effect, I mean that the cause contains the perfections of the effect with a higher degree of excellence than does the effect itself. See also Axiom 8.

5. Every thing in which there is something that we perceive as immediately inhering in a subject,[29] or through which there exists something that we perceive (i.e., some property, quality or attribute whose real idea is in us), is called *substance*. For of substance itself, taken precisely, we have no

---

26. Spinoza holds a similar position: an idea is not "some dumb thing like a picture on a tablet" (E2P43Schol; E2P49Schol).
27. Cf. Med3, 27–28 (AT7, 40–41). The reader will note that the terms 'objective' and 'objectively' are used by Spinoza (and his contemporaries) in a very different sense from that of modern practice. In fact, in an opposite sense. [Tr.] See the next note.
28. Descartes discusses these terms more fully at Med3, 27–28 (AT7, 40–41). For Descartes, the 'formal' reality of an object is what we might call its 'real' being—what is really there. The 'objective' reality of a thing is the existence or 'reality' the thing has as it exists as an idea we have of it, that is, as a mental object in our mind. Thus, though the president of the United States has formal reality and Santa Claus does not, both have objective reality in that both are the objects of an idea I now have. Formal and objective reality also come in degrees so that the blush on the president's cheek has less formal reality than the president himself, and my idea of an infinite being (because it is infinite—that it has no formal reality is of no consequence here) has more objective reality than my idea of any finite being (even if the finite being has formal reality).
29. Note that 'subject' (*subjectum*) = that which underlies. [Tr.]

other idea than that it is a thing in which there exists formally or eminently that something which we perceive (i.e., that something which is objectively in one of our ideas).[30]

6. Substance in which thought immediately inheres is called *Mind* (*Mens*).[31] I here speak of 'Mind' rather than 'Soul' (*anima*) because the word 'soul' is equivocal, and is often used to mean a corporeal thing.[32]

7. Substance that is the immediate subject of extension and of accidents that presuppose extension, such as figure, position, and local motion, is called *Body*.

Whether what is called Mind and what is called Body is one and the same substance, or two different substances, is something to be enquired into later.

8. Substance that we understand through itself to be supremely perfect, and in which we conceive nothing at all that involves any defect or limitation of perfection, is called *God*.

9. When we say that something is contained in the nature or conception of some thing, that is the same saying that it is true of that thing or can be truly affirmed of it.[33]

10. Two substances are said to be distinct in reality when each one can exist without the other.[34]

We have here omitted the Postulates of Descartes because in what follows we do not draw any conclusions from them. But we earnestly ask readers to read them through and to think them over carefully.[35]

---

30. This definition of substance follows that in the "Replies to the Second Set of Objections." Later (PPC2Def2) Spinoza will give a second definition modeled on PPH1A51–52. For the differences between the two definitions see our introduction. For Spinoza's own definition, see E1Def3.

31. In the *Ethics*, Spinoza will abandon the notion of inherence in favor of the concept of mind as a dynamic complex of ideas (see E2Def3).

32. For example, it is not a "rarified I-know-not-what" (Med2, 18 [AT7, 26]).

33. In each of the preceding eight definitions a word or phrase has been italicized to indicate the definiendum, but in this definition and the next there is no text italicized. It appears reasonable to assume that Def9 has as definiendum *contained in the nature or conception of some thing* and Def10 *distinct in reality*.

34. Spinoza provides an extended critique of the Cartesian doctrine of a plurality of substances in E1P10Schol.

35. The seven postulates (AT7, 162–164) or *demandes* in the French version (AT9, 125–127) are not postulates in the Euclidean sense but are requests from Descartes to his readers to ponder carefully what can be doubted, the preceding definitions, and especially the distinction between clear, distinct perception and obscure, confused perception.

Axioms.[36]

1. We arrive at the knowledge and certainty of some unknown thing only through the knowledge and certainty of another thing that is prior to it in certainty and knowledge.
2. There are reasons that make us doubt the existence of our bodies. This has in fact been shown in the Prolegomenon, and so is here posited as an axiom.
3. If we have anything besides mind and body, this is less known to us than mind and body.

It should be noted that these axioms do not affirm anything about things external to us, but only such things as we find within ourselves insofar as we are thinking things.[37]

Proposition 1.

We cannot be absolutely certain of anything as long as we do not know that we exist.

Proof.

This proposition is self-evident; for he who absolutely does not know that he is likewise does not know that he is a being affirming or denying, that is, that he certainly affirms or denies.[38]

Here it should be noted that although we may affirm or deny many things with great certainty while not attending to the fact that we exist, unless this is presupposed as indubitable, everything could be called into doubt.

36. The first three axioms are not taken from Descartes, but Meyer, in his preface, has mentioned that Spinoza would expound Descartes's opinions and demonstrations "just as they are found in his writings, or such as should validly be deduced from the foundations laid by him." We shall see that the claim that Spinoza follows Descartes's teachings "just as they are found in his writings" is not entirely true.
37. The stipulation that axioms should contain no existential assumptions probably originates in PPH1A10 and PPH1A49. In Ep10 Spinoza appears to accept the assumption, but it is violated by many axioms in the *Ethics*.
38. Cf. TIE47.

Proposition 2.

'I am' must be self-evident.

Proof.

If this be denied, it will therefore be known only through something else, the knowledge and certainty of which will be prior in us to the statement 'I am' (Ax. 1). But this is absurd. (Prop. 1). Therefore it must be self-evident. Q.E.D.

Proposition 3.

'I am', insofar as the 'I' is a thing consisting of body, is not a first principle and is not known through itself.

Proof.

There are certain things that make us doubt the existence of our body. (Ax. 2). Therefore (Ax. 1) we shall not attain certainty of this except through the knowledge and certainty of something else that is prior to it in knowledge and certainty. Therefore the statement 'I am', insofar as 'I' am a thing consisting of body, is not a first principle and is not known through itself. Q.E.D.

Proposition 4.

'I am' cannot be the first known principle except insofar as we think.

Proof.

The statement 'I am a corporeal thing, or a thing consisting of body' is not a first-known principle (Prop. 3), nor again am I certain of my existence insofar as I consist of anything other than mind and body. For if we consist of anything different from mind and body, this is less well known to us than body (Ax. 3). Therefore 'I am' cannot be the first known thing except insofar as we think. Q.E.D.

Corollary.

From this it is obvious that mind, or a thinking thing, is better known than body.

But for a fuller explanation read Part 1 of the *Principia* Arts. 11 and 12.

Scholium.

Everyone perceives with the utmost certainty that he affirms, denies, doubts, understands, imagines, etc., or that he exists as doubting, understanding, affirming, etc.—in short, as thinking. Nor can this be called into doubt. Therefore the statement 'I think' or 'I am, as thinking' is the unique (Prop. 1) and most certain basis of all philosophy. Now in order to achieve the greatest certainty in the sciences, our aim and purpose can be no other than this, to deduce everything from the strongest first principles and to make the inferences as clear and distinct as the first principles from which they are deduced. It therefore clearly follows that we must consider as most certainly true everything that is equally evident to us and that we perceive with the same clearness and distinctness as the already discovered first principle, and also everything that so agrees with this first principle and so depends on it that we cannot doubt it without also having to doubt this first principle.

But to proceed with the utmost caution in reviewing these matters, at the first stage I shall admit as equally evident and equally clearly and distinctly perceived by us only those things that each of us observes in himself insofar as he is engaged in thinking. Such are, for example, that he wills this or that, that he has definite ideas of such-and-such a kind, and that one idea contains in itself more reality and perfection than another—namely, that the one that contains objectively the being and perfection of substance is far more perfect than one that contains only the objective perfection of some accident, and, finally, that the idea of a supremely perfect being is the most perfect of all. These things, I say, we perceive not merely with equal sureness and clarity but perhaps even more distinctly; for they affirm not only that we think but also how we think.

Further, we shall also say that those things that cannot be doubted without at the same time casting doubt on this unshakable foundation of ours are also in agreement with this first principle. For example, if anyone should doubt whether something can come from nothing, he will be able at the same time to doubt whether we, as long as we are thinking, are. For if I can affirm something of nothing—in effect, that nothing can be the cause of something—I can at the same time and with the same right affirm thought of nothing, and say that I, as long as I am thinking, am nothing. Because I find this impossible, it will also be impossible for me to think that something may come from nothing.

With these considerations in mind, I have decided at this point to list here in order those things that at present seem to us necessary for future progress, and to add to the number of axioms. For these are indeed set forth by Descartes as axioms at the end of his "Reply to the Second Set of Objections," and I do not aim at greater accuracy than he. However, not to depart from the order we have been pursuing, I shall try to make them somewhat clearer, and to show how one depends on another and all on this one first principle, 'I am, while thinking', or how their certainty and reasonableness is of the same degree as that of the first principle.

Axioms taken from Descartes.

4. There are different degrees of reality or being; for substance has more reality than accident or mode, and infinite substance, more than finite substance. Therefore there is more objective reality in the idea of substance than in the idea of accident, and in the idea of infinite substance than in the idea of finite substance.[39]

This axiom is known simply from contemplating our ideas, of whose existence we are certain because they are modes of thinking. For we know how much reality or perfection the idea of substance affirms of substance, and how much the idea of mode affirms of mode.[40] This being so, we also necessarily realize that the idea of substance contains more objective reality than the idea of some accident, etc. See Scholium Prop. 4.

5. A thinking thing,[41] if it knows of any perfections that it lacks, will immediately give these to itself, if they are within its power.[42]

This everyone observes in himself insofar as he is a thinking thing. Therefore (Scholium Prop. 4) we are most certain of it. And for the same reason, we are just as certain of the following:

6. In the idea or concept of every thing, there is contained either possible or necessary existence. (See Axiom 10, Descartes.)

Necessary existence is contained in the concept of God, or a supremely

---

39. Cf. Med3, 27–28 (AT7, 40–42).
40. This explanation in fact is contrary to Descartes's claim that ideas do not contain an element of affirmation (see Med4, 38 [AT7, 56]), but is in agreement with Spinoza's reinterpretation of the notion of 'idea' and his denial of the distinction between intellect and will (see E2P49Cor).
41. Here Spinoza does not exactly follow Descartes, whose text reads, "The *will* of a thinking thing . . ." [emphasis ours]; see AT7, 166.
42. Cf. Med3, 32–33 (AT7, 48).

perfect being; for otherwise he would be conceived as imperfect, which is contrary to what is supposed to be conceived. Contingent or possible existence is contained in the concept of a limited thing.

7. No thing, nor any perfection of a thing actually existing, can have nothing, or a nonexisting thing, as the cause of its existence.

I have demonstrated in the Scholium Prop. 4 that this axiom is as clear to us as is 'I am, when thinking'.

8. Whatever there is of reality or perfection in any thing exists formally or eminently in its first and adequate cause.[43]

By 'eminently' I understand: when the cause contains all the reality of the effect more perfectly than the effect itself. By 'formally': when the cause contains all the reality of the effect equally perfectly.

This axiom depends on the preceding one. For if it were supposed that there is nothing in the cause, or less in the cause than in the effect, then nothing in the cause would be the cause of the effect. But this is absurd (Ax. 7). Therefore it is not the case that anything whatsoever can be the cause of a certain effect; it must be precisely a thing in which there is eminently or at least formally all the perfection that is in the effect.

9. The objective reality of our ideas requires a cause in which that same reality is contained not only objectively but also formally or eminently.[44]

This axiom, although misused by many, is universally admitted, for when somebody conceives something new, everyone wants to know the cause of this concept or idea. Now when they can assign a cause in which is contained formally or eminently as much reality as is contained objectively in that concept, they are satisfied. This is made quite clear by the example of a machine, which Descartes adduces in Art. 17 Part 1 *Principia*.[45] Similarly, if anyone were to ask whence it is that a man has the ideas of his thought and of his body, no one can fail to see that he has them from himself, as containing formally everything that his ideas contain objectively. Therefore if a man were to have some idea that contained more of objective reality than he himself contained of formal reality, then of necessity we should be driven by the natural light to seek another cause outside the man himself, a cause that contained all that perfection formally or eminently. And apart from that cause no one has ever assigned any other cause that he has conceived so clearly and distinctly.

---

43. Cf. Med3, 28 (AT7, 40–41).
44. Cf. Med3, 28 (AT7, 41–42).
45. Cf. Rep1, AT7, 104–106.

Furthermore, as for the truth of this axiom, it depends on the previous ones. By Axiom 4 there are different degrees of reality or being in ideas. Therefore (Ax. 8) they need a more perfect cause in accordance with their degree of perfection. But because the degrees of reality that we observe in ideas are not in the ideas insofar as they are considered as modes of thinking but insofar as one presents substance and another merely a mode of substance—or, in brief, insofar as they are considered as images of things— hence it clearly follows that there can be granted no other first cause of ideas than that which, as we have just shown, all men understand clearly and distinctly by the natural light, namely, one in which is contained formally or eminently the same reality that the ideas have objectively.[46]

To make this conclusion more clearly understood, I shall illustrate it with one or two examples. If anyone sees some books (imagine one to be that of a distinguished philosopher and the other to be that of some trifler) written in one and the same hand, and if he pays no attention to the meaning of the words (i.e., insofar as they are symbols) but only to the shape of the writing and the order of the letters, he will find no distinction between them such as to compel him to seek different causes for them. They will appear to him to have proceeded from the same cause and in the same manner. But if he pays attention to the meaning of the words and of the language, he will find a considerable distinction between them. He will therefore conclude that the first cause of the one book was very different from the first cause of the other, and that the one cause was in fact more perfect than the other to the extent that the meaning of the language of the two books, or their words considered as symbols, are found to differ from one another.

I am speaking of the first cause of books, and there must necessarily be one although I admit—indeed, I take for granted—that one book can be transcribed from another, as is self-evident.

The same point can also be clearly illustrated by the example of a portrait, let us say, of some prince. If we pay attention only to the materials of which it is made, we shall not find any distinction between it and other portraits such as to compel us to look for different causes. Indeed, there will be nothing to prevent us from thinking that it was copied from another likeness, and that one again from another, and so *ad infinitum*. For we shall be quite satisfied that there need be no other cause for its production. But

---

46. We are also certain of this because we experience it ourselves insofar as we are thinking. See preceding Scholium. [Spinoza]

if we attend to the image insofar as it is the image of something, we shall immediately be compelled to seek a first cause such as formally or eminently contains what that image contains representatively. I do not see what more need be said to confirm and elucidate this axiom.

10. To preserve a thing, no lesser cause is required than to produce it in the first place.

From the fact that at this moment we are thinking, it does not necessarily follow that we shall hereafter be thinking. For the concept that we have of our thought does not involve, or does not contain, the necessary existence of the thought. I can clearly and distinctly conceive the thought even though I suppose it not to exist.[47] Now the nature of every cause must contain in itself or involve the perfection of its effect (Ax. 8). Hence it clearly follows that there must be something in us or external to us that we have not yet understood, whose concept or nature involves existence, and that is the reason why our thought began to exist and also continues to exist. For although our thought began to exist, its nature and essence does not on that account involve necessary existence any the more than before it existed, and so in order to persevere in existing it stands in need of the same force that it needs to begin existing. And what we here say about thought must be said about every thing whose essence does not involve necessary existence.

11. Of every thing that exists, it can be asked what is the cause or reason why it exists. See Descartes, Axiom 1.

Because to exist is something positive, we cannot say that it has nothing for its cause (Ax. 7). Therefore we must assign some positive cause or reason why it exists. And this must be either external (i.e., outside the thing itself) or else internal (i.e., included in the nature and definition of the existing thing itself).

The four propositions that follow are taken from Descartes.

Proposition 5.

The existence of God is known solely from the consideration of his nature.

Proof.

To say that something is contained in the nature or concept of a thing is the

---

47. This is something everyone discovers in himself, insofar as he is a thinking thing. [Spinoza]

same as to say that it is true of that thing (Def. 9). But necessary existence is contained in the concept of God (Ax. 6). Therefore it is true to say of God that there is necessary existence in him, or that he exists.[48]

Scholium.

From this proposition there follow many important consequences. Indeed, on this fact alone—that existence pertains to the nature of God, or that the concept of God involves necessary existence just as the concept of a triangle involves its three angles being equal to two right angles, or that his existence, just like his essence, is an eternal truth—depends almost all knowledge of the attributes of God through which we are brought to love of him and to the highest blessedness. Therefore it is much to be desired that mankind should come round to our opinion on this subject.[49]

I do indeed admit that there are some prejudices that prevent this from being so easily understood by everyone.[50] If anyone, moved by goodwill and by the simple love of truth and his own true advantage, comes to look at the matter closely and to reflect on what is contained in the Fifth Meditation and the end of "Replies to the First Set of Objections," and also on what we say about Eternity in Chapter 1 Part 2 of our Appendix, he will undoubtedly understand the matter quite clearly and will in no way be able to doubt whether he has an idea of God (which is, of course, the first foundation of human blessedness). For when he realizes that God is completely different in kind from other things in respect of essence and existence, he will at once see clearly that the idea of God is far different from the ideas of other things.[51] Therefore there is no need to detain the reader any longer on this subject.

Proposition 6.

The existence of God is proved a posteriori from the mere fact that the idea of him is in us.

48. Cf. Med5, 43–46 (AT7, 65–69); E1P11Dem1; KV1/1/1–2.
49. For Spinoza's opinion on this subject, see E2P49Schol, 100; Ep21, 155.
50. Read *Principia* Part 1 Art. 16. [Spinoza]
51. A more radical development of this Cartesian claim is argued by Spinoza in E1P17Schol, in dealing with the intellect and will of God.

Proof.

The objective reality of any of our ideas requires a cause in which that same reality is contained not just objectively but formally or eminently (Ax. 9). Now we do have the idea of God (Defs. 2 and 8), and the objective reality of this idea is not contained in us either formally or eminently (Ax. 4), nor can it be contained in anything other than God himself (Def. 8). Therefore this idea of God, which is in us, requires God for its cause, and therefore God exists (Ax. 7).[52]

Scholium.

There are some who deny that they have any idea of God, and yet, as they declare, they worship and love him. And though you were to set before them the definition of God and the attributes of God, you will meet with no more success than if you were to labor to teach a man blind from birth the differences of colors as we see them. However, except to consider them as a strange type of creature halfway between man and beast, we should pay small heed to their words. How else, I ask, can we show the idea of some thing than by giving its definition and explaining its attributes? Because this is what we are doing in the case of the idea of God, there is no reason for us to be concerned over the words of men who deny the idea of God simply on the grounds that they cannot form an image of him in their brain.

Furthermore, we should note that when Descartes quotes Axiom 4 to show that the objective reality of the idea of God is not contained in us either formally or eminently, he takes for granted that everyone knows that he is not an infinite substance, that is, supremely intelligent, supremely powerful, etc., and this he is entitled to do. For he who knows that he thinks, also knows that he doubts many things and that he does not understand everything clearly and distinctly.

Finally, we should note that it also follows clearly from Definition 8 that there cannot be a number of Gods, but only one God, as we clearly demonstrate in Proposition 11 of this Part, and in Part 2 of our Appendix, Chapter 2.

52. Cf. Med3, 28–31 (AT7, 40–45). Compare to Spinoza's own a posteriori proofs at KV1/1/3 and E1P11Dem3.

Proposition 7.

The existence of God is also proved from the fact that we ourselves exist while having the idea of him.

Proof.

If I had the force to preserve myself, I would be of such a nature that I would involve necessary existence (Lemma 2). Therefore (Corollary Lemma 1) my nature would contain all perfections. But I find in myself, insofar as I am a thinking thing, many imperfections—as that I doubt, desire, etc.—and of this I am certain (Scholium Prop. 4). Therefore I have no force to preserve myself. Nor can I say that the reason I now lack those perfections is that I now will to deny them to myself, for this would be clearly inconsistent with Lemma 1, and with what I clearly find in myself (Ax. 5).

Further, I cannot now exist, while I am existing, without being preserved either by myself—if indeed I have that force—or by something else that does have that force (Axioms 10 and 11). But I do exist (Scholium Prop. 4), and yet I do not have the force to preserve myself, as has just now been proved. Therefore I am preserved by something else. But not by something else that does not have the force to preserve itself (by the same reasoning whereby I have just demonstrated that I am not able to preserve myself). Therefore it must be by something else that has the force to preserve itself; that is (Lemma 2), something whose nature involves necessary existence, that is (Corollary Lemma 1) something that contains all the perfections that I clearly understand to pertain to a supremely perfect being. Therefore a supremely perfect being exists; that is (Def. 8), God exists. Q.E.D.[53]

Scholium.

To demonstrate this proposition Descartes assumes the following two axioms:

1. That which can effect what is greater or more difficult can also effect what is less.

53. Cf. Spinoza's proof: E1P11Dem3.

2. It is a greater thing to create or (Ax. 10) to preserve substance than the attributes or properties of substance.

What he means by these axioms I do not know. For what does he call easy, and what difficult? Nothing is said to be easy or difficult in an absolute sense, but only with respect to its cause. So one and the same thing can be said at the same time to be easy and difficult in respect of different causes.[54] Now if, of things that can be effected by the same cause, he calls those difficult that need great effort and those easy that need less (e.g., the force that can raise fifty pounds can raise twenty-five pounds twice as easily) then surely the axiom is not absolutely true, nor can he prove from it what he aims to prove. For when he says, "If I had the force to preserve myself, I should also have the force to give myself all the perfections that I lack" (because this latter does not require as much power), I would grant him that the strength that I expend on preserving myself could effect many other things far more easily had I not needed it to preserve myself, but I deny that, as long as I am using it to preserve myself,[55] I can direct it to effecting other things however much easier, as can clearly be seen in our example.

And the difficulty is not removed by saying that, because I am a thinking thing, I must necessarily know whether I am expending all my strength in preserving myself, and whether this is also the reason why I do not give myself the other perfections. For—apart from the fact that this point is not at issue, but only how the necessity of this proposition follows from this axiom—if I knew this, I should be a greater being and perhaps require greater strength than I have so as to preserve myself in that greater perfection. Again, I do not know whether it is a greater task to create or preserve substance than to create or preserve its attributes. That is, to speak more clearly and in more philosophic terms, I do not know whether a substance, so as to preserve its attributes, does not need the whole of its virtue and essence with which it may be preserving itself.

But let us leave this and examine further what our noble Author here intends; that is, what he understands by 'easy' and what by 'difficult'. I do

---

54. Take as only one example the spider, which easily weaves a web that men would find very difficult to weave. On the other hand, men find it quite easy to do many things that are perhaps impossible for angels. [Spinoza]
55. I have diverged from the punctuation of Gebhardt. [Tr.]

not think, nor can I in any way be convinced, that by 'difficult' he understands that which is impossible (and therefore cannot be conceived in any
way as coming into being), and by 'easy', that which does not imply any
contradiction (and therefore can readily be conceived as coming into being)—although in the "Third Meditation" he seems at first glance to mean
this when he says: "Nor ought I to think that perhaps those things that I
lack are more difficult to acquire than those that are already in me. For on
the contrary it is obvious that it was far more difficult for me, a thinking
thing or substance, to emerge from nothing than . . .", etc.[56] This would not
be consistent with the Author's words nor would it smack of his genius. For,
passing over the first point, there is no relationship between the possible
and the impossible, or between the intelligible and the nonintelligible, just
as there is no relationship between something and nothing, and power has
no more to do with impossible things than creation and generation, with
nonentities; so there can be no comparison between them. Besides, I can
compare things and understand their relationship only when I have a clear
and distinct conception of them all. So I deny that it follows that he who
can do the impossible can also do the possible. What sort of conclusion, I
ask, would this be? That if someone can make a square circle, he will also be
able to make a circle wherein all the lines drawn from the center to the
circumference are equal. Or if someone can bring it about that 'nothing'
can be acted upon, and can use it as material to produce something, he will
also have the power to make something from something. For, as I have said,
there is no agreement, or analogy, or comparison or any relationship whatsoever between these things and things like these. Anyone can see this, if
only he gives a little attention to the matter. Therefore I think this quite
irreconcilable with Descartes's genius.

But if I attend to the second of the two axioms just now stated, it appears
that what he means by 'greater' and 'more difficult' is 'more perfect', and
by 'lesser' and 'easier', 'less perfect'. Yet this, again, seems very obscure, for
there is here the same difficulty as before. As before, I deny that he who can
do the greater can, at the same time and with the same effort (as must be
supposed in the proposition), do the lesser.

Again, when he says: "It is a greater thing to create or preserve substance
than its attributes," surely he cannot understand by attributes that which is
formally contained in substance and differs from substance itself only by
conceptual abstraction. For then it would be the same thing to create

56. Cf. Med3, 32–33 (AT7, 48).

substance as to create attributes. Nor again, by the same reasoning, can he mean the properties of substance which necessarily follow from its essence and definition.[57] Far less can he mean—and yet he appears to—the properties and attributes of another substance. For instance, if I say that I have the power to preserve myself, a finite thinking substance, I cannot for that reason say that I also have the power to give myself the perfections of infinite substance, which differs totally in essence from my essence. For the force or essence whereby I preserve myself in my being is quite different in kind from the force or essence whereby absolutely infinite substance preserves itself, and from which its powers and properties are distinguishable only by abstract reason.[58] So even though I were to suppose that I preserve myself, if I wanted to conceive that I could give myself the perfections of absolutely infinite substance, I should be supposing nothing other than this, that I could reduce my entire essence to nothing and create an infinite substance anew. This would be much more, surely, than merely to suppose that I can preserve myself, a finite substance.

Therefore, because by the terms 'attributes' or 'properties' he can mean none of these things, there remain only the qualities that substance itself contains eminently (as this or that thought in the mind, which I clearly perceive to be lacking in me), but not the qualities that another substance contains eminently (as this or that motion in extension; for such perfections are not perfections for me, a thinking thing, and therefore they are not lacking to me). But then what Descartes wants to prove—that if I am preserving myself, I also have the power to give myself all the perfections that I clearly see as pertaining to a most perfect being—can in no way be concluded from this axiom, as is quite clear from what I have said previously. However, not to leave the matter unproved, and to avoid all confusion, I have thought it advisable first of all to demonstrate the following Lemmas, and thereafter to construct on them the proof of Proposition 7.

57. In PPH1A62 Descartes maintains that the distinction between substance and attributes is one of reason only. This objection and the one given in the next paragraph are quite close to those made by Burman (AT5, 154–155), but we have no evidence to suggest that Spinoza was familiar with the *Conversation with Burman*. Spinoza distinguishes between substance and attributes: see E1Defs3–4.
58. Note that the force by which substance preserves itself is nothing but its essence, differing from it only in name. This will be a particular feature of our discussion in the Appendix, concerning the power of God. [Spinoza]

Lemma 1.

The more perfect a thing is by its own nature, the greater the existence it involves, and the more necessary is the existence. Conversely, the more a thing by its own nature involves necessary existence, the more perfect it is.

Proof.

Existence is contained in the idea or concept of every thing (Ax.6). Then let it be supposed that A is a thing that has ten degrees of perfection. I say that its concept involves more existence than if it were supposed to contain only five degrees of perfection. Because we cannot affirm any existence of nothing (see Scholium Prop. 4), in proportion as we in thought subtract from its perfection and therefore conceive it as participating more and more in nothing, to that extent we also deny the possibility of its existence. So if we conceive its degrees of perfection to be reduced indefinitely to nought or zero, it will contain no existence, or absolutely impossible existence. But, on the other hand, if we increase its degrees of perfection indefinitely, we shall conceive it as involving the utmost existence, and therefore the most necessary existence.[59] That was the first thing to be proved. Now since these two things can in no way be separated (as is quite clear from Axiom 6 and the whole of Part 1 of this work), what we proposed to prove in the second place clearly follows.

Note 1. Although many things are said to exist necessarily solely on the grounds that there is given a cause determined to produce them, it is not of this that we are here speaking; we are speaking only of that necessity and possibility that follows solely from consideration of the nature or essence of a thing, without taking any account of its cause.[60]

Note 2. We are not here speaking of beauty and other 'perfections', which, out of superstition and ignorance, men have thought fit to call perfections; by perfection I understand only reality or being.[61] For example, I perceive that more reality is contained in substance than in modes or accidents. So I understand clearly that substance contains more necessary and more perfect existence than is contained in accidents, as is well established from Axioms 4 and 6.

59. Cf. E1P10Schol; KV1/2/1–ff.
60. See a similar passage in TIE97.
61. For Spinoza's view of 'perfection', see E2Def6; E4Pref; Ep19.

Corollary.

Hence it follows that whatever involves necessary existence is a supremely perfect being, or God.

Lemma 2.

The nature of one who has the power to preserve himself involves necessary existence.

Proof.

He who has the force to preserve himself has also the force to create himself (Ax. 10); that is (as everyone will readily admit), he needs no external cause to exist, but his own nature alone will be a sufficient cause of his existence, either possibly (Ax. 10) or necessarily. But not possibly; for then (through what I have demonstrated with regard to Axiom 10) from the fact that he now existed it would not follow that he would thereafter exist (which is contrary to the hypothesis). Therefore necessarily; that is, his nature involves necessary existence. Q.E.D.

Corollary.

God can bring about every thing that we clearly perceive, just as we perceive it.

Proof.

All this follows clearly from the preceding proposition. For there God's existence was proved from the fact that there must exist someone in whom are all the perfections of which there is an idea in us. Now there is in us the idea of a power so great that by him alone in whom it resides there can be made the sky, the earth, and all the other things that are understood by me as possible. Therefore, along with God's existence, all these things, too, are proved of him.

Proposition 8.

Mind and body are distinct in reality.

Proof.

Whatever we clearly perceive can be brought about by God just as we perceive it (Corollary Prop. 7). But we clearly perceive mind, that is (Def. 6), a thinking substance, without body, that is (Def. 7), without any extended substance (Props. 3 and 4); and conversely we clearly perceive body without mind, as everyone readily admits. Therefore, at least through divine power, mind can be without body and body without mind.[62] Now substances that can be without one another are distinct in reality (Def. 10). But mind and body are substances (Defs. 5, 6, and 7) that can exist without one another, as has just been proved. Therefore mind and body are distinct in reality.

See Proposition 4 at the end of Descartes's "Replies to the Second Set of Objections," and the passages in *Principia* Part 1 from Arts. 22–29. For I do not think it worthwhile to transcribe them here.[63]

Proposition 9.

God is a supremely understanding being.

Proof.

If you deny this, then God will understand either nothing or not everything, that is, only some things. But to understand only some things and to be ignorant of the rest supposes a limited and imperfect intellect, which it is absurd to ascribe to God (Def. 8). And that God should understand nothing either indicates a lack of intellection in God—as it does with men who understand nothing—and involves imperfection (which, by the same definition, cannot be the case with God), or else it indicates that it is incompatible with God's perfection that he should understand something. But because intellection is thus completely denied of God, he will not be

---

62. Cf. Med6, 51 (AT7, 78).
63. The sections not cited are those where Descartes deals with the limits of the human intellect—the mysteries of the Incarnation and Trinity, the indefinite (but not, apparently, infinite) extension of the physical universe, and God's goal in creating it. See Meyer's preface for Spinoza's disagreement with and disregard of these.

able to create any intellect (Ax. 8). Now because intellect is clearly and distinctly perceived by us, God can be its cause (Cor. Prop. 7). Therefore it is far from true that it is incompatible with God's perfection for him to understand something. Therefore he is a supremely understanding being. Q.E.D.[64]

Scholium.

Although it must be granted that God is incorporeal, as is demonstrated in Prop. 16, this must not be taken to mean that all the perfections of extension are to be withdrawn from him. They are to be withdrawn from him only to the extent that the nature and properties of extension involve some imperfection. The same point is to be made concerning God's intellection, as is admitted by all who seek wisdom beyond the common run of philosophers, and as will be fully explained in our Appendix Part 2 Chapter 7.

Proposition 10.

Whatever perfection is found in God, is from God.

Proof.

If you deny this, suppose that there is in God some perfection that is not from God. It will be in God either from itself, or from something different from God. If from itself, it will therefore have necessary existence, not merely possible existence (Lemma 2 Prop. 7), and so (Corollary Lemma 1 Prop. 7) it will be something supremely perfect, and therefore (Def. 8) it will be God. So if it be said that there is in God something that is from itself, at the same time it is said that this is from God. Q.E.D. But if it be from something different from God, then God cannot be conceived through himself as supremely perfect, contrary to Definition 8. Therefore whatever perfection is found in God, is from God. Q.E.D.

Proposition 11.

There cannot be more than one God.

---

64. Spinoza notes that God is a supremely understanding being, *not* that God has supreme understanding.

Proof.

If you deny this, conceive, if you can, more than one God (e.g., A and B). Then of necessity (Prop. 9) both A and B will have the highest degree of understanding; that is, A will understand everything, himself and B, and in turn B will understand himself and A. But because A and B necessarily exist (Prop. 5), therefore the cause of the truth and the necessity of the idea of B, which is in A, is B; and conversely the cause of the truth and the necessity of the idea of A, which is in B, is A. Therefore there will be in A a perfection that is not from A, and in B a perfection that is not from B. Therefore (Prop. 10) neither A nor B will be a God, and so there cannot be more than one God. Q.E.D.

Here it should be noted that, from the mere fact that some thing of itself involves necessary existence—as is the case with God—it necessarily follows that it is unique.[65] This is something that everyone can see for himself with careful thought, and I could have demonstrated it here, but not in a manner as comprehensible to all as is done in this proposition.

Proposition 12.

All things that exist are preserved solely by the power of God.

Proof.

If you deny this, suppose that something preserves itself. Therefore (Lemma 2 Prop. 7) its nature involves necessary existence. Thus (Corollary Lemma 1 Prop. 7) it would be God, and there would be more than one God, which is absurd (Prop. 11). Therefore everything that exists is preserved solely by the power of God. Q.E.D.

Corollary 1.

God is the creator of all things.

---

65. On Spinoza's arguments for the uniqueness of substance, see E1P10Schol; E1P14; E1P14Cor1; Ep34; Ep35, 204–205; Ep50, 259–260.

Proof.

God preserves all things (Prop. 12); that is (Ax. 10), he has created, and still continuously creates, everything that exists.

Corollary 2.

Things of themselves do not have any essence that is the cause of God's knowledge. On the contrary, God is also the cause of things with respect to their essence.

Proof.

Because there is not to be found in God anything of perfection that is not from God (Prop. 10), things of themselves will not have any essence that can be the cause of God's knowledge. On the contrary, because God has created all things wholly, not generating them from something else (Prop. 12 with Cor. 1), and because the act of creation acknowledges no other cause but the efficient cause (for this is how I define 'creation'), which is God, it follows that before their creation things were nothing at all, and therefore God was also the cause of their essence. Q.E.D.

It should be noted that this corollary is also evident from the fact that God is the cause or creator of all things (Cor. 1) and that the cause must contain in itself all the perfections of the effect (Ax. 8), as everyone can readily see.

Corollary 3.

Hence it clearly follows that God does not sense, nor, properly speaking, does he perceive. For his intellect is not determined by anything external to himself; all things derive from him.

Corollary 4.

God is prior in causality to the essence and existence of things, as clearly follows from Corollaries 1 and 2 of this Proposition.

Proposition 13.

God is supremely truthful, and not at all a deceiver.[66]

Proof.

We cannot attribute to God anything in which we find any imperfection (Def. 8); and because (as is self-evident) all deception or will to deceive proceeds only from malice or fear, and fear supposes diminished power while malice supposes privation of goodness, no deception or will to deceive is to be ascribed to God, a being supremely powerful and supremely good. On the contrary, he must be said to be supremely truthful and not at all a deceiver. Q.E.D. See "Replies to the Second Set of Objections," No. 4.[67]

Proposition 14.

Whatever we clearly and distinctly perceive is true.

Proof.

The faculty of distinguishing true from false, which is in us (as everyone can discover in himself, and as is obvious from all that has already been proved) has been created and is continuously preserved by God (Prop. 12 with Cor.), that is, by a being supremely truthful and not at all a deceiver (Prop. 13), and he has not bestowed on us (as everyone can discover in himself) any faculty for holding aloof from, or refusing assent to, those things that we clearly and distinctly perceive. Therefore if we were to be deceived in regard to them, we should be deceived entirely by God, and he would be a deceiver, which is absurd (Prop. 13). So whatever we clearly and distinctly perceive is true. Q.E.D.

---

66. I have not included this axiom among the axioms because it was not at all necessary. I had no need of it except for the proof of this proposition alone, and furthermore, as long as I did not know God's existence, I did not wish to assume as true anything more than what I could deduce from the first known thing, 'I am', as I said in the Scholium to Proposition 4. Again, I have not included among my definitions the definitions of fear and malice because everyone knows them, and I have no need of them except for this one proposition. [Spinoza]
67. AT7, 142–147.

Scholium.

Because those things to which we must necessarily assent when they are clearly and distinctly perceived by us are necessarily true, and because we have a faculty for withholding assent from those things that are obscure or doubtful or are not deduced from the most certain principles—as everyone can see in himself—it clearly follows that we can always take precautions against falling into error and against ever being deceived (a point that will be understood even more clearly from what follows), provided that we make an earnest resolution to affirm nothing that we do not clearly and distinctly perceive or that is not deduced from first principles clear and certain in themselves.

Proposition 15.

Error is not anything positive.

Proof.

If error were something positive, it would have as its cause only God, by whom it must be continuously created (Prop. 12). But this is absurd (Prop. 13). Therefore error is not anything positive. Q.E.D.[68]

Scholium.[69]

Because error is not anything positive in man, it can be nothing else than the privation of the right use of freedom (Schol. Prop. 14). Therefore God must not be said to be the cause of error, except in the sense in which we say that the absence of the sun is the cause of darkness, or that God, in making a child similar to others except for sight, is the cause of blindness. He is not to be said to be the cause of error in giving us an intellect that extends to only a few things. To understand this clearly, and also how error depends solely on the misuse of the will, and, finally, to understand how we may guard against error, let us recall to mind the modes of thinking that we

68. Cf. E2P33.
69. The account of error about to be explained is very different from that of Spinoza found at E2P47Schol; E2P48; E2P48Schol; E2P49Schol; Ep21, 154–158.

possess, namely, all modes of perceiving (sensing, imagining, and pure understanding) and modes of willing (desiring, misliking, affirming, denying, and doubting); for they can all be subsumed under these two headings. Now with regard to these modes we should note, first, that insofar as the mind understands things clearly and distinctly and assents to them, it cannot be deceived (Prop. 14); nor again can it be deceived insofar as it merely perceives things and does not assent to them. For although I may now perceive a winged horse, it is certain that this perception contains nothing false as long as I do not assent to the truth that there is a winged horse, nor again as long as I doubt whether there is a winged horse. And because to assent is nothing but to determine the will, it follows that error depends only on the use of the will.

To make this even clearer, we should note, secondly, that we have the power to assent not only to those things that we clearly and distinctly perceive but also to those things that we perceive in any other way. For our will is not determined by any limits. Everyone can clearly see this if only he attends to the following point, that if God had wished to make infinite our faculty of understanding, he would not have needed to give us a more extensive faculty of willing than that which we already possess in order to enable us to assent to all that we understand. That which we already possess would be sufficient for assenting to an infinite number of things.[70] And in fact experience tells us, too, that we assent to many things that we have not deduced from sure first principles. Furthermore, these considerations make it clear that if the intellect extended as widely as the faculty of willing, or if the faculty of willing could not extend more widely than the intellect, or if, finally, we could restrict the faculty of willing within the limits of the intellect, we would never fall into error (Prop. 14).

But the first two possibilities lie beyond our power, for they would involve that the will should not be infinite and the intellect created finite. So it remains for us to consider the third possibility, namely, whether we have the power to restrict our faculty of willing within the limits of the intellect. Now because the will is free to determine itself, it follows that we do have the power to restrict the faculty of assenting within the limits of the intellect, therefore bringing it about that we do not fall into error. Hence it is quite manifest that our never being deceived depends entirely on the use of the freedom of the will. That our will is free is demonstrated in Art. 39

70. Cf. Med4, 38 (AT7, 56–57).

Part 1 of the *Principia* and in the "Fourth Meditation,"[71] and is also shown at some length by me in the last chapter of my Appendix. And although, when we perceive a thing clearly and distinctly, we cannot refrain from assenting to it, that necessary assent depends not on the weakness but simply on the freedom and perfection of the will. For to assent to the truth is a perfection in us (as is self-evident), and the will is never more perfect and more free than when it completely determines itself.[72] Because this can occur when the mind understands something clearly and distinctly, it will necessarily give itself this perfection at once (Ax. 3). Therefore we by no means understand ourselves to be less free because we are not at all indifferent in embracing truth. On the contrary, we take it as certain that the more indifferent we are, the less free we are.

So now it remains only to be explained how error is nothing but privation with respect to man, whereas with respect to God it is mere negation. This will easily be seen if we first observe that our perceiving many things besides those that we clearly understand makes us more perfect than if we did not perceive them. This is clearly established from the fact that, if it were supposed that we could perceive nothing clearly and distinctly but only confusedly, we should possess nothing more perfect than this perceiving things confusedly, nor would anything else be expected of our nature. Furthermore, to assent to things, however confused, insofar as it is also a kind of action, is a perfection. This will also be obvious to everyone if he supposes, as previously, that it is contrary to man's nature to perceive things clearly and distinctly. For then it will become quite clear that it is far better for a man to assent to things, however confused, and to exercise his freedom, than to remain always indifferent, that is (as we have just shown), at the lowest grade of freedom. And if we also turn our attention to the needs and convenience of human life, we shall find this absolutely necessary, as experience teaches each of us every day.

Therefore, because all the modes of thinking that we possess are perfect insofar as they are regarded in themselves alone, to that extent that which constitutes the form of error cannot be in them. But if we attend to the way in which modes of willing differ from one another, we shall find that some are more perfect than others in that some render the will less indifferent

71. This is not literally true. Neither in PPH nor in the *Meditations* does Descartes attempt any demonstration of freedom of will, but rather claims that it is a datum of our ordinary experience; see Med4, 38–39 (AT7, 57).
72. In Spinoza's mature thought, freedom lies not in decision but in necessity and being determined. Cf. Ep58; E1P17, Cors. and Schol.

(i.e., more free) than others. Again, we shall also see that, as long as we assent to confused things, we make our minds less apt to distinguish true from false, thereby depriving ourselves of the highest freedom. Therefore to assent to confused things, insofar as this is something positive, does not contain any imperfection or the form of error; it does so only insofar as we thus deprive our own selves of the highest freedom that is within reach of our nature and is within our power. So the imperfection of error will consist entirely merely in the privation of the highest freedom, a privation that is called error. Now it is called privation because we are deprived of a perfection that is compatible with our nature, and it is called error because it is our own fault that we lack this perfection, in that we fail to restrict the will within the limits of the intellect, as we are able to do. Therefore, because error is nothing else with respect to man but the privation of the perfect or correct use of freedom, it follows that it does not lie in any faculty that he has from God, nor again in any operation of his faculties insofar as this depends on God.[73] Nor can we say that God has deprived us of the greater intellect that he might have given us and has thereby brought it about that we could fall into error. For no thing's nature can demand anything from God, and nothing belongs to a thing except what the will of God has willed to bestow on it. For nothing existed, or can even be conceived, prior to God's will (as is fully explained in our Appendix Part 2 Chapters 7 and 8). Therefore God has not deprived us of a greater intellect or a more perfect faculty of understanding any more than he has deprived a circle of the properties of a sphere, and a circumference of the properties of a spherical surface.

So because none of our faculties, in whatever way it be considered, can point to any imperfection in God, it clearly follows that the imperfection in which the form of error consists is privation only with respect to man. When related to God as its cause, it can be termed not privation, but only negation.

Proposition 16.

God is incorporeal.

73. Med4, 36–39 (AT7, 54–58).

Proof.

Body is the immediate subject of local motion (Def. 7). Therefore if God were corporeal, he would be divided into parts; and this, since it clearly involves imperfection, it is absurd to affirm of God (Def. 8).[74]

Another proof.

If God were corporeal, he could be divided into parts (Def. 7). Now either each single part could subsist of itself, or it could not. If the latter, it would be like the other things created by God, and thus, like every created thing, it would be continuously created by the same force by God (Prop. 10 and Ax. 11), and would not pertain to God's nature any more than other created things, which is absurd (Prop. 5). But if each single part exists through itself, each single part must also involve necessary existence (Lemma 2 Prop. 7), and consequently each single part would be a supremely perfect being (Cor. Lemma 2 Prop. 7). But this, too, is absurd (Prop. 11). Therefore God is incorporeal. Q.E.D.

Proposition 17.

God is a completely simple being.

Proof.

If God were composed of parts, the parts (as all will readily grant) would have to be at least prior in nature to God, which is absurd (Cor. 4 Prop. 12). Therefore he is a completely simple being. Q.E.D.

Corollary.

Hence it follows that God's intelligence, his will or decree, and his power are not distinguished from his essence, except by abstract reasoning.[75]

---

74. On God's indivisibility, see E1P13. On Spinoza's consideration that the divine nature is corporeal, see E1P15Schol.
75. Spinoza would agree that God's will and intelligence are the same (E2P49Cor) and that God's power and essence are one (E1P34).

Proposition 18.

God is immutable.[76]

Proof.

If God were mutable, he could not change in part, but would have to change with respect to his whole essence (Prop. 17). But the essence of God exists necessarily (Props. 5, 6 and 7). Therefore God is immutable. Q.E.D.

Proposition 19.

God is eternal.

Proof.

God is a supremely perfect being (Def. 8), from which it follows that he exists necessarily (Prop. 5). If now we attribute to him limited existence, the limits of his existence must necessarily be understood, if not by us, at any rate by God himself (Prop. 9), because he has understanding in the highest degree. Therefore God will understand himself (i.e. [Def. 8], a supremely perfect being) as not existing beyond these limits, which is absurd (Prop. 5). Therefore God has not a limited but an infinite existence, which we call eternity. See Chapter 1 Part 2 of our Appendix. Therefore God is eternal. Q.E.D.[77]

Proposition 20.

God has preordained all things from eternity.

Proof.

Because God is eternal (Prop. 19), his understanding is eternal, because it pertains to his eternal essence (Cor. Prop. 17). But his intellect is not different in reality from his will or decree (Cor. Prop. 17). Therefore when

---

76. For Spinoza, the immutability of God takes a decidedly un-Cartesian twist; see E1P20Cor2; E1P33Schol2.
77. Cf. E1P19, Dem, Schol.

we say that God has understood things from eternity, we are also saying that he has willed or decreed things thus from eternity. Q.E.D.[78]

Corollary.

From this proposition it follows that God is in the highest degree constant in his works.

Proposition 21.

Substance extended in length, breadth, and depth exists in reality, and we are united to one part of it.

Proof.

That which is extended, as it is clearly and distinctly perceived by us, does not pertain to God's nature (Prop. 16), but it can be created by God (Cor. Prop. 7 and Prop. 8). Furthermore, we clearly and distinctly perceive (as everyone can discover in himself, insofar as he thinks) that extended substance is a sufficient cause for producing in us pleasure, pain, and similar ideas or sensations, which are continually produced in us even against our will. But if we wish to suppose some other cause for our sensations apart from extended substance—say, God or an angel—we immediately destroy the clear and distinct concept that we have. Therefore,[79] as long as we correctly attend to our perceptions so as to allow nothing but what we clearly and distinctly perceive, we shall be altogether inclined, or by no means uninclined, to accept that extended substance is the only cause of our sensations, and therefore to affirm that the extended thing exists, created by God. And in this we surely cannot be deceived (Prop. 14 with Schol.). Therefore it is truly affirmed that substance extended in length, breadth, and depth exists. This was the first point.[80]

Furthermore, among our sensations, which must be produced in us (as we have already proved) by extended substance, we observe a considerable difference, as when I say that I sense or see a tree or when I say that I am thirsty, or in pain, etc. But I clearly see that I cannot perceive the cause of

---

78. Spinoza would agree; see E1P29; E1P33Schol2.
79. See the proof to Proposition 14 and the Scholium to Proposition 15. [Spinoza]
80. Cf. Med6, 51–52 (AT7, 78–80).

this difference unless I first understand that I am closely united to one part of matter, and not so to other parts. Because I clearly and distinctly understand this, and I cannot perceive it in any other way, it is true (Prop. 14 with Schol.) that I am united to one part of matter. This was the second point. We have therefore proved what was to be proved.[81]

Note: Unless the reader here considers himself only as a thinking thing, lacking body, and unless he puts aside as prejudices all the reasons that he previously entertained for believing that body exists, his attempts to understand this proof will be in vain.[82]

End of Part 1.

81. Namely that we (as a thinking thing) are united to matter. See Med6, 52–53 (AT7, 80–81).
82. The demonstration with which Spinoza closes PPC1 is in fact drawn from PPH2A1–2 of Descartes. A2 seems to make the exposition of Cartesian physics depend upon the proof of the union of body and soul—a union that Descartes has already admitted is incomprehensible. By placing this material at the end of PPC1 rather than at the beginning of the physical theory in PPC2, Spinoza may have wished to disassociate the presentation of Cartesian physics from the nongeometrical topics discussed in the first part of the text, allowing the physics to be developed independently of these. See André Lécrivain, "Spinoza et la physique cartésienne (suite): la Partie II des *Principia*," *Cahiers Spinoza* 2 (1978), pp. 93–206, esp. 96–102 for a more extensive discussion of this demonstration and the implications of Spinoza's changes. Henceforth this work is simply referenced as Lécrivain.

The PRINCIPLES OF PHILOSOPHY

demonstrated in the geometric manner.

Part 2.

Postulate.

Here the only requirement is that everyone should attend to his perceptions as accurately as possible, so that he may distinguish what is clear from what is obscure.

Definitions.

1. *Extension* is that which consists of three dimensions. But by extension we do not understand the act of extending, or anything distinct from quantity.[83]

2. By *Substance* we understand that which, in order to exist, needs only the concurrence of God.[84]

3. An *atom* is a part of matter indivisible by its own nature.

4. The *indefinite* is that whose bounds, if it has any, cannot be discovered by human intellect.

5. A *vacuum* is extension without corporeal substance.

6. *Space* is to be distinguished from extension only in thought; there is no difference in reality. Read Art. 10 Part 2 of the *Principia*.

---

83. Extension is here identified with quantity (*quantitas*), the term that Spinoza will use in Ep12 and E1P15Schol to develop his own and different account of extension. The proviso that it does not imply activity (*actus extendendi*) is intended, at least by Descartes, to make local motion (*motus localis*) logically and ontologically distinct from it (see Def8 later). When extension is treated by Spinoza as an infinite attribute, local motion is introduced as an infinite mode, and the notion of *actus extendendi* becomes appropriate. Perhaps this is what Spinoza means in writing to Tschirnhaus (Ep83) that Descartes's definition of extension is completely wrong.

84. This is one of Descartes's two (incompatible) definitions of substance. Spinoza will introduce the other later and make no effort at reconciliation. See our introduction.

45

7. That which in our thinking we understand to be divided is *divisible,* at least potentially.

8. *Local motion* is the transfer of one part of matter, or of one body, from the vicinity of those bodies that are immediately contiguous and are regarded as at rest, to the vicinity of other bodies.
This is the definition used by Descartes to explain local motion. To understand this definition correctly, we should consider:

8.1. That by a part of matter he understands all that which is transferred together, although it may in turn consist of many parts.[85]

8.2. That, to avoid confusion, in this definition he refers only to that which is constantly in the moving thing in motion, that is, its being transferred. So this should not be confused, as is commonly done by others, with the force or action that effects the transfer. This force or action is commonly thought to be required only for motion and not for rest, an opinion that is plainly wrong. For, as is self-evident, the same force that is required to impart fixed degrees of motion to a body that is at rest is again required for the withdrawal of those fixed degrees of motion from the same body, and for bringing it entirely to rest. Indeed, this can also be proved by experience, for we use about the same force to propel a boat that is at rest in still water as to halt it suddenly when it is moving. In fact, it would be exactly the same, were we not helped in halting the boat by the weight and resistance of the water displaced by it.

8.3. That he says that the transfer takes place from the vicinity of contiguous bodies to the vicinity of others, and not from one place to another. For place (as he himself has explained in Art. 13 Part 2) is not something real, but depends only on our thought, so that the same body may be said at the same time to change, and not to change, its place. But it cannot be said at the same time to be transferred, and not to be transferred, from the vicinity of a contiguous body. For only certain definite bodies can, at the same moment of time, be contiguous to the same movable body.

---

85. This is the basis of the Cartesian formulation of the individuation of bodies: an individual body is characterized by those parts that are transferred together in local motion (*id omne quod simul transfertur*). The difficulty is that it makes individuation wholly relative, like local motion itself. Spinoza will later develop a dynamic concept of individuation in response to just this weakness in Descartes's account. See Frederick Ablondi and Steven Barbone, "Individual Identity in Descartes and Spinoza," *Studia Spinozana* 10 (1996), 69–92. For a discussion of the development of Spinoza's critique of Descartes on individuation, see Lécrivain, 110–114.

8.4. That he does not say, without qualification, that the transfer takes place from the vicinity of contiguous bodies, but only from the vicinity of contiguous bodies that are regarded as at rest. For in order that a body A may be moved away from a body B, which is at rest, the same force and action are required on the one side as on the other. This is evident in the example of a boat that is sticking to the mud or sand at the bottom of the water. To push it forward, an equal force must be applied to the bottom as to the boat. Therefore the force by which bodies are to be moved is expended equally on the moved body and on the body at rest. The transfer is indeed reciprocal; if the boat is separated from the sand, the sand is also separated from the boat. Therefore, when bodies separate from one another, if we were to attribute to them without qualification equal motions in opposite directions, refusing to regard one of them as at rest simply on the grounds that there is the same action in the one case as in the other, then we should also be compelled to attribute to bodies that are universally regarded as at rest (e.g., the sand from which the boat is separated) the same amount of motion as to the moving bodies. For, as we have shown, the same action is required on the one side as on the other, and the transfer is reciprocal. But this would be too remote from the normal usages of language. However, although those bodies from which other bodies are separated are regarded as at rest and are also spoken of in this way, we shall remember that everything in the moving body on account of which it is said to move is also in the body at rest.

8.5. Finally, that it is also clear from the definition that each body possesses only one motion peculiar to itself because it is understood to move away only from one set of bodies contiguous to it and at rest. However, if the moving body forms part of other bodies having other motions, we clearly understand that it can also participate in innumerable other motions. But because it is not easy to understand so many motions at the same time, or even to recognize them all, it will be sufficient to consider in each body that unique motion, which is peculiar to it. See Art. 31 Part 2 *Principia.*

9. By a circle of moving bodies we understand only a formation where the last body, in motion because of the impulse of another body, immediately touches the first of the moving bodies, even though the figure formed by all the bodies together through the impulse of a single motion may be very contorted.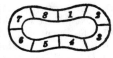

Axioms.[86]

1. To nothing there belong no properties.[87]
2. Whatever can be taken away from a thing without impairing its integrity does not constitute the thing's essence. But that whose removal destroys a thing constitutes its essence.
3. In the case of hardness, our sense indicates to us nothing else, and we clearly and distinctly understand of it nothing else, than that the parts of hard bodies resist the movement of our hands.[88]
4. If two bodies approach each other, or move away from each other, they will not thereby occupy more or less space.
5. A part of matter, whether it gives way or resists, does not thereby lose the nature of body.
6. Motion, rest, figure, and the like cannot be conceived without extension.
7. Apart from its sensible qualities, nothing remains in body but extension and its affections enumerated in Part 1 of *Principia*.
8. Any one space or extension cannot be greater at one time than at another.
9. All extension can be divided, at least in thought.

No one who has learned even the elements of mathematics doubts the truth of this axiom. For the space between a tangent and a circle can always be divided by an infinite number of larger circles. The same point is also made obvious by the asymptotes of the hyperbola.

10. No one can conceive the boundaries of an extension or space without at the same time conceiving other spaces beyond those boundaries, immediately following on that space.
11. If matter is manifold, and one piece is not in immediate contact with another, each piece is necessarily comprehended within boundaries beyond which there is no matter.
12. The most minute bodies readily give way to the movement of our hands.
13. One space does not penetrate another space, nor is it greater at one time than at another.
14. If a hollow pipe A is of the same length as C, and C is twice as wide as A, and if a liquid passes through pipe A at twice the speed at which a

86. For an analysis of the logical relations in Spinoza's restructuring of the Cartesian axioms, see Lécrivain, 114–117.
87. This axiom is the basis of the Cartesian rejection of the existence of a vacuum in nature, a rejection which Spinoza continued to accept. See Ep12, 103.
88. Spinoza's own definition of hard bodies is at E2P13Ax3.

liquid passes through pipe C, the same amount of matter will pass through both pipes in the same space of time. And if in the same time the same amount of matter passes through pipe A as through C, the former will move at twice the speed.

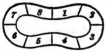

15. Things that agree with a third thing agree with one another; and things that are double a third thing are equal to one another.

16. Matter that moves in diverse ways has at least as many parts, divided in actuality, as there are different degrees of speed to be observed in it at the same time.

17. The shortest line between two points is a straight line.

18. If a body A moving from C toward B is repelled by an opposite impulse, it will move along the same line toward C.

19. When bodies having opposite motions collide with each other, they are both—or at least one of them—compelled to undergo some change.

20. A change in any thing proceeds from a stronger force.

21. When body 1 moves toward body 2 and pushes it, if as a result of this impulse body 8 moves toward body 1, then bodies 1, 2, 3, etc., cannot be in a straight line, and all eight bodies form a complete circle. See Def. 9.

Lemma 1.[89]

Where there is extension or space, there is necessarily substance.

Proof.

Extension or space (Ax. 1) cannot be pure nothing. It is therefore an attribute that must be attributed to some thing, but not to God (Prop. 16 Part 1); therefore it must be attributed to a thing that needs only the concurrence of God to exist (Prop. 12 Part 1), that is (Def. 2 Part 2), to substance. Q.E.D.

---

89. The lemmas are intended to prevent any contamination of intellectual knowledge by the prejudices of imagination. See Lécrivain, 117–118.

Lemma 2.

Rarefaction and condensation are clearly and distinctly conceived by us, although we do not grant that bodies occupy more space in rarefaction than in condensation.

Proof.

Rarefaction and condensation can be clearly and distinctly conceived from the mere fact that parts of a body may move away from, or toward, one another. Therefore (Ax. 4) they will not occupy either more or less space. For if the parts of a body—say, a sponge—by moving toward one another expel the bodies with which its interstices are filled, this in itself will make that body more dense, and its parts will not thereby occupy less space than before (Ax. 4). And if again the parts move away from one another and the gaps are filled by other bodies, there will be rarefaction, but the parts will not occupy more space. And this, which we clearly perceive with the aid of our senses in the case of a sponge, we can conceive with the unaided intellect in the case of all bodies, although their interstices completely escape human sense-perception. Therefore rarefaction and condensation are clearly and distinctly conceived by us, etc. Q.E.D.

I have thought it advisable to set out these Lemmas first, so that the intellect may rid itself of prejudices concerning space, rarefaction, etc., and be rendered apt to understand what is to follow.

Proposition 1.

Although hardness, weight, and the other sensible qualities may be separated from a body, the nature of the body will nevertheless remain unimpaired.[90]

Proof.

In the case of hardness—say, of this stone—our sense-perception indicates

---

90. Lécrivain's comment on the first six propositions, which outline the essence of extension, is worth quoting here: "The author is here producing a reevaluation and critical reelaboration of the significance of the principal Cartesian concepts of extension, which he does without doubt adopt as valid, but only by conferring upon them, by an analysis which is both radical and deep, a new orientation and a different direction" (119, translation ours).

to us nothing else, and we clearly and distinctly understand nothing else, than that the parts of hard bodies resist the movement of our hands (Ax. 3). Therefore (Prop. 14 Part 1) hardness also will be nothing else but this. Indeed, if the said body is reduced to the finest powder, its parts will readily give way (Ax. 12); yet it will not lose the nature of body (Ax. 5). Q.E.D.

In the case of weight and the other sensible qualities, the proof proceeds in the same way.

Proposition 2.

The nature of body or matter consists only in extension.

Proof.

The nature of body is not lost as a result of the loss of sensible qualities (Prop. 1 Part 2). Therefore these do not constitute its essence (Ax. 2). Therefore nothing is left but extension and its affections (Ax. 7). So if extension be taken away, nothing will remain pertaining to the nature of body, and it will be completely annulled. Therefore (Ax. 2) the nature of body consists only in extension. Q.E.D.

Corollary.

Space and body do not differ in reality.

Proof.

Body and extension do not differ in reality (previous Prop.), and also space and extension do not differ in reality (Def. 6). Therefore (Ax. 15) space and body do not differ in reality. Q.E.D.

Scholium.

Although we say that God is everywhere,[91] it is not thereby admitted that God is extended (i.e. [previous Prop.], that God is corporeal). For his ubiquity refers only to God's power and his concurrence whereby he

---

91. On this, see a fuller explanation in Appendix, Part 2, Chapters 3 and 9. [Spinoza]

preserves all things, so that God's ubiquity does not refer to body or extension any more than to angels and human souls. But it should be noted that when we say that his power is everywhere, we do not exclude his essence; for where his power is, there too is his essence (Cor. Prop. 17 Part 1). We intend to exclude only bodily nature; that is, we mean that God is everywhere not by a corporeal power but by his divine power or essence, which serves alike to preserve extension and thinking things (Prop. 17 Part 1). The latter he certainly could not have preserved if his power, that is, his essence, were corporeal.[92]

Proposition 3.

That there should be a vacuum is a contradiction.

Proof.

By a vacuum is understood extension without corporeal substance (Def. 3); that is (Prop. 2 Part 2), body without body, which is absurd.

For a fuller explanation, and to correct prejudice concerning the vacuum, read Articles 17 and 18 Part 2 of the *Principia*, where it should be particularly noted that bodies between which nothing lies must necessarily touch one another, and also that to nothing there belong no properties.[93]

Proposition 4.

One part of a body does not occupy more space at one time than at another; and, conversely, the same space does not contain more body at one time than at another.

92. This scholium summarizes the principal themes of the correspondence between Descartes and Morus, the latter refusing to identify matter with extension and following the general analysis of Cambridge Platonists such as Henry More in distinguishing divine from material extension. Spinoza's own position will be in disagreement with both Descartes and Morus by making material extension an attribute of God. See E2P2; Lécrivain, 123–127.

93. On Spinoza's thoughts on the possibility of a vacuum, see E1P15Schol, 42; Ep13, 112–113; Jonathan Bennett, "Spinoza's Vacuum Argument," *Midwest Studies in Philosophy* 5 (1980), 99–106.

Proof.

Space and body do not differ in reality (Cor. Prop. 2 Part 2). Therefore when we say that a space is not greater at one time than at another (Ax. 13), we are also saying that a body cannot be greater (i.e., occupy more space) at one time than at another, which was our first point. Furthermore, from the fact that space and body do not differ in reality, it follows that when we say that body cannot occupy more space at one time than at another, we are also saying that the same space cannot contain more body at one time than at another. Q.E.D.

Corollary.

Bodies that occupy equal space—say, gold and air—have the same amount of matter or corporeal substance.

Proof.

Corporeal substance consists not in hardness (e.g., of gold) nor in softness (e.g., of air) nor in any of the sensible qualities (Prop. 1 Part 2), but only in extension (Prop. 2 Part 2). Now because, by hypothesis, there is the same amount of space or (Def. 6) extension in the one as in the other; therefore there will also be the same amount of corporeal substance. Q.E.D.

Proposition 5.

There are no atoms.

Proof.

Atoms are parts of matter that are, by their own nature, indivisible (Def. 3). But because the nature of matter consists in extension (Prop. 2 Part 2), which by its own nature is divisible, however small it be (Ax. 9 and Def. 7); therefore however small a part of matter may be, it is by its own nature divisible. That is, there are no atoms, or parts of matter that are by their own nature indivisible. Q.E.D.

Scholium.

The question of atoms has always been a difficult and complicated one.

Some assert that there must be atoms, arguing from the impossibility of an infinite being greater than another infinite; and if two quantities—say A and its double—are infinitely divisible, they can also be divided in actuality into an infinite number of parts by the power of God, who understands their infinitely many parts with a single intuition. Therefore, because one infinite cannot be greater than another infinite, as has been said, quantity A will be equal to its double, which is absurd. Then again, they ask whether half an infinite number is also infinite, and whether it is even or odd, and other such questions. To all this Descartes replied that we must not reject what comes within the scope of our intellect, and is therefore clearly and distinctly conceived, because of other things that exceed our intellect or grasp, and that are therefore only perceived very inadequately by us. Now the infinite and its properties exceed the human intellect because that is by nature finite.[94] And so it would be foolish to reject as false, or to doubt, what we clearly and distinctly conceive concerning space, on the grounds that we do not comprehend the infinite. And for this reason Descartes considers as indefinite those things in which we can see no boundaries, such as the extension of the world, the divisibility of the parts of matter, etc. Read Art. 26 Part 1 of the *Principia*.

Proposition 6.

Matter is indefinitely[95] extended, and the matter of the heavens and the earth is one and the same.

Proof.

1. We cannot imagine the boundaries of extension, that is (Prop. 2 Part 2)

94. Spinoza, of course, rejects the claim that infinity exceeds the human intellect and also the claim that one infinite quantity cannot be greater than another (see Ep12). He appears to be following Galileo rather than Descartes, but his reasoning for the existence of infinities of different magnitudes is different from that of Galileo. See Alexandre Koyré, "Bonaventura Cavalieri et la géométrie des continus," in *Etudes d'Histoire de la Pensée Scientifique* (Paris: Presses Universitaires de France, 1978), 297–324; Lee Rice, "Spinoza's Infinite Extension," *History of European Ideas* 22 (1996b), 33–43.
95. The notion of the indefinite was Descartes's hedge against attributing to nature a property (infinity) customarily reserved for God. See Steven Barbone, "Infinity in Descartes," *Philosophical Inquiry* 17 (1995a), 297–307.

of matter, without conceiving other spaces immediately following or beyond them (Ax. 10), that is, without conceiving extension or matter (Def. 6)
beyond them, and so on indefinitely. This was the first point.
   2. The essence of matter consists in extension (Prop. 2 Part 2), and this is
indefinite (first part of this proof); that is, it cannot be conceived by the
human intellect as having any boundaries. Therefore (Ax. 11) it is not a
manifold but everywhere one and the same. That was the second point.

Scholium.

So far we have been dealing with the nature or essence of extension. The
fact that it exists such as we conceive it, created by God, we have proved in
the last Proposition of Part 1, and from Prop. 12 Part 1, it follows that it is
now preserved by the same power by which it was created. Then again, in
that same last Proposition of Part 1, we proved that, insofar as we are
thinking things, we are united to some part of matter, by whose help we
perceive that there are in actuality all those variations whereof, by merely
contemplating matter, we know it to be capable. Such are divisibility and
local motion or movement of one part from one place to another, which we
clearly and distinctly perceive provided that we understand that other parts
of matter take the place of those that move. And this division and motion
are conceived by us in infinite ways, and therefore infinite variations of
matter can also be conceived. I say that they are clearly and distinctly
conceived by us as long as we conceive them as modes of extension, not as
things distinct in reality from extension, as is fully explained in *Principia*
Part 1. And although philosophers have fabricated any number of other
motions, because we admit nothing but what we clearly and distinctly
conceive, and because we do not clearly and distinctly understand extension to be capable of any motion except local motion, nor does any other
motion even come within the scope of our imagination, we must not admit
any other motion but local motion.
   But Zeno,[96] so it is said, denied local motion and did so for various
reasons that Diogenes the Cynic refuted in his own way, by walking about
the school where Zeno was teaching these doctrines and disturbing his
listeners with his perambulations. When he saw that he was being held by

96. For a brief overview of Spinoza's treatment of Zeno, which is not derived from
Descartes, see our introduction. Lécrivain (131–144) provides a more detailed analysis, with Spinoza's possible sources.

one of the audience so as to prevent his wanderings, he rebuked him, saying: Why have you thus dared to refute your master's arguments? However, it may be that someone could be deceived by Zeno's arguments into thinking that the senses reveal to us something—in this case, motion—entirely opposed to the intellect, with the result that the mind may be deceived even concerning those things that it perceives clearly and distinctly with the aid of the intellect. To prevent this, I shall here set forth Zeno's principal arguments, showing that they rest only on false prejudices because he had no true conception of matter.

In the first place, then, he is reported to have said that, if local motion were granted, the motion of a body moving with a circular motion at the 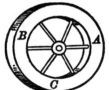 highest speed would be no different from a state of rest. But the latter is absurd; therefore so is the former. He proves the consequence as follows. A body whose every point remains constantly in the same place is at rest. But all the points of a body moving with a circular motion at the highest speed remain constantly in the same place; therefore, etc. He is said to have explained this by the example of a wheel, say, ABC. If the wheel were to move about its center at a certain speed, point A would complete a circle through B and C more quickly than if it were to move at a slower speed. So suppose, for example, that it begins to move slowly, and that after an hour it is in the same place from which it began. Now if it be supposed that it moves at twice that speed, it will be in the same place from which it began after half an hour; and if at four times the speed, after quarter of an hour. And if we conceive the speed to be infinitely increased and the time to be reduced to moments, then the point A at its highest speed will be at all moments, or constantly, in the place from which it began to move, and so it always remains in the same place. And what we understand about point A must also be understood about every point of the wheel. Therefore at the highest speed, all points remain constantly in the same place.

Now, in reply, it should be noted that this is an argument directed against motion's highest speed rather than against motion itself. But we shall not here examine the validity of Zeno's argument; we shall rather disclose the prejudices whereon all this argument depends insofar as it claims to attack motion. In the first place, he supposes that bodies can be conceived to move so quickly that they cannot move more quickly. Secondly, he supposes time to be made up of moments, just as others have conceived quantity to be

made up of indivisible points. Both of these suppositions are false. For we
can never conceive a motion so fast that we cannot at the same time
conceive a faster. It is contrary to our intellect to conceive a motion so fast,
however short be its course, that there can be no faster motion.

And the same holds true in the case of slowness. To conceive a motion so
slow that there cannot be a slower, involves a contradiction. And regarding
time, too, which is the measure of motion, we make the same assertion, that
it is clearly contrary to our intellect to conceive a time other than which
there can be none shorter.

To prove all this, let us follow in Zeno's footsteps. Let us suppose, with
him, that a wheel ABC moves about its center at such a speed that the point
A is at every mo-
ment in the posi-
tion A from which
it moves. I say that
I clearly conceive
a speed indefinite-
ly greater than this,

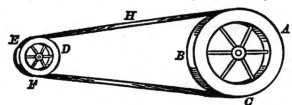

and consequently moments that are infinitely less. For let it be supposed
that while the wheel ABC moves about its center, with the help of a belt H
it causes another wheel, DEF, half its size, to move about its center. Now
because the wheel DEF is supposed to be half the size of the wheel ABC, it
is plain that the wheel DEF moves at twice the speed of the wheel ABC, and
consequently the point D is at every half-moment again in the same place
from which it began to move. Then if we assign the motion of the wheel
DEF to the wheel ABC, DEF will move four times faster than the original
speed, and if we again assign this last speed of the wheel DEF to the wheel
ABC, then DEF will move eight times as fast, and so *ad infinitum*.

But this is quite clear merely from the concept of matter. For the essence
of matter consists in extension, or ever-divisible space, as we have proved,
and there is no motion without space. We have also demonstrated that one
part of matter cannot occupy two spaces at the same time; for that would be
the same as saying that one part of matter is equal to its double, as is evident
from what has already been demonstrated. Therefore if a part of matter
moves, it moves through some space, a space that, however small it is
imagined to be, is nevertheless divisible, and consequently so is the time
through which the motion is measured. Consequently the duration of that
motion, or its time, is divisible, and is so to infinity. Q.E.D.

Let us now proceed to another fallacious problem, said to have been propounded by Zeno,[97] which is as follows. If a body moves, it moves either in the place in which it is, or in a place in which it is not. But not in a place in which it is; for if it is in any place, it must be at rest. Nor again in a place in which it is not. Therefore the body does not move. But this line of argument is just like the previous one, for it also supposes that there is a time other than which there is no shorter. If we reply that a body moves not in, but from, the place in which it is to a place in which it is not, he will ask whether it has not been in any intermediate places. We may reply by making a distinction: if by 'has been' he means 'has rested', we deny that it has been in any place while it was moving; but if by 'has been' is understood 'has existed', we say that it has necessarily existed while it was moving. He will again ask where it has existed while it was moving. We may once more reply that if by 'where it has existed' he means 'what place it has stayed in' while it was moving, we say that it did not stay in any place; but if he means 'what place it has changed', we say that it has changed all those places that he may wish to assign as belonging to the space through which it was moving. He will go on to ask whether at the same moment of time it could occupy and change its place. To this we finally reply by making the following distinction. If by a moment of time he means a time other than which there can be none shorter, he is asking an unintelligible question, as we have adequately shown, and thus one that does not deserve a reply. But if he takes time in the sense that I have explained previously (i.e., its true sense), he can never assign a time so short that in it a body cannot occupy and change place, even though the time is supposed to be able to be shortened indefinitely; and this is obvious to one who pays sufficient attention. Hence it is quite evident, as we said previously, that he is supposing a time so short that there cannot be a shorter, and so he proves nothing.

Besides these two arguments, there is yet another argument of Zeno's in circulation, which can be read, together with its refutation, in Descartes's *Letters* Vol. l, penultimate letter.[98]

I should like my readers here to observe that I have opposed Zeno's reasonings with my own reasonings, and so I have refuted him by reason,

97. Some commentators suggest that this is the "flying arrow" paradox, but Spinoza's presentation is too brief to be certain of its structure or origin. Cf. Aristotle *Physics* 6, 9, 239b5, 30–32.

98. Spinoza probably refers to the Dutch translation of Descartes's letters: *Brieven*, tr. J.H. Glazemaker, Amsterdam, 1661. The letter mentioned is probably to Clerselier, June/July 1646, AT4, 445–447.

not by the senses, as did Diogenes. For the senses cannot produce for the seeker after truth anything other than the phenomena of Nature, by which he is determined to investigate their causes; they can never show to be false what the intellect clearly and distinctly grasps as true. This is the view we take, and so this is our method, to demonstrate our propositions with reasons clearly and distinctly perceived by the intellect, disregarding whatever the senses assert when that seems contrary to reason. The senses, as we have said, can do no more than determine the intellect to enquire into one thing rather than another; they cannot convict the intellect of falsity when it has clearly and distinctly perceived something.

Proposition 7.

No body moves into the place of another body unless at the same time that other body moves into the place of another body.

Proof. (See diagram of next Proposition.)

If you deny this, suppose, if it is possible, that a body A moves into the place of a body B, which I suppose to be equal to A and which does not give way from its own place. Therefore the space that contained only B, by hypothesis, now contains A and B, and so contains twice the amount of corporeal substance as it contained before, which is absurd (Prop. 4 Part 2). Therefore no body moves into the place of another, . . . , etc. Q.E.D.

Proposition 8.

When a body moves into the place of another body, at the same moment of time the place quitted by it is occupied by another body immediately contiguous to it.

Proof.

If a body B moves toward D, bodies A and C at the same moment of time will either move toward each other and touch each other, or they will not. If they move toward each other and touch each other, what we have proposed is granted. If they do not move toward each other and the entire space quitted by B lies between A and C, then a body equal to B (Cor. Prop. 2 Part 2 and Cor. Prop. 4 Part 2) lies between. But, by hypothesis, this is not B. Therefore it is another

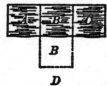

body, which at the same moment of time moves into B's place. And because it moves into B's place at the same moment of time, it can be none other than that which is immediately contiguous, according to Scholium Prop. 6 Part 2. For there we demonstrated that there can be no motion from one place to another such that it does not require a time other than which there is always a shorter time. From this it follows that the space of body B cannot be occupied at the same moment of time by another body that would have to move through some space before it moved into B's space. Therefore only a body immediately contiguous to B moves into its place at the same moment of time. Q.E.D.

Scholium.

Because the parts of matter are in reality distinct from one another (Art. 61 *Principia* Part 1), one can exist without another (Cor. Prop. 7 Part 1), and they do not depend on one another. So all those fictions about Sympathy and Antipathy must be rejected as false. Furthermore, because the cause of an effect must always be positive (Ax. 8 Part 1), it must never be said that a body moves to avoid there being a vacuum. It moves only through the impulse of another body.

Corollary.

In every motion, a complete circle of bodies moves at the same time.[99]

Proof.

At the time when body 1 moves into the place of body 2, body 2 must move into the place of another body, say, body 3, and so on (Prop. 7 Part 2). Again, at the same moment of time as body 1 moves into the place of body 2, the place quitted by body 1 must be occupied by another body (Prop. 8 Part 2), let us say body 8 or another body immediately contiguous to body 1. Because this oc-

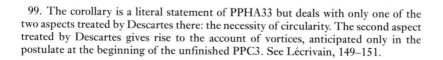

99. The corollary is a literal statement of PPHA33 but deals with only one of the two aspects treated by Descartes there: the necessity of circularity. The second aspect treated by Descartes gives rise to the account of vortices, anticipated only in the postulate at the beginning of the unfinished PPC3. See Lécrivain, 149–151.

curs only through the impulse of another body (Schol. to this Prop.), which is here supposed to be body 1, all these moving bodies cannot be in the same straight line (Ax. 21) but (Def. 9) form a complete circle. Q.E.D.

Proposition 9.

If a circular tube ABC is full of water and is four times as wide at A as at B, then at the time that the water (or any other fluid body) at A begins to move toward B, the water at B will move at four times that speed.

Proof.

When all the water at A moves toward B, the same amount of water must at the same time move into its place from C, which is immediately contiguous to A (Prop. 8 Part 2). And from B the same amount of water will have to move into the place of C (same Prop.). Therefore (Ax. 14) it will move at four times that speed. Q.E.D.

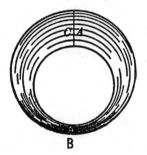

What we say about the circular tube must also apply to all unequal spaces through which bodies moving at the same time are compelled to pass; for the proof will be the same in the other cases.

Lemma.

If two semicircles A and B are described about the same center, the space between their circumferences will be everywhere the same. But if two semicircles C and D are described about different centers, the space between their circumferences will be everywhere unequal.

The proof is evident merely from the definition of a circle.[100]

---

100. This lemma underlines the mathematico-geometrical structure of the entire Cartesian theory of motion. Spinoza makes use of the same considerations in Ep12 (101–107). A detailed commentary on the model implied by the lemma is given by Martial Gueroult, *Spinoza, Dieu (Ethique I)* (Paris: Editions Aubier-Montaigne, 1968b), Appendix #9, 500–528.

Proposition 10.

The fluid body that moves through the tube ABC (of Prop. 9) receives an indefinite number of degrees of speed.

Proof.

The space between A and B is everywhere unequal (previous Lemma). Therefore (Prop. 9 Part 2) the speed at which the fluid body passes through the tube ABC will be unequal at all points. Furthermore, because we conceive in thought an indefinite number of spaces ever smaller and smaller between A and B (Prop. 5 Part 2), we shall also conceive its inequalities of speed, which are at all points, as indefinite. Therefore (Prop. 9 Part 2) the degrees of speed will be indefinite in number. Q.E.D.

Proposition 11.

The matter that flows through the tube ABC (of Prop. 9) is divided into an indefinite number of particles.

Proof.

The matter that flows through the tube ABC acquires at the same time an indefinite number of degrees of speed (Prop. 10 Part 2). Therefore (Ax. 16) it has an indefinite number of parts into which it is in reality divided. Q.E.D. Read Arts. 34 and 35 Part 2 of the *Principia*.

Scholium.

So far we have been dealing with the nature of motion. We should now enquire into its cause, which is twofold: (1) the primary or general cause, which is the cause of all the motions in the world, and (2) the particular cause, whereby it comes about that individual parts of matter acquire motions that they did not have before. As to the general cause, because we must admit nothing (Prop. 14 Part 1 and Schol. Prop. 15 Part 1)[101] but what we clearly and distinctly perceive, and because we clearly and distinctly understand no other cause than God, the creator of matter, it is obvious that

---

101. Here I deviate from Gebhardt to follow Hubbeling's emendation. [Tr.]

no other general cause but God must be admitted. And what we here say about motion must also be understood about rest.

Proposition 12.

God is the principal cause of motion.[102]

Proof.

See the immediately preceding Scholium.

Proposition 13.

God still preserves by his concurrence the same quantity of motion and rest that he originally gave to matter.

Proof.

Because God is the cause of motion and rest (Prop. 12 Part 2), he continues to preserve them by that same power by which he created them (Ax. 10 Part 1), the quantity also remaining the same as when he first created them (Cor. Prop. 20 Part 1). Q.E.D.

Scholium.

1. Although in theology it is said that God does many things at his own good pleasure and with the purpose of displaying his power to men, nevertheless, because those things that depend merely on his good pleasure are known by no other means than divine revelation, to prevent philosophy from being confused with theology, they are not to be admitted in philosophy, where enquiry is restricted to what reason tells us.[103]

2. Although motion is nothing but a mode of moving matter, it nevertheless has a fixed and determinate quantity. How this is to be understood will become evident from what follows. Read Art. 36 Part 2 of the *Principia*.

---

102. Propositions 12 to 37 provide a deductive derivation of the principal laws and rules of motion for Cartesian mechanics. These are based upon the principle of conservation of quantity of motion and rest (P11–P13) and the law of inertia (P14–P17).
103. This remark is probably a muted critique of Descartes: see PPH1A76.

Proposition 14.

Each single thing, insofar as it is simple and undivided and is considered only in itself, always perseveres in the same state, as far as in it lies.[104]

Many take this proposition as an axiom, but we shall demonstrate it.

Proof.

Because every thing is in a certain state only by the concurrence of God (Prop. 12 Part 1) and God is in the highest degree constant in his works (Cor. Prop. 20 Part 1), if we pay no attention to any external causes (i.e., particular causes) but consider the thing only in itself, we must affirm that as far as in it lies, it always perseveres in the state in which it is. Q.E.D.

Corollary.

A body that is once in motion always continues to move unless it is checked by external causes.

Proof.

This is obvious from the preceding proposition. But to correct prejudice concerning motion, read Arts. 37 and 38 Part 2 of the *Principia*.

Proposition 15.

Every body in motion tends of itself to continue to move in a straight line, not in a curved line.

This proposition could well be considered as an axiom, but I shall demonstrate it from the preceding, as follows.

---

104. See PPH2A37. The phrase, "as far as in it lies" (*quantum in se est*), is used by both Descartes and Newton in defining inertial force. Spinoza uses the same phrase in his definition of *conatus*: see E3P6 and Lee C. Rice, "Emotion, Appetition, and Conatus in Spinoza," *Revue Internationale de Philosophie* 31 (1977), 101–116. A detailed analysis of Spinoza's development of a dynamic notion of *conatus* in opposition to Descartes is also provided by Lécrivain, 158–165.

Proof.

Motion, having only God for its cause (Prop. 12 Part 2), never has of itself
any force to exist (Ax. 10 Part 1), but at every moment continues, as it were,
to be created by God (by what is demonstrated in connection with the
Axiom just cited). Therefore, although we attend only to the nature of the
motion, we can never attribute to it, as pertaining to its nature, a duration
that can be conceived as greater than another duration.[105] But if it is said
that it pertains to the nature of a moving body to describe by its movement
a curve, we should be attributing to the nature of motion a longer duration
than when it is supposed to be in the nature of a moving body to tend to
continue to move in a straight line (Ax. 17). Now because (as we have just
proved) we cannot attribute such duration to the nature of motion, then
neither can we posit that it is of the nature of a moving body to continue to
move in a curve; it must continue to move only in a straight line. Q.E.D.

Scholium.

Perhaps many will think that this proof is equally effective in showing that
it does not pertain to the nature of motion to describe a straight line as in
showing that it does not pertain to the nature of motion to describe a curved
line, and that this is so because there cannot be posited a straight line other
than which there is no shorter, whether straight or curved, nor any curved
line other than which there is no shorter curve. However, although I have
this in mind, I nevertheless hold that the proof proceeds correctly, because
it concludes what was required to be proved solely from the universal
essence of lines, that is, their essential specific difference, and not from the
length of individual lines, that is, their accidental specific difference. But to
avoid making more obscure, by my proof, a thing that is through itself quite
clear, I refer my readers to the simple definition of motion, which affirms
of motion nothing other than its being the transfer of one part of matter
from the vicinity . . ., etc., to the vicinity of other . . ., etc. So unless we
conceive this transfer in its simplest form—that is, as proceeding in a
straight line—we are attaching to motion something not contained in its
essence or definition, and so not pertaining to its nature.

---

105. Spinoza's proof is quite different from that given by Descartes in PPH2A30,
which seems to deny the intelligibility of the notion of motion at an instant.

Corollary.

From this Proposition it follows that every body that moves in a curve is continuously deviating from the line along which it would continue to move of itself, and this is through the force of an external cause (Prop. 14 Part 2).

Proposition 16.

Every body that moves in a circle (e.g., a stone in a sling) is continuously determined to continue in motion at a tangent to that circle.[106]

Proof.

A body that moves in a circle is continuously prevented by an external force from continuing to move in a straight line (Cor. previous Prop.). If this force ceases, the body will of itself proceed to move in a straight line (Prop. 15). Furthermore, I say that a body that moves in a circle is determined by an external cause to proceed to move at a tangent to the circle. If you deny

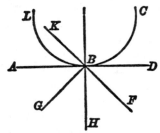

this, suppose that a stone at B is determined (e.g., by a sling) to move not along the tangent BD but along another line conceived as drawn without or within the circle from the same point. When the sling is supposed to be coming from L toward B, let this line be BF. If on the other hand the sling is supposed to be coming from C toward B, let this line be BG. If BH is the line drawn from the center through the circumference, which it cuts at B, I understand the angle GBH to be equal to the angle FBH. But if the stone at B is determined to proceed to move toward F by the sling moving in a circle from L toward B, then it necessarily follows (Ax. 18) that when the sling moves with a contrary determination from C toward B, the stone will be determined to proceed to move in line with BF with a contrary determination and will therefore tend not toward G but toward K. This is contrary to

---

106. Spinoza's argument here is much more elaborate than anything suggested by Descartes and may not even be consistent with Descartes. Spinoza treats the sling as cause of the stone's tangential tendency, whereas Descartes treats it as an impediment to rectilinear motion.

our hypothesis. And because no line except a tangent can be drawn through point B making equal adjacent angles, DBH, ABH, with the line BH,[107] there can be no line but a tangent that can preserve the same hypothesis, whether the sling moves from L to B or from C to B. And so the stone can tend to move along no line but the tangent. Q.E.D.

Another Proof.

Instead of a circle,[108] conceive a hexagon ABH inscribed in a circle, and a body C at rest on one side, AB. Then conceive that a ruler DBE, whose one end I suppose to be fixed at the center D while the other end is free, moves about the center D, continuously cutting the line AB. It is evident that if the ruler DBE, conceived to move in this way, meets the body C just when the ruler cuts the line AB at right angles, by its impact the ruler will determine the body C to proceed to move along the line FBAG toward G, that is, along the side AB produced indefinitely. But because we have chosen a hexagon at random, the same must be affirmed of any other figure that we conceive can be inscribed in a circle, namely, that when a body C, at rest on one side of the figure, is struck by the ruler DBE just when the ruler cuts that side at right angles, it will be determined by that ruler to proceed to move along that side produced indefinitely. Let us conceive, then, instead of a hexagon, a rectilinear figure having an infinite number of sides—that is, by Archimedes's definition, a circle. It is evident that, whenever the ruler DBE meets the body C, it always meets it just when it cuts some side of such a figure at right angles, and thus will never meet the body C without at the same time determining it to proceed to move along that side produced indefinitely. And because any side produced in either direction must always fall outside the figure, that side produced indefinitely will be the tangent to a figure of an infinite number of sides, that is, a circle. If, then, instead of a ruler we conceive a sling

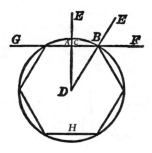

---

107. This is evident from Propositions 18 and 19 of Book 3 of the *Elements*. [Spinoza]
108. Spinoza's diagram is mislabeled. 'A' must be at the corner of the hexagon between B and G. In this alternative proof Spinoza substitutes the Archimedean concept of a circle for the Euclidean and provides a direct proof rather than a *reductio* argument. See Lécrivain, 169–170.

moving in a circle, this will continuously determine the stone to proceed to move at a tangent. Q.E.D.

It should here be noted that both of these proofs can be adapted to any curvilinear figure.

Proposition 17.

Every body that moves in a circle endeavors[109] to move away from the center of the circle that it describes.[110]

Proof

As long as a body moves in a circle, it is being compelled by some external cause; and if this ceases, it at once proceeds to move at a tangent to the

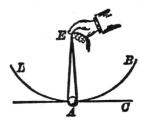

circle (previous Prop.). All the points of this tangent, except that which touches the circle, fall outside the circle (Prop. 16 Book 3 *Elements*) and are therefore further distant from the center. Therefore when a stone moving in a circle in a sling EA is at a point A, it endeavors to continue in a line, all of whose points are farther distant from the center E than any points on the circumference LAB. And this is nothing other than to endeavor to move away from the center of the circle that it describes. Q.E.D.

Proposition 18.

If a body A moves toward a body B, which is at rest, and B loses nothing of its state of rest in spite of the impetus of body A, then neither will A lose anything of its motion, but will retain entirely the same quantity of motion that it had before.

---

109. Spinoza replaces Descartes's *tendere* with *conari* here, another sign of the importance that the concept of *conatus* is to later assume in his own physics and psychology.

110. In the following proof, Spinoza follows Descartes in characterizing tangential motion as a combination of rectlinear centrifugal motion and circular motion. This analysis is also at the basis of Descartes's account of the vortices (see PPHA56–A59).

Proof.

If you deny this, suppose that body A loses some of its motion without transferring the lost motion to something else, say, to B. When this happens, there will be in Nature a smaller quantity of motion than before, which is absurd (Prop. 13 Part 2). The proof proceeds in the same way with respect to the state of rest of body B, therefore if the one body does not transfer anything to the other body, B will retain all its rest, and A, all its motion. Q.E.D.

Proposition 19.

Motion, regarded in itself, is different from its determination toward a certain direction; and there is no need for a moving body to be for any time at rest in order that it may travel or be repelled in an opposite direction.

Proof.

Suppose, as in the preceding proposition, that a body A moves in a straight line toward a body B and is prevented by body B from continuing further. Therefore (preceding Prop.) A will retain its motion undiminished, and it will not be at rest for even the smallest space of time. However, because it continues to move, it does not move in the same direction as before, for it is supposed to be prevented by B. Therefore, with its motion remaining undiminished and its previous determination lost, it will move in the opposite direction, and not any other (see what is said in Chapter 2 *Dioptrics*).[111] Therefore (Ax. 2) determination does not pertain to the essence of motion but is different from it,[112] and a moving body that is repelled is not at rest for any time. Q.E.D.

Corollary.

Hence it follows that motion is not contrary to motion.

---

111. Cf. E2P13Ax2.
112. See PPH2A41 and *Dioptrics* 2 (AT6, 94–96). The distinction between motion and its determination or direction is critical to Cartesian physics.

Proposition 20.

If a body A collides with a body B and takes it along with it, A will lose as much of its motion as B acquires from A because of its collision with A.

Proof.

If you deny this, suppose that B acquires more or less motion from A than A loses. All this difference must be added to or subtracted from the quantity   of motion in the whole of Nature, which is absurd (Prop. 13 Part 2). Therefore, because body B can acquire neither more nor less motion, it will acquire just as much motion as A loses. Q.E.D.

Proposition 21. *(See preceding diagram.)*

If a body A is twice as large as B and moves with equal speed, A will also have twice as much motion as B, or twice as much force for retaining a speed equal to Bs.

Proof.

Suppose that instead of A there are two Bs; that is, by hypothesis, one A divided into two equal parts. Each B has a force for remaining in the state in which it is (Prop. 14 Part 2), and this force is equal in both Bs (by hypothesis). If now these two Bs are joined together, their speed remaining the same, they will become one A, whose force and quantity will be equal to two Bs, or twice that of one B. Q.E.D.

Note that this follows simply from the definition of motion. For the greater the moving body, the more the matter that is being separated from other matter. Therefore there is more separation, that is (Def. 8), more motion. See Note 4 regarding the definition of motion.

Proposition 22. *(See diagram Prop. 20.)*

If a body A is equal to a body B, and A is moving at twice the speed of B, the force or motion in A will be twice that in B.

Proof.

Suppose that B, when it first acquired a certain force of motion has acquired four degrees of speed. If now nothing is added to this, it will continue to move (Prop. 14 Part 2) and persevere in its state. Suppose that it now acquires an additional force from a further impulse equal to the former. As a result, it will acquire another four degrees of speed in addition to the previous four degrees, which it will also preserve (same Prop.), that is, it will move twice as fast (i.e., as fast as A), and at the same time it will have twice the force (i.e., a force equal to A's). Therefore the motion in A is twice that of B. Q.E.D.

Note that by force in moving bodies we here understand quantity of motion. This quantity must be greater in equal bodies in proportion to their speed of motion, insofar as by that speed equal bodies become more separated in the same time from immediately contiguous bodies than if they were to move more slowly. Thus they also have more motion (Def. 8). But in bodies at rest, we understand by 'force of resistance' the quantity of rest.[113] Hence it follows:

Corollary 1.

The more slowly bodies move, the more they participate in rest.

For they offer more resistance to more swiftly moving bodies that collide with them and have less force than they, and they also are less separated from immediately contiguous bodies.

Corollary 2.

If a body A moves twice as fast as a body B, and B is twice as great as A, there is the same amount of motion in the greater body B as in the smaller body A, and therefore there is also an equal force.

Proof.

Let B be twice the size of A, and let A move with twice the speed of B; then

---

113. Descartes does not explicitly identify inertia with resistance to motion by a body at rest, so this development is Spinoza's. It is a step toward the Newtonian concept of 'inertial mass'.

let C be half the size of B and move with half the speed of A. Therefore B (Prop. 21 Part 2) will have a motion twice that of C's, and A (Prop. 22 Part 2) will have a motion twice that of C's. Therefore (Ax. 15) B and A will have equal motion; for the motion of each is twice that of the third body C. Q.E.D.

Corollary 3.

Hence it follows that motion is distinct from speed. For we conceive that, of bodies possessing equal speed, one can have more motion than another (Prop. 21 Part 2), and on the other hand, bodies possessing unequal speed can have equal motion (previous Cor.). This can also be deduced merely from the definition of motion, for it is nothing but the transfer of one body from the vicinity . . ., etc.

But here it should be noted that this third corollary is not inconsistent with the first. For we conceive speed in two ways—either insofar as a body is more or less separated in the same time from immediately contiguous bodies (and to that extent it participates to a greater or lesser degree in motion or rest), or insofar as it describes in the same time a longer or shorter line (and to that extent is distinct from motion).

I could here have added other propositions for a fuller explanation of Prop. 14 Part 2 and could have explained the forces of things in any state whatsoever, as we have here done with regard to motion. But it will suffice to read through Art. 43 Part 2 of the *Principia* and to add only one more proposition, which is necessary for the understanding of what is to follow.

Proposition 23.

When the modes of a body are compelled to undergo variation, that variation will always be the least that can be.[114]

Proof.

This proposition follows quite clearly from Prop. 14 Part 2.

---

114. Descartes states this principle of least variation most directly in his letter to Clerselier of 17 February 1645 (AT4, 185), which appears to be Spinoza's source, since it does not appear directly in PPH.

Proposition 24, Rule 1. (See diagram Prop. 20.)[115]

If two bodies, A and B, should be completely equal and should move in a straight line toward each other with equal velocity, on colliding with each other they will both be reflected in the opposite direction with no loss of speed.[116]
In this hypothesis it is evident that, in order that the contrariety of these two bodies should be removed, either both must be reflected in the opposite direction or the one must take the other along with it. For they are contrary to each other only in respect of their determination, not in respect of motion.

Proof.

When A and B collide, they must undergo some variation (Ax. 19). But because motion is not contrary to motion (Cor. Prop. 19 Part 2), they will not be compelled to lose any of their motion (Ax. 19). Therefore there will be change only in determination. But we cannot conceive that only the determination of the one, say B, is changed, unless we suppose that A, by which it would have to be changed, is the stronger (Ax. 20). But this would be contrary to the hypothesis. Therefore because there cannot be a change of determination in only the one, there will be a change in both, with A and B changing course in the opposite direction—but not in any other direction (see what is said in Chap. 2 *Dioptrics*)[117]—and preserving their own motion undiminished. Q.E.D.

Proposition 25, Rule 2. (See diagram Prop. 20.)

If A and B are unequal in mass, B being greater than A, other conditions being as previously stated, then A alone will be reflected, and each will continue to move at the same speed.

115. P24–P31 restate the Cartesian laws of impact. There is no hint of the criticism that Spinoza will later direct at Rule 6 in Ep32, nor of any departure from the interpretation that Descartes gives of the laws. See Lécrivain, 179–192.
116. See PPH2A46. Descartes prefaces these rules (actually the laws of impact) with a warning that they are idealizations, whereas Spinoza defers the warning to PPC2P31Schol. In 1665 (see Ep30) Spinoza was expressing a limited disagreement with these laws; whereas, by 1676 (see Ep81), he was prepared to criticize them globally. See our introduction for a discussion of Spinoza's developing criticism.
117. In PPH the laws of impact are stated without demonstrations. Spinoza appears to be following the demonstrations that Descartes does provide in the *Dioptrics*.

Proof.

Because A is supposed to be smaller than B, it will also have less force than B (Prop. 21 Part 2). But because in this hypothesis, as in the previous one, there is contrariety only in the determination, and so, as we have demonstrated in the previous proposition, variation must occur only in the determination, it will occur only in A and not in B (Ax. 20). Therefore only A will be reflected in the opposite direction by the stronger B, while retaining its speed undiminished. Q.E.D.

Proposition 26. (See diagram Prop. 20.)

If A and B are unequal in mass and speed, B being twice the size of A and the motion in A being twice the speed of that in B, other conditions being as before stated, they will both be reflected in the opposite direction, each retaining the speed that it possessed.

Proof.

When A and B move toward each other, according to the hypothesis, there is the same amount of motion in the one as in the other (Cor. 2 Prop. 22 Part 2). Therefore the motion of the one is not contrary to the motion of the other (Cor. Prop. 19 Part 2), and the forces are equal in both (Cor. 2 Prop. 22 Part 2). Therefore this hypothesis is exactly similar to the hypothesis of Proposition 24 Part 2 and so, according to the same proof, A and B will be reflected in opposite directions, retaining their own motion undiminished. Q.E.D.

Corollary.

From these three preceding propositions it is clear that to change the determination of one body requires equal force as to change its motion.[118] Hence it follows that a body that loses more than half its determination and more than half its motion undergoes more change than one that loses all its determination.

---

118. In fact, Descartes explicitly denies this claim. See *Dioptrics* 2 (AT11, 94).

Proposition 27, Rule 3.

If A and B are equal in mass but B moves a little faster than A, not only will A be reflected in the opposite direction, but also B will transfer to A half the difference of their speeds, and both will proceed to move in the same direction at the same speed.

Proof.

By hypothesis, A is opposed to B not only by its determination but also by its slowness, insofar as it participates in rest (Cor. 1 Prop. 22 Part 2). Therefore, even though it is reflected in the opposite direction and only its determination is changed, not all the contrariety of these two bodies is thereby removed. Hence (Ax. 19) there must be a variation both in determination and in motion. But because B, by hypothesis, moves faster than A, B will be stronger than A (Prop. 22 Part 2). Therefore a change (Ax. 20) will be produced in A by B, by which it will be reflected in the opposite direction. That was the first point.

Secondly, as long as it moves more slowly than B, A is opposed to B (Cor. 1 Prop. 22 Part 2). Therefore a variation must occur (Ax. 19) until it does not move more slowly than B. Now in this hypothesis there is no cause strong enough to compel it to move faster than B. So because it can move neither more slowly nor faster than B when it is impelled by B, it will proceed to move at the same speed as B. Again, if B transfers less than half its excess of speed to A, then A will proceed to move more slowly than B. If it transfers more than half, then A will proceed to move more quickly than B. But both these possibilities are absurd, as we have just demonstrated. Therefore a variation will occur until a point is reached when B has transferred to A half its excess of speed, which B must lose (Prop. 20 Part 2). And so both will proceed to move with equal speed in the same direction without any contrariety. Q.E.D.

Corollary.

Hence it follows that, the greater the speed of a body, the more it is determined to move in the same straight line, and conversely, the more slowly it moves, the less its determination.

Scholium.[119]

Lest my readers should here confuse the force of determination with the force of motion, I think it advisable to add a few words wherein the force of determination is explained as distinct from the force of motion. If bodies A and C are conceived as equal and moving in a straight line toward each other at equal speed, these two bodies (Prop. 24 Part 2) will be reflected in opposite directions, each preserving its own motion undiminished. But if body C is at B, and moving at an oblique angle toward A, it is clear that it is now less determined to move along the line BD or CA. So although it possesses motion equal to A's, yet the force of C's determination when it

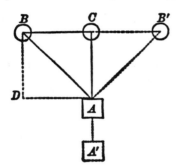

moves from directly opposite toward A— a force that is equal to body A's force of determination—is greater than C's force of determination when it moves from B toward A; and it is greater in proportion as the line BA is greater than the line CA. For in proportion as BA is greater than CA, so much more time does B require (with B and A moving at the same speed, as is here supposed) to be able to move along the line BD or CA, along which it

opposes the determination of body A. So when C moves from B to meet A at an oblique angle, it will be determined as if it were to proceed to move along the line AB' toward B' (which I suppose, it being at a point where the line AB' cuts BC produced, to be the same distance from C as C is from B). But A, retaining its original motion and determination, will proceed to move toward C, and will push body B along with it, because B, as long as it is determined to motion along the diagonal AB' and moves with the same speed as A, requires more time than A to describe by its motion any part of the line AC. And to that extent it is opposed to the determination of body A, which is the stronger. But in order for C's force of determination in moving from B to A, insofar as it participates in the direction CA, may be equal to C's force of determination in moving directly toward A (or, by hypothesis, equal to A's force of determination), B will have to have degrees of motion in excess of A in proportion as the line BA is greater than the line

---

119. A difficulty with the following explanation is that Spinoza takes 'B' to mean: position B; body C at position B, and body B (which is body C).

CA. And then, when it meets body A at an oblique angle, A will be reflected in the opposite direction toward A' and B toward B', both retaining their original motion. But if the excess of B over A is more than the excess of the line BA over the line CA, then B will repel A toward A', and will impart to it as much of its motion as will make the ratio of the motions of B to A the same as the ratio of the line BA to the line CA, and, losing as much motion as it has transferred to A, it will proceed to move in its original direction. For example, if the line AC is to the line AB as 1 to 2, and the motion of body A is to that of body B as 1 to 5, then B will transfer to A one degree of its motion and will repel it in the opposite direction, and B with four remaining degrees of motion will continue to move in its original direction.

Proposition 28, Rule 4. (See diagram Prop. 20.)[120]

If a body A is completely at rest and is a little larger than B, with whatever speed B moves toward A it will never move A, but will be repelled by A in the opposite direction, retaining its original motion.

Note[121] that the contrariety of these bodies is removed in three ways. (1) When one takes the other along with it, and they thereafter proceed to move at the same speed in the same direction. (2) When one is reflected in the opposite direction and the other retains its original rest. (3) When one is reflected in the opposite direction and transfers some of its motion to the other, which was at rest. There can be no fourth possibility (from Prop. 13 Part 2). So we must now demonstrate (by Prop. 23 Part 2) that according to our hypothesis the least change occurs in these bodies.

Proof.

If B were to move A until they both proceeded to move at the same speed, it would have to transfer to A as much of its motion as A acquires (Prop. 20 Part 2) and would have to lose more than half of its motion (Prop. 21 Part 2), and consequently (Cor. Prop. 27 Part 2) more than half of its determination as well. And so (Cor. Prop. 26 Part 2) it would undergo more change than if it were merely to lose its determination. And if A were to lose some

---

120. Corrected from Prop. 27.
121. This note and the note immediately following P29 are set in smaller type in the first edition, indicating that they were additions that Spinoza made in proof (see Ep15).

of its rest, but not so much that it finally proceeded to move with equal speed with B, then the opposition of these two bodies would not be removed. For A by its slowness, insofar as that participates in rest, will be opposed to B's speed (Cor. 1 Prop. 22 Part 2). And so B will still have to be reflected in the opposite direction and will lose all its determination and part of its motion, which it has transferred to A. This, too, is a greater change than if it were merely to lose its determination. Therefore, because the change is only in the determination, in accordance with our hypothesis, it will be the least that there can be in these bodies, and therefore (Prop. 23 Part 2) no other change will occur. Q.E.D.

It should be noted that, in the proof of this proposition and also in the case of other proofs, we have not quoted Prop. 19 Part 2, in which it is demonstrated that the whole determination can be changed while yet the motion remains unaltered. Yet attention should be paid to this proposition, so that the force of the proof may be rightly perceived. For in Prop. 23 Part 2 we did not say that the variation will always be the least absolutely, but the least that there can be. But that there can be such a change as we have supposed in this proof, one consisting solely in determination, is evident from Props. 18 and 19 with Cor. Part 2.

Proposition 29, Rule 5. (See diagram Prop. 30.)

If a body A at rest is smaller than B, then however slowly B moves toward A, it will move it along with it, transferring to it such a part of its motion that both bodies thereafter move at the same speed. (Read Art. 50 Part 2 of the Principia.*)*

In this rule as in the previous one, only three cases could be conceived in which this opposition would be removed. But we shall demonstrate that, according to our hypothesis, the least change occurs in these bodies. And so (Prop. 23 Part 2) their variation, too, must occur in this way.

Proof.

According to our hypothesis B transfers to A (Prop. 21 Part 2) less than half of its motion and (Cor. Prop. 27 Part 2)[122] less than half of its determina-

---

122. I accept Hubbeling's emendation of 17 to 27. [Tr.]

tion. Now if B were not to take A along with it but were to be reflected in the opposite direction, it would lose all its determination, and a greater variation would occur (Cor. Prop. 26 Part 2). And even greater would be the variation if it lost all its determination and at the same time a part of its motion, as is supposed in the third case. Therefore the variation, in accordance with our hypothesis, is the least. Q.E.D.

Proposition 30, Rule 6.

If a body A at rest were exactly equal to a body B, which is moving toward it, to some degree A would be impelled by B, and to some degree B would be repelled by A in the opposite direction.

Here again, as in the preceding Prop., only three cases could be conceived. And so it must be demonstrated that we are here positing the least variation that there can be.

Proof.

If body B takes body A along with it until both are proceeding to move at the same speed, then there will be the same amount of motion in the one as in the other (Prop. 22 Part 2), and (Cor. Prop. 27 Part 2) B will have to lose half its determination and also (Prop. 20 Part 2) half its motion. But if it is repelled by A in the opposite direction, then it will lose all its determination and will retain all its motion (Prop. 18   Part 2). This variation is equal to the former (Cor. Prop. 26 Part 2). But neither of these possibilities can occur. For if A were to retain its own state and could change the determination of B, it would necessarily be stronger than B (Ax. 20), which would be contrary to the hypothesis. And if B were to take A along with it until they were both moving at the same speed, B would be stronger than A, which is also contrary to the hypothesis. Because both of these cases are ruled out, the third case will occur; B will give a slight impulse to A[123] and will be repelled by A. Q.E.D. Read Art. 51 Part 2 of the *Principia*.

---

123. See PPH1A51. Descartes claims that if B approaches A with four degrees of velocity, it will transfer one of these to A and be deflected by three degrees. This is the law to which Spinoza takes specific exception in Ep30 and Ep32.

Proposition 31, Rule 7. (See diagram Prop. 30.)

If B and A are moving in the same direction, A more slowly and B following it more quickly so that it finally overtakes A, and if A is bigger than B, but B's excess of speed is greater than A's excess of magnitude, then B will transfer to A so much of its motion that both will thereafter move at the same speed in the same direction. But if, on the other hand, A's excess of magnitude should be greater than B's excess of speed, B would be reflected by it in the opposite direction, retaining all its motion.

Read Art. 52 Part 2 of the *Principia*. Here again, as in the preceding propositions, only three cases can be conceived.

Proof.

Part 1. B being supposed to be stronger than A (Props. 21 and 22 Part 2) cannot be reflected in the opposite direction by A (Ax. 20). Therefore, because B is stronger, it will take A along with it, and in such a way that they proceed to move at the same speed. For then the least change will occur, as can easily be seen from the preceding propositions.

Part 2. B being supposed to be less strong than A (Props. 21 and 22 Part 2) cannot impel A (Ax. 20), nor give it any of its own motion. Thus (Cor. Prop. 14 Part 2) it will retain all its motion, but not in the same direction, for it is supposed to be impeded by A. Therefore (according to Chap. 2 *Dioptrics*) it will be reflected in the opposite direction, not in any other direction, retaining its original motion (Prop. 18 Part 2). Q.E.D.

Note that here and in the preceding propositions we have taken as proved that any body meeting from the opposite direction another body by which it is absolutely impeded from advancing further in the same direction, must be reflected in the opposite direction, not in any other direction. For the understanding of this, read Chap. 2 *Dioptrics*.

Scholium.

Up to this point, to explain the changes of bodies resulting from their impact on each other, we have considered the two bodies as though isolated from all other bodies, that is, without taking into account bodies that surround them on all sides. But now we shall consider their state and their changes while taking into account bodies that surround them on all sides.[124]

Proposition 32.

If a body B is surrounded on all sides by particles in motion, which at the same time are impelling it with equal force in all directions, as long as no other cause occurs it will remain unmoved in the same place.[125]

Proof.

This proposition is self-evident. For if it were to move in any direction through the impulse of particles coming from one direction, the particles that move it would be impelling it with greater force than other particles that at the same time are impelling it in the opposite direction, with no effect (Ax. 20).[126] This would be contrary to the hypothesis.

Proposition 33.

Body B, under the conditions stated previously, can be moved in any direction by any additional force, however small.

Proof.

Because all bodies immediately contiguous to B are in motion (by hypothesis), and B (Prop. 32) remains unmoved, as soon as they touch B they will be reflected in another direction while retaining their original motion (Prop. 28 Part 2). Thus body B is all the time automatically being left by immediately contiguous bodies. And so, whatever magnitude is assigned to B, no action is required to separate it from immediately contiguous bodies (Note 4 of Def. 8). So any external force striking against it, however small it is imagined to be, is bound to be greater than the force that B possesses

---

124. This remark reflects the transition to an account of the nature and properties of fluids (PPH2A56), and Meyer notes in his introduction that it requires further elaboration than Spinoza provided. For Descartes the distinction depends on the fact that the particles of fluid bodies are in motion, whereas those of solids are at rest.
125. P32–P37 deal with the role of surrounding bodies and provide the basis for Descartess account of equilibrium of change in a field. See Lécrivain, 192–200.
126. Here I follow the generally accepted emendation of 29 to 20. [Tr.]

for remaining in the same place (for we have just demonstrated that B possesses no force for adhering to its immediately contiguous bodies), and, when added to the impulse of those particles that together with it are impelling B by external force in the same direction, it is also bound to be greater than the force of other particles impelling B in the opposite direction (for, disregarding this external force, the one force was supposed to be equal to the other). Therefore (Ax. 20) body B will be moved in any direction by this external force, however small it be imagined. Q.E.D.

Proposition 34.

Body B, under the same conditions as previously, cannot move more quickly than it is impelled by the external force, even though the particles by which it is surrounded are in much swifter motion.

Proof.

Although the particles that, together with the external force, are impelling B in the same direction are in much swifter motion than the external force can move B, yet because (by hypothesis) they have no more force than the bodies that are repelling B in the opposite direction, they will use up all the power of their determination merely in resisting these, without imparting any speed to B (Prop. 32 Part 2). Therefore, because no other circumstances or causes are supposed, B will not receive any amount of speed from any cause other than the external force, and therefore (Ax. 8 Part 1) it cannot move more quickly than it is impelled by the external force. Q.E.D.

Proposition 35.

When body B is thus moved by an external impulse, it receives the greatest part of its motion from the bodies by which it is constantly surrounded, and not from the external force.[127]

---

127. Leibniz notes that this rule is both vague and inexact. See his *Animadversiones*, in *Philosophische Schriften*, ed. Carl Gebhardt, vol. 4, tr. P. Schrecker (Paris: Vrin, 1980), 74–75.

Proof.

Even though body B is imagined to be very large, it must be moved by even the smallest impulse (Prop. 33 Part 2). Let us then conceive B as four times as large as the external body by whose force it is impelled. Therefore, because both must move at the same speed (preceding Prop.), there will be four times as much motion in B as in the external body by which it is impelled (Prop. 21 Part 2). Therefore (Ax. 8 Part 1) it does not have the principal part of its motion from the external cause. And because, apart from this cause, no causes are supposed other than the bodies by which it is constantly surrounded (for B is supposed to be not moving of itself), then it is only from the bodies by which it is surrounded (Ax. 7 Part 1) that it receives the principal part of its motion, and not from the external cause. Q.E.D.

Note that here we cannot say, as previously, that the motion of particles coming from one direction is required in order to resist the motion of particles coming from the opposite direction. For bodies moving toward each other with equal motion (as these are supposed) are contrary only by determination,[128] and not by motion (Cor. Prop. 19 Part 2). And so in resisting one another they use up only their determination, and not their motion. Therefore body B can receive no determination, and consequently (Cor. Prop. 27 Part 2) no speed—insofar as that is distinct from motion—from adjacent bodies. But it can receive motion; indeed, when the extra force is added, it must necessarily be moved by them, as we have demonstrated in this proposition and as can be clearly seen from the manner of the proof of Proposition 33.

Proposition 36.

If any body (e.g., our hand) can move in any direction whatsoever with equal motion without offering any resistance to any bodies or meeting with any resistance from any other bodies, then in that space through which it would thus move there must necessarily be as many bodies moving in one direction as there are bodies moving in any other direction, their force of speed being equal to one another's and to that of the hand.

128. See Prop. 24 Part 2, where it is demonstrated that two bodies, in resisting one another, expend their determination, not their motion. [Spinoza]

Proof.

Any space through which a body can move is bound to be full of bodies (Prop. 3 Part 2). I therefore say that the space through which our hand can thus move is filled with bodies which will move in the manner I have already described. For if you deny this, let them be supposed to be at rest, or to move in a different way. If they are at rest, they will necessarily resist the motion of the hand until its motion is communicated to them (Prop. 14 Part 2), so that finally they will move together with it in the same direction at the same speed (Prop. 20 Part 2). But in the hypothesis they are supposed not to resist; therefore these bodies are in motion. This was the first point to be proved.

Furthermore, they must be moving in all directions. If you deny this, suppose that there is some direction in which they are not moving, say from A toward B. Therefore if the hand is moving from A toward B, it will necessarily meet moving bodies (by the first part of this proof), bodies, by your hypothesis, with a determination different from that of the hand. Therefore they will resist it (Prop. 14 Part 2) until they move along with the hand in the same direction (Prop. 24 and Schol. Prop. 27 Part 2). But, by hypothesis, they do not resist the hand. Therefore they will be moving in all directions. That was the second point.

Again, these bodies will be moving in all directions equaling one another in force of speed. For if they were supposed not to be moving with equal force of speed, suppose that those that are moving from A toward B are not moving with as much force of speed as those that are moving from A toward C. Therefore if the hand (for it is supposed to be able to move with equal motion in all directions without resistance) were to move from A toward B with the same speed with which bodies are moving from A toward C, the bodies moving from A toward B will resist the hand (Prop. 14 Part 2) until they move with a force of speed equal to that of the hand (Prop. 31 Part 2). But this is contrary to the hypothesis. Therefore they will move with equal force of speed in all directions. That was the third point.

Finally, if the bodies are not moving with the same force of speed as the hand, then the hand will either move more slowly, with less force of speed, or more quickly, with greater force of speed, than the bodies. If the former, the hand will resist the bodies that are following it in the same direction (Prop. 31 Part 2). If the latter, the bodies that the hand is following and with which it is moving in the same direction will resist it (same Prop.). Each of these is contrary to the hypothesis. Therefore, because the hand can move neither more slowly nor more quickly than the bodies, it will move with the same force of speed as the bodies. Q.E.D.

If you ask why I say 'with equal force of speed' and not simply 'with equal speed', read Scholium Cor. Prop. 27 Part 2. If you then ask whether the hand, while moving (e.g., from A toward B), does not resist bodies that are moving at the same time with equal force from B toward A, read Prop. 33 Part 2, from which you will understand that their force is balanced by the force of the bodies moving together with the hand at the same time from A toward B (for, by the third part of this Prop., these two forces are equal).

Proposition 37.

If a body A can be moved in any direction whatsoever by any force, however small, it must necessarily be surrounded by bodies that are moving at the same speed as one another.

Proof.

Body A must be surrounded on all sides by bodies (Prop. 6 Part 2), bodies that are moving equally in all directions. For if they were at rest, body A could not be moved, as is supposed, in any direction whatsoever by any force, however small, but only by such force as could at least be able to move along with itself the bodies immediately contiguous to A (Ax. 20 Part 2). Again, if the bodies by which A is surrounded were moving with greater force in one direction than in another—say, with greater force from B toward C than from C toward B—then because it is surrounded on all sides by moving bodies (as we have just now demonstrated), the bodies moving from B toward C would necessarily take A along with them in the same direction (by what we have demonstrated in Prop. 33). So it is not any force, however small, that will suffice to move A toward B; it must be exactly such as would counterbalance the excess of motion of the bodies coming from B toward C (Ax. 20). Therefore they must be moving with equal force in all directions. Q.E.D.

Scholium.

Because this is the case with bodies called fluid, it follows that fluid bodies are those that are divided into many tiny particles moving with equal force in all directions. And although those particles cannot be seen by any eye, even a lynx's, one must not deny what we have now clearly demonstrated. For from our previously stated Props. 10 and 11, a minuteness of nature such as cannot be determined or attained by any thought, not to say the senses, is sufficiently proved. Furthermore, because it is also well established from what has preceded that bodies resist other bodies merely by their rest, and that we, as our senses indicate, perceive of hardness nothing more than that the parts of hard bodies resist the motion of our hands, we clearly infer that those bodies are hard, all of whose particles are at rest in close proximity to one another. Read Arts. 54, 55, 56 Part 2 of the *Principia*.

End of Part 2.

THE PRINCIPLES OF PHILOSOPHY

demonstrated in the geometric manner.

Part 3.

Having thus set forth the most universal principles of natural things, we must now go on to explain what follows from them. However, because the things that follow from these principles exceed all that our mind can ever survey in thought, and because we are not determined by them to consider some in particular rather than others, we should first of all present a brief account of the most important phenomena whose causes we shall here be investigating. But this you have in Arts. 5–15 Part 3 of the *Principia*. And in Arts. 20–43 is set out the hypothesis that Descartes judges most suitable not only for understanding the phenomena of the heavens but also for seeking out their natural causes.[129]

Then again, because the best way to understand the nature of Plants or Man is to consider in what way they gradually come into existence and are generated from their seeds, we must devise such principles as are the simplest and easiest to know, from which we may demonstrate that the stars, the earth, in short, everything we observe in this visible world, could have arisen as from certain seeds—although we may well know that they never did thus arise. For in this way we shall explain their nature far better than if we were to describe them only as they are now.

I say that we seek principles that are simple and easy to know; for unless they are such, we shall not be in need of them. The only reason why we assign seeds to things is to get to know their nature more easily and, like mathematicians, to ascend from the clearest to the more obscure and from the simplest to the more complex.[130]

---

129. Cf. DIE57, note y.
130. In PPH3A45 Descartes uses this argument to excuse his departure from creationism.

Next, we say that the principles we seek are such that we may demonstrate that from them the stars, the earth, etc., could have arisen. For we do not seek causes that suffice only to explain the phenomena of the heavens, as is the common practice of astronomers, but such as may also lead us to knowledge of the things on earth. For we hold that everything we observe to happen above the earth should be counted as phenomena of nature. Now to discover these causes, the following are the requirements of a good hypothesis.

1. Considered only in itself, it must not imply any contradiction.

2. It must be the simplest that can be.

3. Following from (2), it must be very easy to know.

4. Everything that is observed in the whole of nature must be able to be deduced from it.[131]

We have said, finally, that it is allowable for us to assume a hypothesis from which we can deduce, as from a cause, the phenomena of nature, even though we well know that they did not arise in that way. For this to be understood, I shall make use of the following example. If someone were to find drawn on a sheet of paper the curved line we call a parabola and wished to enquire into its nature, it would make no difference whether he were to suppose that the line was first cut from a cone and then imprinted on the paper, or that the line was described as a result of the motion of two straight lines, or that it arose in some other way, provided that his supposition enabled him to demonstrate all the properties of a parabola. Indeed, even though he may know that it originated from the imprinting of a conic section on the paper, he can nevertheless assume any other cause he pleases that seems to him most convenient for explaining all the properties of a parabola. So too, in order to explain the features of nature, we are permitted to assume any hypothesis we please, provided we deduce from it by mathematical inference all the phenomena of nature. And a more important point to note is this, that there is hardly any assumption we can make from which the same effects cannot be deduced—although perhaps with more trouble—from the laws of nature explained previously. For because, by the operation of those laws, matter assumes successively all the forms of which it is capable, if we consider those forms in due order, we shall finally be able to

---

131. Cf. Spinoza's criteria for a good definition at TIE96–97.

arrive at the form that is the form of this world. So one need fear no error from a false hypothesis.

Postulate.

It is requested that the following be taken for granted. All the matter of which this visible world is composed was in the beginning divided by God into particles as near as possible equal to one another. These were not spherical because a number of tiny spheres joined together do not fill a continuous space. These parts were of different shapes and medium size; that is, of a size intermediate between all those of which the heavens and the stars are now composed. The parts possessed in themselves the same amount of motion as is now found in the world and moved with equal speed. Individually, they moved about their own centers, each independently of the others, so as to compose a fluid body such as we think the heavens to be. Many also moved in unison around certain other points, equidistant from one another and arranged in the same way as are now the centers of the fixed stars. Others, again, moved about a somewhat greater number of other points that are equal to the number of the planets, thus forming as many different vortices as there now are stars in the world. See the diagram in Art. 47 Part 3 of the *Principia.*

This hypothesis, regarded in itself, implies no contradiction, for it ascribes to matter nothing except divisibility and motion, modifications that we have already shown to exist in reality in matter; and because we have shown that matter is boundless, and one and the same in the heavens and on earth, we can suppose these modifications to have been in the whole of matter without any danger of contradiction.

Again, this hypothesis is the simplest because it supposes no inequality or dissimilarity in the particles into which matter was divided in the beginning, nor yet in their motion. From this it follows that this hypothesis is also very easy to know. This is also evident from the fact that by this hypothesis nothing is supposed to have been in matter except what everyone immediately knows from the mere concept of matter, divisibility, and local motion.

That everything observed in nature can be deduced from this hypothesis, we shall try to show as far as possible in actual fact, adopting the following order. First, we shall deduce from it the fluidity of the heavens, explaining how this is the cause of light. Then we shall proceed to the nature of the sun, and at the same time to what is observed in the fixed stars. After that we shall speak of comets, and lastly of the planets and their phenomena.

Definitions.

1. By *ecliptic* we understand that part of a vortex that, in rotating about its axis, describes the greatest circle.

2. By *poles* we understand the parts of a vortex that are farthest away from the ecliptic or that describe the smallest circles.

3. By *conatus to motion* we understand, not some thought, but that a part of matter is so situated and stirred to motion that it would in fact be going in some direction if it were not impeded by any cause.

4. By *angle* we understand whatever in any body projects beyond a spherical shape.

Axioms.

1. A number of small spherical bodies joined together cannot occupy a continuous space.

2. A portion of matter divided into angular parts, if its parts are moving about their own centers, requires more space than if its parts were all at rest and all their sides were immediately contiguous to one another.

3. The smaller a part of matter is, the more easily it is divided by the same force.

4. Parts of matter that are moving in the same direction and in that motion do not withdraw from one another are not in actuality divided.

Proposition 1.

The parts into which matter was first divided were not round but angular.

Proof.

All matter was in the beginning divided into equal and similar parts (Postulate). Therefore (Ax. 1 and Prop. 2 Part 2) they were not round; and so (Def. 4) they were angular. Q.E.D.

Proposition 2.

The force that brought it about that the particles of matter should move about their own centers, at the same time brought it about that the angles of the particles should be worn away by collision with one another.

Proof.

In the beginning, all matter was divided into equal (Postulate) and angular (Prop. 1 Part 3) parts. Therefore, if their angles had not been worn away as soon as they began to move about their own centers, then of necessity (Ax. 2) the whole of matter would have had to occupy more space than when it was at rest. But this is absurd (Prop. 4 Part 2). Therefore their angles were worn away as soon as they began to move. Q.E.D.

The rest is lacking.

APPENDIX

containing the
METAPHYSICAL THOUGHTS

in which are briefly explained the more difficult
questions that arise in both the general and special
parts of Metaphysics with regard to Being and its
modifications, God and his Attributes, and the Human Mind.

Author
Benedict de Spinoza.

Amsterdam.

APPENDIX CONTAINING METAPHYSICAL THOUGHTS.

Part 1.

In which are briefly explained the principal questions
that commonly arise in the general part of Metaphysics,
with regard to Being and its modifications.[1]

Chapter 1.

Of Real Being, Fictitious Being, and Being of Reason.

I shall say nothing about the definition of this Science, nor about its subject matter. My intention here is only to explain matters that are rather obscure and are commonly treated by writers on metaphysics.

[*Definition of Being.*] Let us begin, then, with Being, by which I understand 'Everything which, when it is clearly and distinctly perceived, we find to exist necessarily or at least possibly.'

[*The Chimera, the Fictitious Being and the Being of Reason are not beings.*] From this definition, or, if you prefer, description, it follows that a Chimera, a Fictitious Being and a Being of Reason can in no way be classed as beings. For a Chimera, of its own nature, cannot exist. (N.B. By the term 'Chimera', here and in what follows, is to be understood that whose nature involves open contradiction, as is more fully explained in Chapter 3). A Fictitious Being excludes clear and distinct perception, because a man merely according to his fancy—and not unknowingly, as in the case of the false, but knowingly and wittingly—joins together what he wants to join and separates what he wants to separate.[2] Finally, a Being of Reason is nothing but a mode of thinking, which serves the more easily to retain, explain, and imagine things that are understood. Here it should be noted

---

1. The end and purpose of this Part is to show that ordinary Logic and Philosophy serve only to exercise and strengthen the memory, enabling us to keep in mind things that are presented to us through the senses at random, without order or connection, and insofar as we can be affected by them only through the senses; but they do not serve to exercise the intellect. [Balling]
2. Spinoza provides a lengthy discussion of fiction or fictitious being in TIE57–67.

that by a mode of thinking we understand, as we explained in Schol. Prop. 15 Part 1, all modifications of thought, such as intellect, joy, imagination, etc.

[*By what modes of thinking we retain things.*] That there are certain modes of thinking that serve to retain things more firmly and more easily, and, when we wish, to recall them to mind or to set them before the mind, is an accepted fact for all those who make use of that well-known rule of memory. By this rule, in order to retain something that is quite new and impress it on the memory, we have recourse to another thing, familiar to us, that has something in common with it either in name or in actuality. Similarly, philosophers have arranged all natural things in fixed classes, to which they have recourse when they encounter something new. These classes they call genus, species, etc.

[*By what modes of thinking we explicate things.*] Again, we have modes of thinking for explicating a thing by determining it in comparison with another thing. The modes of thinking by which we do this are called time, number, measure, and such others as there are. Of these, time serves to explicate duration, number (discrete quantity), and measure (continuous quantity).[3]

[*By what modes of thinking we imagine things.*] Finally, because we are also accustomed to depict in our fantasy images of all the things that we understand, it comes about that we imagine nonbeings positively as beings. For the mind, considered only in itself, because it is a thinking thing, has no greater power to affirm than to deny. But because to imagine is nothing other than to sense those traces found in the brain from the motion of the spirits, which is excited in the senses by objects, such a sensing can only be a confused affirmation.[4] Hence it comes about that we imagine as beings all the modes that the mind uses to negate, such as blindness, extremity or limit, boundary, and darkness.

[*Why beings of reason are not ideas of things, and yet are taken to be such.*] Hence it is evident that these modes of thinking are not ideas of things and can in no way be classed as ideas. So they also have no object (*ideatum*) that exists of necessity or that can exist. The reason why these modes of thinking are taken for ideas of things is that they originate and arise so immediately from real beings that they are easily confused with them by those who

3. On time, see Ep12, 103–105.
4. The claim that imagination involves awareness of traces of the animal spirits in the brain originates in Descartes, but Spinoza's claim that such an awareness also involves affirmation or belief is contrary to Descartes and follows his own account of belief (which does not require an act of will). See our introduction.

do not pay careful attention. Hence they have even given them names as if to signify beings existing outside our mind; and these beings, or rather nonbeings, they have called beings of reason.[5]

[*Being is wrongly divided into Real Being and Being of Reason.*] And so it is easy to see how absurd is that division whereby being is divided into real being and being of reason, for they are dividing being into being and nonbeing, or into being and a mode of thinking. Still, I am not surprised that verbal or grammatical philosophers fall into errors like these, for they judge things from words, not words from things.

[*In what way a Being of Reason can be termed a mere nothing, and in what way it may be termed Real Being.*] No less absurdly does he speak who says that a being of reason is not a mere nothing.[6] For if he seeks outside the intellect what is meant by those words, he will find it is mere nothing, whereas if he understands them as modes of thinking, they are true real beings. For when I ask what is species, I am only enquiring into the nature of that mode of thinking that is in fact a being and is distinct from another mode of thinking. However, these modes of thinking cannot be termed ideas nor can they be said to be true or false, just as love cannot be called true or false, but only good or bad. So when Plato said that man is a featherless biped creature,[7] he erred no more than those who said that man is a rational creature. For Plato knew no less than others that man is a rational creature, but he referred man to a certain class so that, when he wanted to think about man, by having recourse to the class that was easy for him to remember, he could immediately come to think of man. Indeed, it was Aristotle who was gravely at fault if he thought that by that definition of his he had adequately explained human essence. As to whether Plato was right, that is another question; but this is not the place for these matters.

[*In the investigation of things Real Beings should not be confused with Beings of Reason.*] From all that has been said already, it is obvious that there is no agreement between real being and the objects (*ideata*) of a being of reason. Hence it is also easy to see how carefully, in our investigation of things, we must beware of confusing real beings with beings of reason. For it is one thing to enquire into the nature of things, and quite another to enquire into the modes by which we perceive things. If these are confused, we shall not

5. Spinoza uses a similar device for explaining the origin of general or universal ideas in E2P40Schol1; TIE89. See also PPH1A57–58.
6. Spinoza may have Heereboord in mind here. See his *Meletemata philosophica* (Amsterdam, 1680), 221–223.
7. See Plato, *Statesman*, 266e.

be able to understand either modes of perceiving or nature itself. Indeed—and this is a point of greatest importance—it will be the cause of our falling into grave errors, as has happened to many before us.[8]

[*How a Being of Reason and Fictitious Being are to be distinguished.*] It should also be noted that many people confuse a being of reason with a fictitious being, for they think that a fictitious being is also a being of reason because it has no existence outside the mind. But if attention is correctly paid to the definitions just given of being of reason and fictitious being, a considerable difference will be found between them both from consideration of their cause and also from their own nature without regard to cause. For we defined fictitious being as the connecting of two terms by mere act of will without any guidance of reason, and therefore a fictitious being can chance to be true. But a being of reason neither depends solely on the will nor does it consist of any terms joined together, as is quite obvious from the definition. So if someone asks whether a fictitious being is a real being or a being of reason, we should reply by repeating what we have just said, namely, that to divide being into real being and being of reason is a mistake, and so the question as to whether fictitious being is real being or being of reason is based on error. For it presupposes that all being is divided into real being and being of reason.

[*The division of Being.*] But let us return to our theme, from which we now seem to have digressed somewhat. From the definition, or, if you prefer, the description of being already given, it is easy to see that being should be divided into being that exists necessarily of its own nature (i.e., whose essence involves existence) and being whose essence involves only possible existence. This last is divided into Substance and Mode, whose definitions are given in Arts. 51, 52, and 56 of Part 1 *Princ. Philosoph.*; so it is not necessary to repeat them here. But concerning this division I want only this to be noted, that we expressly say that being is divided into Substance and Mode, not Substance and Accident. For Accident is nothing more than a mode of thinking, inasmuch as it denotes only a relation [*respectum*]. For example, when I say that a triangle moves, motion is not a mode of the triangle, but of the body that moves. So motion is called accident in relation to the triangle, whereas in relation to body it is a real being or mode. For motion cannot be conceived without body, though it can without a triangle.[9]

---

8. Cf. E1App.
9. See PPH1A61.

Furthermore, for the better understanding of what has already been said and also of what is to come, we shall try to explain what it is that should be understood by the terms 'essence', 'existence', 'idea', and 'potency'. In so doing we are also motivated by the ignorance of some people who do not recognize any distinction between essence and existence, or, if they do recognize it, they confuse what essence is with what idea is or what potency is. So for their sake and the sake of truth, we shall explain the matter as distinctly as possible in what follows.

Chapter 2.

What Essence is, what Existence is, what Idea is, and what Potency is.

So that one may clearly grasp what should be understood by these four terms, it is only necessary to reflect upon what we have said about un-created substance or God, to wit:

[*Creatures are in God eminently.*] 1. God contains eminently what is to be found formally in created things; that is, God possesses attributes of such a kind that in them are contained in a more eminent way all created things. See Part 1 Ax. 8 and Cor. 1 Prop. 12. For example, we clearly conceive extension without any existence, and so, because it has of itself no force to exist, we have demonstrated that it is created by God (last Prop. of Part 1.) And because there must be at least as much perfection in the cause as in the effect, it follows that all the perfections of extension are in God. But because we then saw that an extended thing is of its own nature divisible, that is, it contains imperfection, we therefore could not attribute extension to God (Prop. 16 Part 1), and so we were compelled to take the view that there is an attribute in God that contains in a more excellent way all the perfections of matter (Schol. Prop. 9 Part 1) and that can fulfil the role of matter.[10]

2. God understands himself and all other things, too; that is, he also has in himself all things in the form of thought (Prop. 9 Part 1).

3. God is the cause of all things, and he acts from absolute freedom of will.

[*What Essence is, what Existence is, what Idea is, what Potency is.*][11] From

---

10. Spinoza here follows Descartes, as he did in the propositions cited from the PPC. His own rejection of this argument is given in E1P15Schol.
11. See Heereboord, *Meletemata philosophica*, 342–345.

this, therefore, it can clearly be seen what must be understood by those four things. First, that which is essence is nothing other than the way in which created things are comprehended in the attributes of God. That which is idea refers to the manner in which all things are contained in the idea of God in the form of thought. That which is potency has reference only to the potency of God, whereby from absolute freedom of will he could have created all things not already existing. Finally, that which is existence is the essence of things outside God when considered in itself and is attributed to things after they have been created by God.

[*These four are distinguished from one another only in creatures.*] From this it is evident that these four are distinguished from one another only in created things, but not at all in God. For we do not conceive God to have been in potency in another thing, and his existence and his intellect are not distinguished from his essence.

[*A reply to certain questions concerning Essence.*] From this we can readily reply to the questions that are commonly raised regarding essence. These questions are as follows: whether essence is distinct from existence; if so, whether it is something different from idea, and if that is the case, whether it has any being outside the intellect. To this last question we must surely give assent. Now to the first question we reply by making this distinction, that in God essence is not distinct from existence, because the former cannot be conceived without the latter, but that in other things essence differs from existence, seeing that it can be conceived without existence. To the second question we say that a thing that is clearly and distinctly (i.e., truly) conceived outside the intellect is something different from an idea. But then there is the further question as to whether this being outside the intellect is self-generated or whether it is created by God. To this we reply that formal essence is not self-generated nor again is it created—for both of these would presuppose that it is a thing existing in actuality—but it depends on the divine essence alone, in which all things are contained. And so in this sense we agree with those who say that the essences of things are eternal. It could still be asked how we, not yet understanding the nature of God, understand the essences of things, because they depend on the nature of God alone, as we have just said. In reply I say that this arises from the fact that things are already created. If they had not been created, I would entirely agree that it would be impossible to understand them except after an adequate knowledge of the nature of God, just as it is impossible—indeed, even less possible—to know the nature of the coordinates of a parabola without yet knowing the nature of a parabola.

[*Why in his definition of essence the Author has recourse to the attributes of*

God.] Furthermore, it should be noted that although the essences of nonexisting modes are comprehended in their substances, and that which is their essence is in their substances, we have nevertheless chosen to have recourse to God so as to give a general explanation of the essence of modes and substances. Another reason for this procedure is that the essence of modes has been in their substances only since the creation of the substances, and what we were seeking was the eternal being of essences.

[*Why the Author has not reviewed the definitions of others.*] In this connection I do not think it worthwhile to refute those writers whose views differ from ours, nor again to examine their definitions or descriptions of essence and existence; for we would thus be obscuring what is clear. What can be clearer than our understanding of what essence is and what existence is, seeing that we cannot give the definition of any thing without at the same time explaining its essence?

[*How the distinction between essence and existence is easily learned.*] Finally, if any philosopher still doubts whether essence is distinguished from existence in created things, he need not toil away over definitions of essence and existence in order to remove that doubt. For if he merely approaches a sculptor or a woodcarver, they will show him how they conceive in set order a nonexistent statue and thereafter bring it into existence for him.

Chapter 3.

Concerning the Necessary, the Impossible, the Possible, and the Contingent.

[*What is here to be understood by affections.*] Now that the nature of being, insofar as it is being, has been explained, we pass on to the explanation of some of its affections. It should be noted that by affections we here understand what elsewhere, in Art. 52 Part 1 *Princ. Philosoph.*, Descartes has termed attributes. For being, insofar as it is being, does not affect us through itself alone, as substance, and has therefore to be explained through some attribute, from which, however, it is distinguished only by reason. Hence I cannot sufficiently wonder at the subtlety of mind of those who have sought, not without great harm to truth, something that is between being and nothing.[12] But I shall waste no time in refuting their error, because they themselves, in struggling to provide definitions of such affections, disappear from sight in their own vain subtlety.

---

12. See Heereboord, *Meletemata philosophica*, 225.

[*Definition of Affections.*] We shall therefore continue on our way, and we say that the affections of being are certain attributes under which we understand the essence or existence of each individual thing, although these attributes are distinguished from the thing only by reason.[13] I shall here attempt to explain some of these affections (for I do not undertake to deal with them all) and to set them apart from those designations that are not affections of any being. And in the first place I shall deal with the Necessary and the Impossible.

[*In how many ways a thing is said to be necessary or impossible.*] There are two ways in which a thing is said to be necessary or impossible, either with respect to its essence or with respect to its cause.[14] With respect to essence we know that God necessarily exists, for his essence cannot be conceived without existence; whereas, with respect to the contradiction involved in its essence, a chimera is incapable of existence. With respect to cause, things (e.g., material things) are said to be either impossible or necessary. For if we have regard only to their essence, we can conceive that clearly and distinctly without existence; therefore they can never exist through the force and necessity of their essence, but only through the force of their cause, God, the creator of all things. So if it is in the divine decree that a thing should exist, it will necessarily exist; if not, it will be impossible for it to exist. For it is self-evident that if a thing has no cause for existence—either an internal or an external cause—it is impossible for it to exist. Now in this second hypothesis a thing is supposed to be such that it cannot exist either by force of its own essence—which I understand to be an internal cause— or by force of the divine decree, the unique external cause of all things. Hence it follows that it is impossible for things, as we suppose them to be in the second hypothesis, to exist.

[*A Chimera is properly called a verbal being.*] Here it should be noted that: 1. Because a chimera is neither in the intellect nor in the imagination, we may properly call it a verbal being, for it can be expressed only in words. For example, we can express a square circle in words, but we cannot in any way imagine it, far less understand it. Therefore a chimera is nothing but a word; and so impossibility cannot be counted among the affections of being, for it is mere negation.

[*Created things depend on God for their essence and existence.*] 2. Not only the existence of created things but also, as we shall later on demonstrate

---

13. Cf. Ep10.
14. See Heereboord, *Meletemata philosophica,* 99.

with the greatest certainty in Part 2, their essence and their nature depend solely on God's decree. Hence it clearly follows that created things have no necessity of themselves; for they have no essence of themselves, nor do they exist of themselves.[15]

[*The necessity that is in created things from their cause is either of essence or of existence; but these two are not distinguished in God.*] 3. Finally, the necessity such as is in created things by virtue of their cause is so called either with respect to their essence or with respect to their existence; for these two are distinct in created things, the former depending on the eternal laws of nature, the latter on the series and order of causes. But in God, whose essence is not distinguished from his existence, the necessity of essence is likewise not distinguished from the necessity of existence. Hence it follows that if we were to conceive the entire order of nature, we should find that many things whose nature we clearly and distinctly perceive—that is, whose essence is necessarily such as it is—could in no way exist. For we should find that the existence of such things in nature is just as much impossible as we now see it to be impossible that a huge elephant should pass through the eye of a needle, although we clearly perceive the nature of both. Hence the existence of those things would be only a chimera, which we could neither imagine nor understand.

[*The Possible and the Contingent are not affections of things.*] So much for necessity and impossibility, to which I have thought it advisable to add a few remarks concerning the possible and the contingent. For these two are regarded by some as affections of things, whereas they are in fact nothing but a failure of our intellect, as I shall clearly show when I explain what is to be understood by these two terms.

[*What is the Possible, and what the Contingent.*] A thing is said to be possible when we understand its efficient cause but do not know whether the cause is determined. Hence we can also consider it as possible, but not as either necessary or impossible. But if we attend simply to the essence of the thing and not to its cause, we shall call the thing contingent; that is, we shall consider it as midway between God and a chimera, so to speak, because on the side of essence we find in it no necessity to exist, as in the case of the divine essence, nor again any inconsistency or impossibility, as in the case of a chimera. Now if anyone wishes to call contingent what I call possible, or possible what I call contingent, I shall not oppose him, for it is not my custom to argue about words. It will be enough if he grants us that

15. Cf. E1P25.

these two are only the defect of our perception, and not anything real.[16]

[*The Possible and the Contingent are only the defect of our intellect.*] If anyone wishes to deny this, his error can be demonstrated to him with no trouble. For if he attends to nature and the way it depends on God, he will find nothing contingent in things, that is, nothing that can either exist or not exist on the part of the thing, or is a real contingency, as it is commonly called. This is readily apparent from our teaching in Axiom 10 Part 1, to wit, that the same force is required in creating a thing as in preserving it. So no created thing affects anything by its own force, just as no created thing began to exist by its own force. From this it follows that nothing happens except by the power of the all-creating cause—that is, God—who by his concurrence at every moment continues to create all things. Now because nothing happens except by the divine power alone, it is easy to see that those things that happen do so by the force of God's decree and will. But because there is in God no inconstancy or variability (by Prop. 18 and Cor. Prop. 20 Part 1), he must have resolved from eternity to produce those things that he is now producing. And because nothing has a more necessary existence than that which God has decreed should exist, it follows that the necessity to exist has been from eternity in all created things. Nor can we say that those things are contingent because God could have decreed otherwise. For because in eternity there is no when or before or after or any affection of time, it follows that God never existed prior to those decrees so as to be able to decree otherwise.[17]

[*To reconcile the freedom of our will with God's predestination surpasses human understanding.*] As to the freedom of the human will, which we asserted to be free in Schol. Prop. 15 Part 1, this too is preserved by the

16. See Spinoza's comments on possibility and contingency at E1P33Schol.
17. In order that this proof may be well understood, attention should be given to what is indicated in the second part of the Appendix concerning the will of God, to wit, that God's will or constant decree is understood only when we conceive the thing clearly and distinctly. For the essence of the thing, considered in itself, is nothing other than God's decree, or his determinate will. But we are also saying that the necessity of existence is no different from the necessity of essence (Chapter 9 of Part 2); that is, when we say that God has decreed that the triangle should exist, we are saying nothing other than that God has so arranged the order of nature and of causes that the triangle should necessarily exist at a particular time. So if we were to understand the order of causes as established by God, we should find that the triangle must exist at a particular time with the same necessity as we now find, when we attend to the triangle's nature, that its three angles are equal to two right angles. [Balling]

concurrence of God, nor does any man will or perform anything except what God has decreed from eternity that he should will or perform. How this can be while saving human freedom is beyond our capacity to understand. Yet we must not reject what we clearly perceive because of what we do not know, for if we attend to our nature, we clearly and distinctly understand that we are free in our actions, and that we reach decisions on many things simply on account of our will to do so. Again, if we attend to the nature of God, as we have just shown, we clearly and distinctly perceive that all things depend on him, and that nothing exists except that whose existence God has decreed from eternity. But how the human will continues to be created by God at every moment in such a way as to remain free, we do not know.[18] For there are many things that exceed our grasp and that nevertheless we know to have been brought about by God—for example, the real division of matter into indefinite particles, clearly demonstrated by us in Prop. ll Part 2, although we do not know how that division comes about.[19]

Note that we here take for granted that those two notions, the possible and the contingent, signify merely the defectiveness of our knowledge regarding the existence of a thing.

Chapter 4.

Of Duration and Time.

[*What is Eternity, Duration, and Time.*] From our previous division of being into being whose essence involves existence and being whose essence involves only possible existence, there arises the distinction between eternity and duration. Of eternity we shall speak later at greater length. Here we say only that it is the attribute under which we conceive the infinite existence of God. Duration is the attribute under which we conceive the existence of created things, insofar as they persevere in their actuality.[20] From this it clearly follows that duration is distinguished only by reason from the total existence of a thing. For as much as you take away from the duration of a

---

18. Spinoza here follows Descartes: see PPH1A40–41.
19. As noted in Meyer's preface, Spinoza often takes a Cartesian attitude even though he holds the contrary. In his own writing, he especially lashed out against those who, unable to explain some event, sought refuge in that "sanctuary of ignorance," that is, the will of God (E1App, 60). See all of E1App; E3P2Schol; E5Pref.
20. Spinoza tends to speak of time as the measure of (in modern terms, the metric field imposed upon) duration.

thing, so much you necessarily take away from its existence. Now in order that duration may be determined, we compare it with the duration of other things that have a fixed and determinate motion, and this comparison is called time. Therefore time is not an affection of things, but a mere mode of thinking, or, as we have previously called it, a being of reason; for it is a mode of thinking serving to explicate duration. Here with regard to duration we should note something that will be useful to us later when we speak about eternity, to wit, that it is conceived as longer and shorter and as if composed of parts, and, secondly, that it is an attribute of existence only, not of essence.[21]

Chapter 5.

Of Opposition, Order, etc.

[*What are Opposition, Order, Agreement, Difference, Subject, Adjunct, etc.*][22] From our comparing things with one another there arise certain notions that are nevertheless nothing outside things themselves but modes of thinking. This is shown by the fact that if we wish to consider them as things having a place outside thought, we immediately render confused the otherwise clear conception we have of them. Such notions are opposition, order, agreement, difference, subject, adjunct, and any others like these. These notions, I say, are quite clearly perceived by us insofar as we conceive them not as something different from the essences of the things that are opposed, ordered, etc., but merely as modes of thinking whereby we more easily retain or imagine the things themselves. I therefore do not consider it necessary to speak of them at greater length, but pass on to the terms commonly called transcendental.

Chapter 6.

Of the One, the True, and the Good.

These terms are considered by almost all metaphysicians as the most general

21. See PPH1A55–57. For Spinoza's thoughts on eternity, duration, and time, see E1Def8; E2Def5; Ep12.
22. The scholastic author from whom Spinoza appears to derive the order and much of the content in this section is Burgersdijck (*Institutiones logicarum*, chaps. 19–23, and *Institutiones metaphysicarum*, chaps. 15–19).

affections of being; for they say that every being is one, true and good even though this may not be in anyone's thought. But we shall see what is to be understood regarding these terms when we examine each of them separately.[23]

[*What Unity is.*] Let us begin, then, with the first, to wit, the one. They say that this term signifies something real outside the intellect. But they cannot explain what this adds to being, and this is a clear indication that they are confusing beings of reason with real being and are thereby rendering confused that which they clearly understand. But we on our part say that unity is in no way distinct from the thing itself or additional to being and is merely a mode of thinking whereby we separate a thing from other things that are similar to it or agree with it in some respect.[24]

[*What plurality is, and in what respect God can be called one, and in what respect unique.*] The opposite of unity is plurality, which likewise obviously adds nothing to things, nor is it anything but a mode of thinking, just as we clearly and distinctly understand. Nor do I see what more remains to be said regarding a thing so clear, except that here it should be noted that, insofar as we separate God from other beings, he can be said to be one; but insofar as we conceive that there cannot be more than one of the same nature, he is called unique. In truth, if we wished to look into the matter more rigorously, we might perhaps show that God is only improperly called one and unique. But this question is of little importance—indeed, it is of no importance—to those who are concerned with things rather than words. Therefore we leave this and pass on to the second term, at the same time explaining what the false is.

[*What is the true and what the false, both in the common acceptance and according to philosophers.*] In order that these two, the true and the false, may be correctly perceived, we shall begin with the meaning of words, from which it will be evident that these are only the extrinsic marks of things, and it is only figuratively that they are attributed to things. But because it is

23. These are terms that the scholastics called 'transcendental'. For Thomas Aquinas there were six: 'being', 'thing', 'one', 'something', 'true', and 'good'. Later scholastics limited the list to three: 'one', 'true', and 'good'. See E2P40Schol1 (pp. 88–90) for Spinoza's mature discussion of them as creatures of imagination or blurred sensory cognition.
24. See PPH1A58.

the common people who first invent words that are then used by philosophers, it seems relevant for one who seeks the original meaning of a word to
enquire what it first denoted among common people, especially when other
causes, which might have been derived from the nature of language, are not
available for the investigation. The first meaning of true and false seems to
have had its origin in story-telling, and the tale was said to be true if it was
of something that had occurred in actuality, and false if it was of something
that had nowhere occurred. Later, philosophers made use of this significa-
tion to denote the agreement or disagreement of an idea with its object
(*ideatum*). Therefore an idea is said to be true if it shows us the thing as it is
in itself, false if it shows us the thing otherwise than as it really is. For ideas
are merely mental narrations or accounts of nature. And hence these terms
came to be applied metaphorically to lifeless things, as when we talk about
true or false gold, as if the gold presented before us were telling us something about itself that either is in itself or not.

[*The true is not a transcendental term.*] Therefore those who have held that
'the true' is a transcendental term or an affection of being are quite wrong.
For this term can be applied to things themselves only improperly, or if you
prefer, figuratively.

[*The difference between truth and a true idea.*] If you go on to ask what is
truth other than a true idea, ask also what is whiteness other than a white
body. For the relationship is the same in both cases.

We have already discussed the cause of the true and the cause of the false.
So now there remains nothing to be noted, nor would it have been worthwhile noting even what we have said if writers had not so tied themselves up
in trifles like these that they could not then extricate themselves, always
looking for a difficulty where there is none.

[*What are the properties of truth? Certainty is not in things.*] The properties
of truth, or a true idea, are (1) that it is clear and distinct, (2) that it removes
all doubt, or, in a word, that it is certain. Those who look for certainty in
things themselves are making the same mistake as when they look for truth
in things themselves. And although we may say that a thing is uncertain, we
are figuratively taking the *ideatum* for the idea. In the same way we also call
a thing doubtful, unless perchance in this case by uncertainty we mean
contingency, or a thing that causes us uncertainty or doubt. There is no
need to spend more time on these matters, and so we shall proceed to the
third term, at the same time explaining what is to be understood by its
contrary.

[*Good and Bad are only relative terms.*] A thing is not said to be either
good or bad when considered in isolation, but only in relation to another

thing for which it is useful in gaining what that thing loves, or contrariwise.[25] Thus each single thing can be called good or bad at the same time in different respects. For example, the counsel that Achitophel gave to Absalom is called good in Holy Scripture, but it was very bad for David, being contrived for his death.[26] And many other things are good, which are not good for all. Thus salvation is good for men, but neither good nor bad for animals or plants, for which it has no relevance. God indeed is said to be supremely good because he benefits all, by his concurrence preserving the being of each individual, than which nothing is more desirable. But no absolute evil exists, as is self-evident.

[*Why some have maintained that there is a metaphysical good.*] But those who keep seeking some metaphysical good not qualified by any relation are laboring under a misapprehension, in that they are confusing a distinction of reason with a real or modal distinction. For they are making a distinction between the thing itself and the *conatus* [striving] to preserve its own being, which every thing possesses, although they do not know what they mean by *conatus*. For although the thing and its *conatus* are distinguished by reason, or rather, by words (and this is the main cause of their error), the two are in no way distinct from one another in reality.

[*The distinction between things and the* conatus *by which they endeavor to persevere in their state.*] That this may be clearly understood, we shall take an example of a very simple kind. Motion has force to persevere in its own state. This force is surely nothing else than motion itself, the fact that the nature of motion is such as it is. For if I say that in this body A there is nothing else than a certain quantity of motion, from this it clearly follows that, as long as I am attending to the body A, I must always say that the body is moving. For if I were to say that it is losing its force of motion, I am necessarily ascribing to it something else beyond what we supposed in the hypothesis, something that is causing it to lose its nature. Now if this reasoning seems rather obscure, then let us grant that this *conatus* to motion is something other than the very laws and nature of motion. Because, then, you suppose this *conatus* to be a metaphysical good, this *conatus* will also necessarily have a *conatus* to persevere in its own being, and this again

25. See E1App (esp. 60–61) This is an example of Spinoza's anticipation of his own account of the relativity of value, and is in direct opposition to Descartes. See also E3P9Schol; E4Pref; E4P37Schol2; TP2/23; TTP16, 180; Ep32, 192. See also Lee Rice, "Spinoza's Relativistic Aesthetics," *Tijdschrift voor Filosofie* 58 (1996a), 476–489.
26. 2 Samuel 17:14.

another *conatus,* and so ad infinitum. I cannot imagine anything more absurd than this. Now the reason why they make a distinction between the *conatus* of a thing and the thing itself is that they feel in themselves a wanting to preserve themselves, and they imagine a similar wanting in each individual thing.[27]

[*Whether God can be called good before things were created.*] However, the question is raised as to whether God could be called good before he created things; and it seems to follow from our definition that God did not possess any such attribute because we say that a thing considered in itself alone cannot be called either good or bad. Many will think this absurd, but why I do not know. We attribute to God many attributes of this kind that did not belong to him, except potentially, before things were created, as when he is called creator, judge, merciful, etc. Therefore arguments like this ought not to be a hindrance to us.

[*How perfection may be ascribed in a relative way, and how it may be ascribed absolutely.*] Furthermore, just as good and bad are only relative terms, so too is perfection,[28] except when we take perfection to mean the very essence of a thing. It is in this sense that we previously said that God possesses infinite perfection, that is, infinite essence or infinite being.

It is not my intention to go farther into these matters. The rest of what concerns the general part of Metaphysics I believe to be sufficiently well known, and therefore not worthwhile pursuing any farther.

27. Spinoza holds that *conatus* is the essence of the individual. See E3P4; E3P6; E3P7; E3P9Schol.
28. For Spinoza's view of perfection, see E4Pref.

APPENDIX CONTAINING
METAPHYSICAL THOUGHTS.

Part 2.

In which are briefly explained the main topics that commonly
occur in the special part of Metaphysics,[29]
concerning God, his
attributes, and the human mind.[30]

Chapter 1.

Of God's Eternity.

[*The division of Substance.*] We have already shown that in Nature there is
nothing but substances and their modes.[31] So one should not here expect us
to say anything about substantial forms and real accidents, for these and
things of this type are plainly absurd. We then divided substances into two
general kinds, extension and thought, and we divided thought into created
thought (i.e., the human mind) and uncreated thought (i.e., God). The
existence of God we have demonstrated more than adequately both a
posteriori, from the idea we have of him, and a priori, from his essence as
being the cause of his existence.[32] But because we have treated certain of his

29. The order of exposition used by scholastic authors varies considerably from one
to another. Spinoza appears to be following Burgersdijck in most cases. In his French
translation (p. 436), Appuhn (1964) provides a set of tables comparing Spinoza,
Suarez, Martini, Burgersdijck, and Heereboord on the general division of what
Spinoza here calls 'special metaphysics'.
30. In this section God's existence is explained in a way quite different from that in
which men commonly understand it; for they confuse God's existence with their
own, with the result that they imagine God to be something like a man, and they fail
to note the true idea of God that they possess, or are quite unconscious of possessing
it. And so it comes about that they can neither prove nor conceive God's existence
either a priori (i.e. from his true definition or essence) or a posteriori, from the idea
of him insofar as it is in us. Therefore in this section we shall try to show as clearly as
we can that God's existence is completely different from the existence of created
things. [Balling]
31. See E1P4Dem.
32. See PPC1Defs5–8; PPC1Ax4; PPC1P5–7.

110

attributes more briefly than the importance of the subject requires, we have decided to return to them here, to explain them more fully and also to provide answers to some problems.

[*Duration does not pertain to God.*] The principal attribute that must be considered before all others is God's eternity, whereby we explicate his duration; or rather, to avoid attributing any duration to God, we say that he is eternal. For, as we noted in the first Part, duration is an affection of the existence of things, not of their essence; but we cannot attribute any duration to God, whose existence is of his essence. For whoever attributes duration to God is distinguishing his existence from his essence. There are some, however, who ask whether at this moment God has not been in existence longer than when he created Adam; and it seems to them quite clear that this is so, and thus they hold that duration must in no way be denied to God. But they are guilty of *petitio principii*, in assuming that God's essence is distinct from his existence. They ask whether God, who existed up to the time of Adam, has not existed over more time between the creation of Adam and our time. Thus they are attributing a longer duration to God as each day passes, and they assume that he is, as it were, continuously created by himself. If they did not distinguish God's existence from his essence, they could not possibly attribute duration to God, because duration can in no way pertain to the essences of things. For no one will ever say that the essence of a circle or a triangle, insofar as it is an eternal truth, has lasted longer at this moment than at the time of Adam. Furthermore, because duration is conceived as longer or shorter, or as consisting of parts, it clearly follows that no duration can be attributed to God. For because his being is eternal, that is, there cannot be in it any before or after, we can never attribute duration to God without at the same time destroying the true conception we have of him. That is to say, by attributing duration to him we would be dividing into parts that which of its own nature is infinite and can never be conceived except as infinite.[33]

[*The reasons why writers have attributed duration to God.*] Now the reasons why writers have thus erred are: (1) They have attempted to explain eternity without giving their attention to God, as if eternity could be understood without consideration of the divine essence, or were something other than the divine essence. And this again has arisen because, through poverty of language, we are in the habit of attributing eternity even to things whose

---

33. We are dividing his existence into parts, or conceiving it as divisible, when we attempt to explicate it through duration. See Part 1, 4. [Balling]

essence is distinct from their existence, as when we say that no contradiction is implied in the world having been in existence from eternity; and again when we attribute eternity to the essences of things while we conceive the things as not existing; for we then call the essences eternal. (2) They have been attributing duration to things only insofar as they held them to be subject to continuous variation, and not, as is our practice, in accordance as their essence is distinguished from their existence. (3) Finally, they have distinguished God's essence from his existence, as is the case with created things.

These errors, I say, have led them astray. By reason of the first error they have failed to understand what eternity is, taking it rather to be some kind of duration. The second error made it difficult for them to see the difference between the duration of created things and God's eternity. Finally, because duration is only an affection of existence and they have made a distinction between God's existence and his essence, the third error has led to their attributing duration to God, as we have already said.

[*What is Eternity.*] But for the better understanding of what eternity is, and how it cannot be conceived without the divine essence, attention must be given to what we have said already, namely, that created things—that is, all things besides God—always exist solely by the force or essence of God, and not by their own force. Hence it follows that the present existence of things is not the cause of their future existence. Only God's immutability is the cause, which compels us to say that when God has created a thing in the first place, he will thereafter continuously preserve it, that is, he will continue the same action of creating it. From this we conclude:

1. That a created thing can be said to enjoy existence, on the grounds that existence is not of its essence. But God cannot be said to enjoy existence, for God's existence is God himself, just as is his essence. Hence it follows that created things enjoy existence, but this is not so with God.

2. That all created things, while enjoying present duration and existence, are entirely lacking in future duration and existence, because this has to be continuously attributed to them, whereas nothing of the sort can be said of their essence. But because God's existence is of his essence, we cannot attribute future existence to him. For the same existence that he would then have must even now be attributed to him in actuality; or, to speak more properly, infinite actual existence pertains to God in the same way as infinite actual intellect pertains to him. Now this infinite existence I call eternity, which is to be attributed to God alone and not

to any created thing, even though, I say, its duration is without beginning or end.

So much for eternity. Of God's necessity I say nothing, there being no need now that we have demonstrated his existence from his essence. Let us proceed, therefore, to his unity.

Chapter 2.

Of the Unity of God.[34]

We have often wondered at the futile arguments with which writers attempt to prove the unity of God, arguments such as: If one could have created the world, others would have been superfluous; if all things work together to the same end, they have been produced by one maker, and other arguments like these, drawn from the relationship of things or their extrinsic characteristics.[35] So, dismissing all these arguments, we shall here set out our proof as clearly and as briefly as possible, as follows.[36]

[*God is unique.*] Among God's attributes we have also listed the highest degree of understanding, adding that he possesses all his perfection from himself and not from any other source. If you now say that there are more than one God, or supremely perfect beings, these must all necessarily possess understanding in the highest degree. That this may be so, it is not enough that each should understand only himself; for because each must understand all things, he must understand both himself and the others. From this it would follow that the perfection of the intellect of each one would depend partly on himself and partly on another. Therefore no one of them can be a supremely perfect being, that is, as we have just noted, a being that possesses all its perfection from itself, and not from any other source. Yet we have already demonstrated that God is a most perfect being, and that he exists. So we can now conclude that he exists as one alone; for

---

34. Cf. PPC1P11Dem.
35. The two arguments judged as without merit here are found in Burgersdijck (*Institutiones metaphysicarum,* Book I). Maimonides also used a variant of the first argument in his *Moreh Nebuchim* I, Chap. 75. The second is based on a teleological framework derived from Aristotle's *Metaphysics,* Book XI, Chap. 10.
36. The argument following may derive from Scotus, but it is contrary to the account later developed by Spinoza in E1P31.

if more than one God existed, it would follow that a most perfect being has imperfection, which is absurd.[37] So much for the unity of God.

Chapter 3.

Of the Immeasurableness of God.

[*How God is called infinite, and how immeasurable.*] We have previously shown that no being can be conceived as finite and imperfect (i.e., as participating in nothingness) unless we first have regard to the perfect and infinite being, that is, God. So only God must be said to be absolutely infinite, in that we find him to consist in actual fact of infinite perfection. But he can also be said to be immeasurable or boundless insofar as we have regard to this point, that there is no being by which God's perfection can be limited. From this it follows that the infinity of God, in spite of the form of the word, is something most positive; for it is insofar as we have regard to his essence or consummate perfection that we say that he is infinite. But measurelessness is attributed to God only in a relational way; for it does not pertain to God insofar as he is considered absolutely as a most perfect being, but only insofar as he is considered as a first cause that, even though it were most perfect only in relation to secondary beings, would nevertheless be measureless. For there would be no being, and consequently no being could be conceived, more perfect than he by which he might be limited or measured. (For a fuller discussion, see Axiom 9 Part 1.)[38]

[*What is commonly understood by the immeasurableness of God.*] Yet writers on all sides, in treating of the immeasurableness of God, appear to attribute quantity to God. For from this attribute they wish to conclude that God must necessarily be present everywhere, as if they meant that if there were any place where God was not, his quantity would be limited.[39] This same point is even more clearly apparent from another argument they produce to show that God is infinite or measureless (for they confuse these two terms) and also that he is everywhere. If God, they say, is pure activity, as indeed he is, he is bound to be everywhere and infinite. For if he were not

---

37. Even though this proof is quite convincing, nevertheless it does not explain God's unity. I therefore suggest to the reader that we conclude the unity of God more correctly from the nature of his existence, which is not distinguished from God's essence, or which necessarily follows from his essence. [Balling]
38. Cf. E1Def6; E1P8Schol1; TIE88–89.
39. This is Burgersdijck's argument in the *Institutiones metaphysicarum*, 207.

everywhere, then either he cannot be wherever he wants to be, or else (note this) he must necessarily move about. This clearly shows that they attribute immeasurableness to God insofar as they consider him to be quantitative; for it is from the properties of extension that they derive these arguments for asserting the immeasurableness of God. Nothing could be more absurd.

[*Proof that God is everywhere.*] If you now ask how, then, shall we prove that God is everywhere, I reply that we have abundantly demonstrated this when we showed that nothing can exist even for a moment without being continuously created by God at every single moment.[40]

[*God's omnipresence cannot be explained.*] Now, for God's ubiquity or his presence in individual things to be properly understood, we should necessarily have to have a clear insight into the inmost nature of the divine will whereby he created things and continuously goes on creating them. Because this exceeds human capacity, it is impossible to explain how God is everywhere.[41]

[*Some hold, wrongly, that God's immeasurableness is threefold.*] Some claim that God's immeasurableness is threefold—that of his essence, his power, and his presence. But this is nonsense, for they seem to distinguish between God's essence and his power.[42]

[*God's power is not distinct from his essence.*] Others, too, have said the same thing more openly, asserting that God is everywhere through power, but not through essence, as if God's power were distinct from all his attributes or his infinite essence. But in fact it can be nothing else; for if it were something else, it would either be some creature or something accidental to the divine essence without which the divine essence could be conceived. Both of these alternatives are absurd; for if it were a creature, it would need God's power for its preservation, and this would give rise to an infinite progression. And if it were something accidental, God would not be a most simple being, contrary to what we have demonstrated previously.[43]

---

40. This argument was frequently used by Descartes, and is derived from Aquinas (*Summa theol.* I, q. 8, a. 1) and Scotus (*Disputatio* XXX).
41. Here it should be noted that when ordinary folk say that God is over all, they are depicting him as the spectator of a play. From this it is evident, as we say at the end of this chapter, that men are constantly confusing the divine nature with human nature. [Balling]
42. Cf. PPC1P17Cor; PPC2P2Schol. According to Heereboord (*Meletemata philosphica*, 138), this threefold division comes from Thomas Aquinas (*Summa theol.* I, q. 8, a. 3), who attributes it to Peter Lombard (*Sententiarum* I, d. 37). Spinoza agrees that God's power and essence are identical: E1P34; E3P7; Ep64, 298; TTP6, 74.
43. See also E1P28 for a more developed version of this argument.

[*Nor is his omnipotence.*] Finally, by the immeasurableness of his presence they again seem to mean something besides the essence of God, through which things have been created and are continuously preserved. This is surely a great absurdity, into which they have fallen through confusing God's intellect with human intellect, and frequently comparing his power with the power of kings.

Chapter 4.

Of the Immutability of God.

[*What change is, and what transformation.*] By 'change' we here understand all the variation that can occur in a subject while the essence of the subject remains as it was. But this term is also commonly taken in a broader sense to mean the corruption of things—not an absolute corruption, but such as also includes generation following on the corruption, as when we say that peat is changed into ashes, or men into beasts. But to denote this latter meaning philosophers use yet another word—transformation. Here we are speaking only of that change in which there is no transformation of the subject as when we say that Peter has changed his color, or his character, etc.

[*In God there can be no transformation.*] We must now see whether such changes are applicable to God, for there is no need to say anything about transformation, now that we have shown that God exists necessarily, that is, that God cannot cease to be, or be transformed into another God. For then he would both cease to be, and also there could be more than one God at the same time. Both of these possibilities we have shown to be absurd.

[*What are the causes of change.*] However, for a clearer understanding of what here remains to be said, we must take into consideration that all change proceeds either from external causes, with or without the subject's consent, or from an internal cause and the subject's free choice. For example, that a man becomes darker, falls ill, grows, and the like, all proceed from external causes, the first two against the subject's will, the last in accordance with it. But that he wills, walks, displays anger, etc., proceed from internal causes.

[*God is not changed by something else.*] Now the first-named changes, those that proceed from external causes, cannot possibly apply to God; for he alone is the cause of all things and is not acted on by anyone. Moreover, nothing created has in itself any force to exist, and so far less can it have any force to act on anything outside itself or on its own cause. And although there are many places in Holy Scripture where God has been angry, or sad, etc., because of the sins of men, in these passages the effect is taken as the cause, just as we also say that the sun is stronger and higher in summer than in winter, although it has not changed its position or renewed its strength. And that such is often the teaching even of Holy Scripture is to be seen in Isaiah; for he says in chapter 59, verse 2, when he is rebuking the people: "Your iniquities separate you from your God."

[*Nor again by himself.*] Let us therefore proceed and ask whether any change can come about in God from God himself. We do not grant that there can be such a change in God; indeed, we deny it completely.[44] For every change that depends on the will is designed to change its subject to a better state, and this cannot apply to a most perfect being. Then again, there can be no such change except for the purpose of avoiding something disadvantageous or of acquiring some good that is lacking. In the case of God there can be no place for either of these purposes. Hence we conclude that God is an immutable being.[45] Note that I have here deliberately omitted the commonly accepted divisions of change,[46] although we have also in a sense covered them. For there was no need to deny them individually of God because in Prop. 16 Part 1 we have demonstrated that God is incorporeal, and those commonly accepted divisions refer only to changes in matter.

Chapter 5.

Of the Simplicity of God.

[*The threefold distinction between things: real, modal, and a distinction of reason.*] Let us proceed to the simplicity of God. In order that this attribute of God may be rightly understood, we must recall what Descartes said in *Princip. Philosophiae* Part 1 Arts. 48 and 49, to wit, that in Nature there is

---

44. Cf. E1P20Cor2.
45. Note that this can be much more clearly seen if we attend to the nature of God's will and his decrees. For, as I shall show in due course, God's will, through which he has created things, is not distinct from his intellect, through which he understands them. So to say that God understands that the three angles of a triangle are equal to two right angles is the same as to say that God has willed or decreed that the three angles of a triangle should be equal to two right angles. Therefore, for us to conceive that God can change his decrees is just as impossible as to think that the three angles of a triangle are not equal to two right angles. Furthermore, the fact that there can be no change in God can also be proved in other ways; but, because we aim at brevity, we prefer not to pursue this further. [Balling]
46. Further subdivisions are found in Heereboord (*Meletemata philosophica*, 972).

nothing but substances and their modes, whence in Arts. 60, 61, and 62 he deduces a threefold distinction between things—real, modal, and a distinction of reason.[47] What is called a real distinction is that whereby two substances, whether of different or of the same attribute, are distinguished from one another; for example, thought and extension, or the parts of matter. This distinction is recognized from the fact that each of the two can be conceived, and consequently can exist, without the help of the other. Modal distinction is of two kinds, that between a mode of substance and the substance itself, and that between two modes of one and the same substance. The latter we recognize from the fact that, although either mode can be conceived without the help of the other, neither can be conceived without the help of the substance of which they are modes. The former distinction we recognize from the fact that, although the substance can be conceived without its mode, the mode cannot be conceived without the substance. Finally, what is termed a distinction of reason is that which arises between a substance and its attribute, as when duration is distinguished from extension. And this is also recognized from the fact that such a substance cannot be understood without that attribute.

[*How all composition arises, and how many kinds there are.*] All composition arises from these three kinds of distinction. The first composition is that of two or more substances either of the same attribute, as is the case with all composition of two or more bodies, or of different attributes, as is the case with man. The second composition results from the union of different modes. The third composition is not a composition, but is only conceived by reason as if it were so, in order that a thing may thereby be more easily understood. Whatever is not a composition of the first two kinds must be said to be simple.

[*God is a most simple Being.*][48] It must therefore be shown that God is not a composite thing, from which we can conclude that he is a most simple being; and this we shall easily accomplish. Because it is self-evident that component parts are prior at least by nature to the composite whole, then of necessity those substances from whose coalescence and union God is composed will be prior to God by nature, and each can be conceived through

---

47. This threefold distinction, frequently used by Descartes, has many scholastic roots (see Heereboord, *Meletemata philosophica*, 320).
48. On God's simplicity see PPC1P17 and PPC1P17Cor, with the note that Spinoza provides thereto. The reflections that Spinoza here offer are further developed in the opening propositions of the *Ethics*: see E1P13 (God's indivisibility); E1P15Schol (God's simplicity); Ep12, 103.

itself without being attributed to God. Again, because they are necessarily distinct from one another in reality, then necessarily each of them can also exist through itself without the help of the others. And thus, as we have just said, there could be as many Gods as there are substances from which it was supposed that God is composed. For because each can exist through itself, it must exist of itself, and therefore it will also have the force to give itself all the perfections that we have shown to be in God, as we have already explained fully in Prop. 7 Part 1, where we demonstrated the existence of God. Now because nothing more absurd than this can be said, we conclude that God is not composed of a coalescence and union of substances. That there is also no composition of different modes in God is convincingly proved from there being no modes in God. For modes arise from an alteration of substance—see *Princ.* Part 1 Art. 56. Finally, if someone wishes to imagine another kind of composition, from the essence of things and their existence, we by no means oppose him. But let him remember that we have already sufficiently demonstrated that these two are not distinct in God.

[*God's Attributes are distinguished only by Reason.*] Hence we can clearly conclude that all the distinctions we make between God's attributes are nothing other than distinctions of reason, and that they are not distinct from one another in reality. Understand these distinctions of reason to be such as I have just referred to, namely, distinctions that are recognized from the fact that such-and-such a substance cannot be without that particular attribute. Hence we conclude that God is a most simple being. So now, disregarding the medley of distinctions made by the Peripatetics,[49] we pass on to the life of God.

Chapter 6.

Of the Life of God.

[*What philosophers commonly understand by Life.*] For the correct understanding of this attribute, the life of God, it is necessary to explain in general terms what in the case of each individual thing is meant by its life. We shall first examine the opinion of the Peripatetics. By life they understand 'the continuance of the nutritive soul, accompanied by heat'—see

---

49. Heereboord enumerates and discusses with approval this "medley of distinctions" in *Meletemata philosophica*, 320.

Aristotle *De Respirat.* Book 1 Chapter 8.[50] And because they imagined there
to be three souls, the vegetative, the sensitive, and the intellective, which
they attribute exclusively to plants, animals, and men, it follows, as they
themselves acknowledge, that all else is devoid of life. Even so, they did not
venture to say that minds and God are without life. Perhaps they were
afraid of falling into the contrary view, that if these were without life, they
were dead. So Aristotle in his *Metaphysics* Book 11 Chapter 7 gives yet
another definition of life, applicable only to minds, namely, that life is the
operation of the intellect, and in this sense he attributes life to God, as one
who understands and is pure activity.[51]

However, we shall not spend much effort in refuting these views. For as
regards the three souls that they attribute to plants, animals, and men, we
have already sufficiently demonstrated that these are nothing but fictions,
having shown that in matter there is nothing but mechanical structures and
their operations. As to the life of God, I do not know why in Aristotle it
should be called activity of intellect rather than activity of will, and the like.
However, expecting no reply to this, I pass on to explain, as promised, what
life is.

[*To what things life can be attributed.*] Although this term is often taken in
a figurative sense to mean the character of a man, we shall briefly explain
only what it denotes in a philosophical sense. It should be noted that if life
is also to be attributed to corporeal things, nothing will be devoid of life; but
if only to those things wherein soul is united to body, then it must be
attributed only to men, and perhaps also to animals, but not to minds or to
God. However, because the word 'life' is commonly used in a wider sense,
there is no doubt that it should also be attributed to corporeal things not
united to minds and to minds separated from body.

[*What life is, and what it is in God.*] Therefore by life we for our part
understand the force through which things persevere in their own being.
And because that force is different from the things themselves, we quite
properly say that things themselves have life.[52] But the force whereby God
perseveres in his own being is nothing but his essence, so that those speak
best who call God 'life.' There are some theologians who hold the opinion

---

50. The reference may be to *De respiratione* 474a25, but see also *De anima* 415a23–25.
Similar passages occur in the *Metaphysics*, but Spinoza's interpretation is incorrect
for all three works because in none of them is Aristotle engaged in providing a
definition of 'life' so much as discussing its common features.
51. This is probably a reference to *Metaphysics* XII, vii (1072b27–29).
52. Spinoza holds that all bodies or individuals are animated: see E2P13Schol.

that it is for this reason—that God is life and is not distinct from life—that the Jews when they swore an oath used to say "by the living Jehovah," and not "by the life of Jehovah," as Joseph, when swearing by Pharaoh's life, said "by the life of Pharaoh."[53]

Chapter 7.

Of God's Intellect.[54]

[*God is omniscient.*] We previously listed among the attributes of God omniscience, which quite obviously pertains to God because knowledge implies perfection, and God, as a most perfect being, must not lack any perfection. Therefore knowledge must be attributed to God in the highest degree, that is, a knowledge that does not presume or posit any ignorance or privation of knowledge; for then there would be some imperfection in the attribute itself, that is, in God. From this it follows that God's intellect has never been merely potential, nor does he reach a conclusion by reasoning.[55]

[*The objects of God's knowledge are not things external to God.*] Furthermore, from God's perfection it also follows that his ideas are not defined, as ours are, by objects that are external to God. On the contrary, the things created by God external to God are determined by God's intellect. (N.B. From this it clearly follows that God's intellect, by which he understands created things, and his will and power, by which he has determined them, are one and the same thing.) For otherwise these objects would have their

---

53. The reference is to Genesis 42:15–16.
54. From what is demonstrated in the next three chapters in which we treat of God's intellect, his will and his power, it follows quite clearly that the essences of things and the necessity of their existing from a given cause is nothing other than God's determinate will or decree. Therefore God's will is most apparent to us when we conceive things clearly and distinctly. So it is ridiculous that philosophers, when they are ignorant of the causes of things, take refuge in the will of God. We constantly see this happening when they say that the things whose causes are unknown to them have come about only from God's good pleasure and absolute decree. The common people, too, have found no stronger proof of God's providence and guidance than that which they draw from their ignorance of causes. This clearly shows that they have no knowledge whatever of the nature of God's will, attributing to him a human will that is truly quite distinct from our intellect. This I consider to have been the basic cause of superstition, and perhaps of much roguery. [Balling] Balling follows Spinoza here: see E1App and especially TTPpref, 1–3.
55. Cf. PPC1P9; CM2/2.

own nature and essence through themselves and would be prior, at least by nature, to the divine intellect—which is absurd. And because some people have failed to take careful note of this, they have fallen into gross errors. Some have maintained that external to God there is matter, coeternal with him and existing of itself, and that God, understanding this matter, has, according to some, merely reduced it to order, and according to others, has in addition impressed forms on it. Others again have maintained that things of their own nature are either necessary or impossible or contingent, and so God knows the latter also as contingent and is quite ignorant as to whether they exist or not. Finally, others have said that God knows contingent things from their relation to other things, perhaps because of his long experience. Besides these errors I could here mention others of this kind, did I not consider it to be superfluous, because from what has already been said their falsity makes itself apparent.

[*The object of God's knowledge is God himself.*] Let us therefore return to our theme, that outside God there is no object of his knowledge, but he is himself the object of his knowledge, or rather, he is his own knowledge. Those who think that the world is also the object of God's knowledge are much less discerning than those who would maintain that a building constructed by some distinguished architect is the object of the architect's knowledge. For the builder is forced to seek suitable material outside himself as well, whereas God has not sought any material outside himself. Things have been constructed by his intellect or will, both with regard to their essence and their existence.

[*How God knows sin, entities of reason, etc.*] The question now arises as to whether God knows evil or sin, entities of reason, and things of that kind. We reply that God must necessarily know those things of which he is the cause, especially so because they cannot exist even for a moment except with the divine concurrence. Therefore, because evil and sin have no being in things but only in the human mind when it compares things with one another, it follows that God does not know them as separate from human minds. Entities of reason we have said to be modes of thinking, and it is in this way that they must be understood by God, that is, insofar as we perceive him as preserving and continuing to create the human mind, in whatever way that is constituted. But we are not saying that God has such modes of thinking in himself in order that he may more easily retain what he understands. And if only proper attention is given to these few points we have made, no problem can arise concerning God's intellect that cannot quite easily be solved.

[*How God knows particular things, and how universals.*] But meanwhile we must not pass over the error made by certain people who maintain that God knows nothing but eternal things such as angels and the heavens, which they suppose to be by their own nature not subject to generation and corruption, but that of this world he knows nothing but species, these being likewise not subject to generation and corruption. Such people do indeed seem set on going astray, contriving utter absurdities. For what can be more absurd than to cut off God's knowledge from particular things, which cannot even for a moment be without God's concurrence? Again, they are maintaining that God is ignorant of really existing things, while ascribing to God knowledge of universals, which have no being nor any essence apart from that of particular things. We, on the other hand, attribute to God knowledge of particular things and deny him knowledge of universals except insofar as he understands human minds.

[*In God there is only one simple idea.*] Finally, before bringing this discussion to a close, we ought to deal with the question as to whether there is in God more than one idea or only one most simple idea. To this I reply that God's idea through which he is called omniscient is unique and completely simple. For in actual fact God is called omniscient for no other reason than that he has the idea of himself, an idea or knowledge that has always existed together with God. For it is nothing but his essence and could have had no other way of being.

[*What is God's knowledge concerning created things.*] But God's acquaintance with created things cannot be referred to God's knowledge without some impropriety; for, if God had so willed, created things would have had a quite different essence, and this could have no place in the knowledge that God has of himself.[56] Still, the question will arise as to whether that knowledge of created things, properly or improperly so termed, is manifold or only single. However, in reply, this question differs in no way from those that ask whether God's decrees and volitions are several or not, and whether God's omnipresence, or the concurrence whereby he preserves particular things, is the same in all things. Concerning these matters, we have already said that we can have no distinct knowledge. However, we know with certainty that, just as God's concurrence, if it is referred to God's omnipotence, must be no more than one although manifested in various ways in its effects, so too God's volitions and decrees (for thus we may term his knowledge concerning created things) considered in God are not a plural-

---

56. Spinoza argues in the *Ethics* that God could not have created things any differently: see E1P20; E1P20Cor2; E1P29; E1P33; E1P33Schol2.

ity, even though they are expressed in various ways through created things, or rather, in created things. Finally, if we look to the whole of Nature by analogy, we can consider it as a single entity, and consequently the idea of God, or his decree concerning *Natura naturata,* will be only one.[57]

Chapter 8.

Of God's Will.

[*We do not know how God's essence, his intellect by which he understands himself, and his will by which he loves himself, are distinguished.*][58] God's will, by which he wills to love himself, follows necessarily from his infinite intellect, by which he understands himself, but how these three are distinguished from one another—his essence, his intellect by which he understands himself, and his will by which he wills to love himself—this we fail to comprehend. We are acquainted with the word 'personality', which theologians commonly use to explain this matter. But although we know the word, we do not know its meaning, nor can we form any clear and distinct conception of it, although we firmly believe that in the most blessed vision of God, which is promised to the faithful, God will reveal this to his own.[59]

[*God's will and power, as externally manifested, are not distinguished from his intellect.*] Will and power, as externally manifested, are not distinguished from God's intellect, as is now well established from what has preceded. For we have shown that God has decreed not only that things should exist, but also that they should exist with a certain nature; that is to say, both their essence and existence must have depended on God's will and power. From this we clearly and distinctly perceive that God's intellect and his power and will, whereby he has created, understood, and preserves or loves created things, are in no way distinct from one another save only in respect of our thought.

---

57.   *Natura naturata* or 'nature natured' is Spinoza's term to refer to the whole of produced nature. This unified whole, of course, is the same as *Natura naturans,* or 'nature naturing'. The two are identical but are understood from different vantage points. On these terms, see the introduction to the *Ethics,* p. 11; E1P29Schol; E1P31Schol. On the singleness of nature, see E2P13Schol.
58.   In the notes to his translation (p. 438), Appuhn suggests that the themes developed in this section are more properly those of the mature Spinoza (in the *Ethics*) rather than having any Cartesian source.
59.   Spinoza confesses to Meyer in Ep12A that he does not at all understand this term (*personalitas*); see Ep12A, 109. Meyer apparently had asked Spinoza to better explain this term in the CM.

[*It is improper to say that God hates some things and loves other things.*] Now when we say that God hates some things and loves other things, this is said in the same sense as when Scripture tells us that the earth will vomit forth men, and other things of that kind. But from Scripture itself it can be sufficiently inferred that God is not angry with anyone, and that he does not love things in the way that is commonly believed. For this is in Isaiah, and more clearly in Paul's Epistle to the Romans, Chapter 9: "For the children being not yet born (that is, the sons of Isaac), neither having done any good or evil, that the purpose of God according to election might stand, not of works but of him that calleth, it was said unto her, the elder shall serve the younger, etc."[60] And a little farther on, "Therefore hath he mercy on whom he will, and whom he will he hardeneth. Thou wilt then say unto me, 'Why doth he yet find fault? For who hath resisted his will?' Nay but, O man, who art thou that replieth against God? Shall the thing formed say unto him who formed it, 'Why has thou made me thus?' Hath not the potter power over the clay, of the same lump to make one vessel unto honor, and another unto dishonor? etc."[61]

[*Why God admonishes men, why he does not save without admonition, and why the impious are punished.*] If you now ask why, then, does God admonish men, to this there is a ready answer: the reason why God has decreed from eternity that he would warn men at a particular time is this, that those whom he has willed to be saved might turn from their ways. If you go on to ask whether God could not have saved them without that warning, we reply that he could have done so. "Why then does he not so save them?" you will perhaps again ask. To this I shall reply when you have told me why God did not make the Red Sea passable without a strong east wind, and why he does not bring about all particular motions without other motions, and innumerable other things that God does through mediating causes. You will again ask, why then are the impious punished, since they act by their own nature and in accordance with the divine decree. But I reply, it is also as a result of the divine decree that they are punished. And if only those ought to be punished whom we suppose to be sinning from free-will alone, why do men try to destroy poisonous snakes? For they sin only from their own nature, and can do no other.[62]

60. Romans 9:11–12.
61. Romans 9:18–21. Spinoza also cites this passage in Ep75, 337 and TTP16 note 34, 248–249.
62. On the necessity of sin and its punishment, see Ep19 and Ep78.

[Scripture teaches nothing that is opposed to the natural light.] Finally, whatever other passages there are in Holy Scripture that cause uneasiness, this is not the place to explain them. For here the object of our enquiry is confined to what can be attained most certainly by natural reason, and to demonstrate these things clearly is sufficient to convince us that the Holy Book must be teaching the same. For truth is not opposed to truth, nor can Scripture be teaching the nonsense that is commonly supposed. If we were to find in it anything contrary to the natural light, we could refute it with the same freedom with which we refute the Koran and the Talmud. But far be it from us to think that something can be found in Holy Scripture opposed to the light of Nature.[63]

Chapter 9.

Of God's Power.

[How God's omnipotence should be understood.] That God is omnipotent has already been sufficiently demonstrated. Here we shall attempt only to explain in brief how this attribute is to be understood; for many speak of it without proper piety and not according to truth.[64] They say that, by their own nature and not from God's decree, some things are possible, some things impossible, and some things necessary, and that God's omnipotence is concerned only with the possible. We, however, who have already shown that all things depend absolutely on God's decree, say that God is omnipotent. But having understood that he has decreed some things from the mere freedom of his will, and then that he is immutable, we say now that he cannot act against his own decrees, and that this is impossible simply because it is at variance with God's perfection.

[All things are necessary with respect to God's decree. It is wrong to say that some things are necessary in themselves, and other things with respect to his decree.] But perhaps someone will argue that some things we find necessary only while having regard for God's decree, while on the other hand some things we find necessary without regard for God's decree. Take, for exam-

---

63. Spinoza here follows Maimonides, but later will claim that Scripture does teach things that are contrary to reason. See TTP7. The compatibility between Scripture and reason is debated in the Spinoza/Blyenbergh correspondence: see Ep20–21; Ep22–24.
64. The theme of an 'impious approach' to divine omnipotence is developed by Heereboord (*Meletemata philosophica*, 30–32).

ple, that Josiah burnt the bones of the idolaters on the altar of Jeroboam.[65] If we attend only to Josiah's will, we shall regard the event as a possible one, and in no way having necessarily to happen except from the prophet's having predicted it from God's decree. But that the three angles of a triangle must be equal to two right angles is something that manifests itself.

But surely these people are inventing distinctions in things from their own ignorance. For if men clearly understood the whole order of Nature, they would find all things to be equally as necessary as are the things treated in mathematics. But because this is beyond the reach of human knowledge, certain things are judged by us as possible and not as necessary.[66] Therefore we must say either that God is powerless—because all things are in actual fact necessary—or that God is all-powerful, and that the necessity we find in things has resulted solely from God's decree.[67]

[*If God had made the nature of things other than it is, he would also have had to give us a different intellect.*] Suppose the question is now raised: What if God had decreed things otherwise and had rendered false those things that are now true? Would we still not accept them as quite true? I answer, yes indeed, if God had left us with the nature that he has given us. But he might then, had he so wished, have also given us a nature—as is now the case—such as to enable us to understand Nature and its laws, as they would have been laid down by God. Indeed, if we have regard to his faithfulness, he would have had to do so. This is also evident from the fact, as we have previously stated, that the whole of *Natura naturata* is nothing but a unique entity, from which it follows that man is a part of Nature that must cohere with the rest.[68] Therefore from the simplicity of God's decree it would also follow that if God had created things in a different way, he would likewise have also so constituted our nature that we could understand things as they had been created by God. So although we want to retain the same distinction in God's power as is commonly adopted by philosophers, we are nevertheless constrained to expound it in a different way.

[*The divisions of God's power—absolute, ordered, ordinary, and extraordinary.*][69] We therefore divide God's power into Ordered and Absolute.

---

65. 1 Kings 13:2, 2 Kings 23:16, 20.
66. Cf. E1P29; E1P33Schol1.
67. On the necessity of nature, see E1P33; E1P33Schol2.
68. Man is not exempt from nature's laws: see TP2/5; TTP16, 179.
69. These divisions are found in Thomas Aquinas (*Summa theol.* I, q. 25, a. 5), Duns Scotus (*Ad Lomb.* Sent. I), and Suarez (*Disputatio* XXX), but are found neither in Burgersdijck nor Heereboord.

We speak of God's absolute power when we consider his omnipotence without regard to his decrees. We speak of his ordered power when we have regard to his decrees.

Then there is a further division into the Ordinary and Extraordinary power of God. His ordinary power is that by which he preserves the world in a fixed order. We mean his extraordinary power when he acts beyond Nature's orders—for example, all miracles, such as the ass speaking, the appearance of angels, and the like.[70] Yet concerning this latter power we may not unreasonably entertain serious doubts, because for God to govern the world with one and the same fixed and immutable order seems a greater miracle than if, because of the folly of mankind, he were to abrogate laws that he himself has sanctioned in Nature in the best way and from pure freedom—as nobody can deny unless he is quite blinded. But we shall leave this for the theologians to decide.[71]

Finally, we pass over other questions commonly raised concerning God's power: Does God's power extend to the past? Can he improve on the things that he does? Can he do many other things than he has done?[72] Answers to these questions can readily be supplied from what has already been said.

Chapter 10.

Of Creation.

That God is the creator of all things we have already established; here we shall now try to explain what is to be understood by creation. Then we shall provide solutions as best we can to those questions that are commonly raised regarding creation. Let us then begin with the first subject.

[*What creation is.*] We say that creation is an operation in which no causes concur beyond the efficient cause; or that a created thing is that which presupposes nothing except God for its existence.[73]

[*The common definition of creation is rejected.*] Here we should note that:
1. We omit the words 'from nothing', which are commonly used by philosophers as if 'nothing' were the matter from which things were produced. This usage of theirs arises from the fact that, being accustomed in the

---

70. Numbers 22:28–31.
71. For Spinoza's views on miracles, see TTP6.
72. These questions are developed and answered by Heereboord (*Meletemata philosophica*, 354).
73. Spinoza suppresses the usual phrase accompanying this definition: *ex nihilo.*

case of generated things to suppose something prior to them from which they are made, in the case of creation they were unable to omit the preposition 'from'. The same confusion has befallen them in the case of matter. Seeing that all bodies are in a place and surrounded by other bodies, when they asked themselves where matter as a whole might be, they replied, "In some imaginary space." So there is no doubt that they have not considered 'nothing' as the negation of all reality but have imagined or pictured it as something real.

[*Our own definition is explained.*] 2. I say that in creation no other causes concur beyond the efficient cause. I might indeed have said that creation denies or excludes all causes beyond the efficient cause. However, I have preferred to say 'concur' so as to avoid having to reply to those who ask whether God in creation did not set before himself an end on account of which he created things. Furthermore, for better explanation, I have added this second definition, that a created thing presupposes nothing but God; because if God did set before himself some end, then obviously that end was not external to God. For there is nothing external to God by which he may be urged to act.

[*Accidents and Modes are not created.*] 3. From this definition it clearly follows that there is no creation of accidents and modes. For these presuppose a created substance besides God.

[*There was no time or duration before creation.*] 4. Finally, neither time nor duration can be imagined before creation; these began along with things. For time is the measure of duration; or rather, it is nothing but a mode of thinking. Therefore it presupposes not just some created thing, but, in particular, thinking men. As for duration, it ceases when created things cease to be and begins when created things begin to exist—created things, I say, because we have already shown beyond doubt that to God there pertains not duration but eternity. Therefore duration presupposes, or at least posits, created things. Those who imagine duration and time prior to created things labor under the same misconception as those who suppose a space outside matter, as is self-evident. So much for the definition of creation.

[*God's action is the same in creating the world and in preserving it.*] Again, there is no need for us to repeat here what we have demonstrated in Axiom 10 Part 1, namely, that the same amount of force is required for the creation of a thing as for its preservation; that is, God's action in creating the world is the same as in its preservation.

Having noted these points, let us proceed to what we promised in the second place. First, we must ask what is created and what is uncreated; and

second, whether what is created could have been created from eternity.
[*What created things are.*] To the first question we reply, in brief, that the
created is every thing whose essence is clearly conceived without any existence, and which is nevertheless conceived through itself: for example,
matter, of which we have a clear and distinct conception when we conceive
it under the attribute of extension, and which we conceive just as clearly
and distinctly whether it exists or not.

[*How God's thought differs from ours.*] But perhaps someone will say that
we perceive thought clearly and distinctly without existence, and that we
nevertheless attribute it to God. To this we reply that we do not attribute to
God such thought as is ours, subject to being acted on and confined by the
nature of things, but such as is pure activity and thus involving existence, as
we have already demonstrated at sufficient length. For we showed that
God's intellect and will are not distinct from his power and his essence,
which involves existence.

[*There is not something external to God and coeternal with him.*] So because
every thing whose essence does not involve existence must, in order to exist,
necessarily be created by God and be continuously preserved by the creator
as we have already abundantly explained, we shall spend no time in refuting
the opinion of those who have maintained that the world, or chaos, or
matter stripped of all form, is coeternal with God and thus independent
of him. Therefore we must pass on to the second question and enquire
whether what has been created could have been created from eternity.

[*What is here denoted by the phrase 'from eternity'.*] For this to be rightly
understood, we must examine this phrase 'from eternity', for by this we
here mean something entirely different from that which we explained
previously when we spoke of God's eternity. Here we mean nothing other
than duration without any beginning, or such duration as, even if we were
to multiply it by many years or tens of thousands of years, and this product
again by tens of thousands, we could still never express by any number,
however great.

[*Proof that there could not have been something created from eternity.*][74] But
that there can be no such duration is clearly demonstrated. For if the world
were to go backward again from this point of time, it could never have such

---

74. In this and the following paragraph Spinoza argues against the thesis that there
is something coeternal with God. Similar arguments are found in Heereboord (*Meletemata philosophica*, 105–107). Freudenthal attributes the position argued against to
Pereira.

a duration; therefore neither could the world have reached this point of time from such a beginning. You will perhaps say that for God nothing is impossible; for he is omnipotent, and so can bring about a duration other than which there could be no greater. We reply that God, being omnipotent, will never create a duration other than which a greater cannot be created by him. For the nature of duration is such that a greater or lesser than a given duration can always be conceived, as is the case with number. You will perhaps insist that God has been from eternity and so has endured until the present, and thus there is a duration other than which a greater cannot be conceived. But in this way there is attributed to God a duration consisting of parts, which we have abundantly refuted when we demonstrated that there pertains to God not duration, but eternity. Would that men had thoroughly considered this truth, for then they might very easily have extricated themselves from many arguments and absurdities, and have given themselves up with the greatest delight to the blessed contemplation of this being.

But let us proceed to answer the arguments put forward by certain people, whereby they try to show the possibility of such an infinite duration stretching from the past.

[*From the fact that God is eternal, it does not follow that his effects can also be from eternity.*] First, then, they assert that the thing produced can be contemporaneous with its cause; but because God has been from eternity then his effects could also have been produced from eternity. And then they further confirm this by the example of the son of God, who was produced by the father from eternity. But from what has already been said, one can clearly see that they are confusing duration with eternity, and they are attributing to God merely a duration from eternity, as is also clear from the example they cite. For they hold that the same eternity that they ascribe to the son of God is possible for creatures. Again, they imagine time and duration as prior to the foundation of the world, and they seek to establish a duration without created things, just as others seek to establish an eternity outside God. Both these assertions are already shown to be quite remote from the truth. Therefore we reply that it is quite false that God can communicate his eternity to his creatures, nor is the son of God a creature, but he is, like his father, eternal. So when we say that the father has begotten the son from eternity, we mean simply this, that the father has always communicated his eternity to the son.[75]

---

75. This passage has presumably been edited by Meyer (see Ep12a, 108), who believed that the original would offend theologians.

[*If God acted necessarily, he would not be of infinite potency.*] Secondly, they argue that, when God acts freely, he is no less powerful than when he acts necessarily; but if God acts necessarily, being of infinite potency he must have created the world from eternity. But this argument, too, can be readily met if we examine its basis. These good people suppose that they can entertain quite different ideas of a being of infinite potency. For they conceive God as of infinite potency both when he acts from the necessity of nature and when he acts freely. We, however, deny that God would be of infinite potency if he were to act from the necessity of nature; and this we may well deny—and indeed they have also necessarily to concede it—now that we have demonstrated that the most perfect being acts freely and can be conceived only as unique. Now if they retort that, even if it is impossible it can nevertheless be posited that God, in acting from the necessity of nature, is of infinite potency, we reply that it is no more permissible to suppose this than to suppose a square circle so as to conclude that all the lines from the center to the circumference are not equal. Not to repeat what we said at an earlier stage, this is well established from what we have just said. For we have just demonstrated that there can be no duration whose double, or whose greater or lesser, cannot be conceived, and therefore a greater or lesser than a given duration can always be created by God, who acts freely with infinite potency. But if God were to act from the necessity of nature, this would in no way follow, for only that duration, which resulted from his nature, could be produced by him, not an infinite number of other durations greater than the given.

Therefore we thus argue in brief; if God were to create the greatest duration, one so great that he could not create one greater, he would necessarily be diminishing his own power. But this latter statement is false, for his power does not differ from his essence; therefore, etc. Again, if God were to act from the necessity of nature, he would have to create a duration such that he himself cannot create a greater. But God, in creating such a duration, is not of infinite potency, for we can always conceive a duration greater than the given. Therefore if God acted from the necessity of nature, he would not be of infinite potency.[76]

[*Whence we have the concept of a duration greater than that which belongs to this world.*] At this point someone may find some difficulty in seeing how, since the world was created five thousand years ago (or more, if the calculations of chronologers are correct), we can nevertheless conceive a greater

76. Cf. E1P17Schol.

duration, which we have asserted is not intelligible without created things. This difficulty will be easily removed if he takes note that we understand that duration not simply from the contemplation of created things but from the contemplation of the infinite power of God for creation. For creatures cannot be conceived as existing and having duration through themselves, but only through the infinite power of God, from which alone they have all their duration. See Prop. 12 Part 1 and its Corollary.

Finally, to waste no time here in answering trivial arguments, these points only are to be noted: the distinction between duration and eternity, and that duration is in no way intelligible without created things, nor eternity without God. When these points have been properly perceived, all arguments can very readily be answered; so we think it unnecessary to spend any more time on these matters.

Chapter 11.

Of God's Concurrence.

Little or nothing remains to be said about this attribute, now that we have shown that God continuously creates a thing as if anew at every moment. From this we have demonstrated that things never have any power from themselves to affect anything or to determine themselves to any action,[77] and that this is the case not only with things outside man but also with the human will.[78] Again, we have also replied to certain arguments concerning this matter; and although many other arguments are frequently produced, I here intend to ignore them, as they principally belong to theology.

However, there are many who, accepting God's concurrence, interpret it in a sense quite at variance with what we have expounded. To expose their fallacy in the simplest way, it should here be noted, as has previously been demonstrated, that present time has no connection with future time (see Ax. 10 Part 1), and that this is clearly and distinctly perceived by us. If only proper attention is paid to this, all their arguments, which may be drawn from philosophy, can be answered without any difficulty.

[*How God's preservation is related to his determining things to act.*] Still, so as not to have touched on this problem without profit, we shall in passing

---

77. Cf. E1P27; E1P28.
78. Here is another example of Spinoza's straying from Descartes and expounding his own viewpoint. Cf. E2P48 to PPH141.

reply to the question as to whether something is added to God's preservation when he determines a thing to act. Now when we spoke about motion, we already hinted at the answer to this question. For we said that God preserves the same quantity of motion in Nature; therefore if we consider the nature of matter in its entirety, nothing new is added to it. But with respect to particular things, in a sense it can be said that something new is added to it. Whether this is also the case with spiritual things is unclear, for it is not obvious that they have such mutual interdependence. Finally, because the parts of duration have no interconnection, we can say that God does not so much preserve things as continue to create them. Therefore, if a man has now a determinate freedom to perform an action, it must be said that God has created him thus at that particular time. Nor can it be objected that the human will is often determined by things external to itself, and that all things in Nature are in turn determined to action by one another; for they are also thus determined by God. No thing can determine the will, nor again can the will be determined, except by the power of God alone.[79] But how this is compatible with human freedom, or how God can bring this about while preserving human freedom, we confess we do not know, as we have already remarked on many occasions.[80]

[*The common division of God's attributes is nominal rather than real.*] This, then, I was resolved to say about the attributes of God, having as yet made no division of them. The division generally given by writers, whereby they divide God's attributes into the incommunicable and the communicable, to speak the truth, seems a nominal rather than a real division. For God's knowledge is no more like human knowledge than the Dog, the constellation in the sky, is like the dog, the barking animal, and perhaps even less so.[81]

[*The Author's own division.*] Our division, however, is as follows. There are some of God's attributes that explicate his essence in action, whereas others, unconcerned with action, set forth the manner of his existing. Of the latter kind are unity, eternity, necessity, etc.: of the former kind are understanding, will, life, omnipotence, etc. This division is quite clear and straightforward and includes all God's attributes.[82]

---

79. Appuhn makes the passive reflexive in his translation ("nor can the will determine itself"), which seems to make more sense.
80. See PPH141. Spinoza, on the contrary, believes that human will is determined: see E2P48.
81. Spinoza develops this line of attack on anthropomorphism more extensively in the *Ethics*, using the same analogy: see E1P17Schol.
82. On this division, see Heereboord, *Meletemata philosophica*, 964.

Chapter 12.

Of the Human Mind.

We must now pass on to created substance, which we have divided into extended and thinking substance. By extended substance we understood matter or corporeal substance; by thinking substance we understood only human minds.

[*Angels are a subject for theology, not metaphysics.*] Although Angels have also been created, yet, because they are not known by the natural light, they are not the concern of metaphysics. For their essence and existence are known only through revelation, and so pertain solely to theology; and because theological knowledge is completely other than, or entirely different in kind from, natural knowledge, it should in no way be confused with it. So let nobody expect us to say anything about angels.

[*The human mind does not derive from something else, but is created by God. Yet we do not know when it is created.*][83] Let us then return to human minds, concerning which few things now remain to be said. Only I must remind you that we have said nothing about the time of the creation of the human mind because it is not sufficiently established at what time God creates it, because it can exist without body. This much is clear, that it does not derive from something else, for this applies only to things that are generated, namely, the modes of some substance. Substance itself cannot be generated, but can be created only by the Omnipotent, as we have sufficiently demonstrated in what has gone before.

[*In what sense the human soul is mortal.*] But to add something about its immortality, it is quite evident that we cannot say of any created thing that its nature implies that it cannot be destroyed by God's power; for he who has the power to create a thing has also the power to destroy it. Furthermore, as we have sufficiently demonstrated, no created thing can exist even for a moment by its own nature, but is continuously created by God.

[*In what sense the human soul is immortal.*] Yet, although the matter stands so, we clearly and distinctly see that we have no idea by which we may conceive that substance is destroyed, in the way that we do have ideas of the corruption and generation of modes. For when we contemplate the structure of the human body, we clearly conceive that such a structure can be

---

83. This is the common scholastic doctrine. It is eventually rejected by Spinoza with a new account of mind-body unity in *Ethics* 2.

destroyed; but when we contemplate corporeal substance,[84] we do not equally conceive that it can be reduced to nothing.

Finally, a philosopher does not ask what God can do from the full extent of his power; he judges the nature of things from those laws that God has imparted to them. So he judges to be fixed and sure what is inferred from those laws to be fixed and sure, while not denying that God can change those laws and all other things. Therefore we too do not enquire, when speaking of the soul, what God can do, but only what follows from the laws of Nature.[85]

[*Its immortality is demonstrated.*] Now because it clearly follows from these laws that substance can be destroyed neither through itself nor through some other created substance—as we have abundantly demonstrated over and over again, unless I am mistaken—we are constrained to maintain from the laws of Nature that the mind is immortal. And if we look into the matter even more closely, we can demonstrate with the greatest certainty that it is immortal. For, as we have just demonstrated, the immortality of the soul clearly follows from the laws of Nature. Now those laws of Nature are God's decrees revealed by the natural light, as is also clearly established from the preceding. Then again, we have also demonstrated that God's decrees are immutable. From all this we clearly conclude that God has made known to men his immutable will concerning the duration of souls not only by revelation but also by the natural light.

[*God acts not against Nature but above Nature. How the Author interprets this.*] Nor does it matter if someone objects that God sometimes destroys those natural laws in order to perform miracles. For most of the wiser theologians concede that God never acts contrary to Nature, but above Nature. That is, as I understand it, God has also many laws of operating that he has not communicated to the human intellect; and if they had been communicated to the human intellect, they would be as natural as the rest.[86]

Hence it is quite clearly established that minds are immortal, nor do I see what remains to be said at this point about the human soul in general. Nor yet would anything remain to be said about its specific functioning, if the

84. Descartes is not consistent in his treatment of corporeal substance as one substance or many. Spinoza is anticipating his own developed doctrine here. See E1P15Schol.
85. Once again Spinoza contradicts Descartes's doctrine and moves in the direction of his own account.
86. Spinoza holds that nothing of God can be known from miracles (TTP6, 73). For Spinoza's full treatment of miracles, see TTP6.

arguments of certain writers, trying to make out that they do not see and sense what in fact they do see and sense, did not call upon me to reply to them.

[*Why some think the will is not free.*] Some think they can show that the will is not free but is always determined by something else.[87] And this they think because they understand by will something distinct from soul, something they look on as a substance whose nature consists solely in being indifferent. To remove all confusion, we shall first explicate the matter, and when this is done we shall easily expose the fallacies in their arguments.

[*What the will is.*] We have said that the human mind is a thinking thing. From this it follows that, merely from its own nature and considered only in itself, it can do something, to wit, think, that is, affirm and deny. Now these thoughts are either determined by things external to the mind or by the mind alone, because it is itself a substance from whose thinking essence many acts of thought can and must follow. Those acts of thought that acknowledge no other cause of themselves than the human mind are called volitions. The human mind, insofar as it is conceived as a sufficient cause for producing such acts, is called the will.[88]

[*There is will.*] That the soul possesses such a power, although not determined by any external things, can most conveniently be explicated by the example of Buridan's ass. For if we suppose that a man instead of an ass is placed in such a state of equilibrium, he would have to be considered a most shameful ass, and not a thinking thing, if he were to perish of hunger and thirst.[89] Again, the same conclusion is evident from the fact that, as we previously said, we even willed to doubt all things, and not merely to regard as doubtful but to reject as false those things that can be called into doubt. See Descartes's *Princip.* Part 1 Art. 39.

[*The will is free.*] It should further be noted that although the soul is determined by external things to affirm or deny something, it is nevertheless not so determined as if it were constrained by the external things, but always remains free. For no thing has the power to destroy its essence,[90] and therefore what it affirms or denies, it always affirms or denies freely, as is

---

87. Spinoza is one of these who hold that the will is determined. See E2P48–49. He does not, however, adhere to what follows in this section because he holds that will and the intellect are identical (E2P49).
88. This definition of 'will' is close to the definition of 'action' which Spinoza gives in E3Def2.
89. Cf. E2P49Schol.
90. Cf. E3P4.

well explained in the "Fourth Meditation." So if anyone asks why the soul wills or does not will this or that, we reply that it is because the soul is a thinking thing, that is, a thing that of its own nature has the power to will and not will, to affirm and deny. For that is what it is to be a thinking thing. [*The will should not be confused with appetite.*] Now that these matters have been thus explained, let us look at our opponents' arguments.[91]

1. The first argument is as follows. "If the will can will what is contrary to the final pronouncement of the intellect, if it can want what is contrary to its good as prescribed by the final pronouncement of the intellect, then it will be able to want what is bad for it as such. But this latter is absurd; therefore so is the former." From this argument one can clearly see that they do not understand what the will is. For they are confusing it with the appetite that the soul has when it has affirmed or denied something; and this they have learned from their Master, who defined the will as appetite for what is presented as good.[92] But we say that the will is the affirming that such-and-such is good, or the contrary, as we have already abundantly explained in our previous discussion concerning the cause of error, which we have shown to arise from the fact that the will extends more widely than the intellect. Now if the mind had not affirmed from its very freedom that such-and-such is good, it would not want anything. Therefore we reply to the argument by granting that the mind cannot will anything contrary to the final pronouncement of the intellect; that is, the mind cannot will anything insofar as it is supposed not to will it—for that is what is here supposed when the mind is said to have judged something to be bad for it, that is, not to have willed it. But we deny that it absolutely cannot have willed that which is bad for it, that is, cannot have judged it to be good; for that would be contrary to experience. We judge many things that are bad to be good, and on the other hand many things that are good to be bad.

[*The will is nothing other than the mind.*] 2. The second argument—or, if you prefer, the first, for so far there has been none—is as follows. "If the will is not determined to will by the final judgment of the practical intellect, it therefore will determine itself. But the will does not determine itself, because of itself and by its own nature it is undetermined." From this they go on to argue as follows: "If the will is of itself and by its own nature uncommitted to willing and not willing, it cannot be determined by itself to

---

91. The arguments are from Heereboord, *Meletemata philosophica*, 713.
92. Their "Master" is, of course, Aristotle: see the *Rhetoric* 1369a1–4; *De Anima* 433a21–433b5.

will. For that which determines must be as much determined as that which it determines is undetermined. But the will considered as determining itself is as much undetermined as is the same will considered as that which is to be determined. For our opponents suppose nothing in the determining will that is not likewise in the will that is either to be determined or that has been determined; nor indeed is it possible for anything to be here supposed. Therefore the will cannot be determined by itself to will. And if it cannot be determined by itself, it must be determined by something else."

These are the very words of Heereboord, Professor of Leiden, by which he clearly shows that by will he understands not the mind itself but something else outside the mind or in the mind, like a blank tablet, lacking any thought and capable of receiving any picture, or rather like a balance in a state of equilibrium, which can be pushed in either direction by any weight whatsoever, according to the determination of the additional weight. Or, finally, like something that neither he nor any other mortal can possibly grasp. Now we have just said—indeed, we clearly showed—that the will is nothing but the mind itself, which we call a thinking thing, that is, an affirming and denying thing. And so, when we look only to the nature of mind, we clearly infer that it has an equal power to affirm and to deny; for that, I say, is what it is to think. If therefore, from the fact that the mind thinks, we infer that it has the power to affirm and deny, why do we seek extraneous causes for the doing of that which follows solely from the nature of the thing?

But, you will say, the mind is not more determined to affirm than to deny, and so you will conclude that we must necessarily seek a cause by which it is determined. Against this, I argue that if the mind of itself and by its own nature were determined only to affirm (although it is impossible to conceive this as long as we conceive it to be a thinking thing), then of its own nature alone it could only affirm and never deny, however many causes may concur. But if it be determined neither to affirm nor deny, it will be able to do neither. And finally, if it has the power to do either, as we have just shown it to have, it will be able to do either from its own nature alone, unassisted by any other cause. This will be obvious to all those who consider a thinking thing as a thinking thing, that is, who do not separate the attribute of thought from the thinking thing. This is just what our opponents do, stripping the thinking thing of all thought and making it out to be like the prime matter of the Peripatetics.

Therefore I reply to their argument as follows, addressing their major premise. If by the will they mean a thing deprived of all thought, we grant that the will is from its own nature undetermined. But we deny that the will is something deprived of all thought; on the contrary, we maintain that it is thought, that is, the power both to affirm and to deny; and surely this can mean nothing else than the sufficient cause for both operations. Furthermore, we also deny that if the will were undetermined (i.e., deprived of all thought), it could be determined by any extraneous cause other than God, through his infinite power of creation. For to seek to conceive a thinking thing that is without any thought is the same as to seek to conceive an extended thing that is without extension.

[*Why philosophers have confused mind with corporeal things.*] Finally, to avoid having to review more arguments here, I merely point out that our opponents, in failing to understand the will and in having no clear and distinct conception of mind, have confused mind with corporeal things. This has arisen for this reason, that the words that they are accustomed to use in referring to corporeal things they have used to denote spiritual things, which they did not understand. For they have been accustomed to apply the word 'undetermined' to those bodies that are in equilibrium because they are impelled in opposite directions by equivalent and directly opposed external causes. So when they call the will undetermined, they appear to conceive it also as a body in a state of equilibrium. And because those bodies have nothing but what they have received from external causes (from which it follows that they must always be determined by an external cause), they think that the same thing follows in the case of the will. But we have already sufficiently explained how the matter stands, and so we here make an end.

With regard to extended substance, too, we have already said enough, and besides these two substances we acknowledge no others. As for real accidents and other qualities, they have been disposed of, and there is no need to spend time refuting them. So here we lay down our pen.

The End.

Cross-References of the PPC to the PPH

We provide below the principal sources from which Spinoza drew in Descarte's *Principles of Philosophy* and "Replies to Objections" in constructing the *Principles of Cartesian Philosophy*. Sections of the PPC where Spinoza is probably making use of other sources in Descartes (including the *Meditations* and Correspondence) are mentioned in the notes to the PPC, but are more speculative. Where an entry to the PPC is without cross-reference, Spinoza is engaged in logical reconstruction. For further information, please see our introduction.

Abbreviations (works):
  PPC: *Principles of Cartesian Philosophy* (Spinoza)
  PPH: *Principles of Philosophy* (Descartes)
  Rep: "Replies to Objections" (Descartes)

Abbreviations (internal references):
  A(rticle)
  Ax(iom)
  Cor(ollary)
  Def(inition)
  Lem(ma)
  P(roposition)
  Post(ulate)
  Pref(ace)
  Prol(egomenon)
  Schol(ium)

PPC1Prol	PPH1A1-7	PPC1Def10	Rep2Def10
PPC1Def1	PPH1A9	PPC1Ax1	
	Rep2Def1	PPC1Ax2	
PPC1Def2	Rep2Def2	PPC1Ax3	
PPC1Def3	Rep2Def3	PPC1P1	PPH1A7
PPC1Def4	Rep2Def4	PPC1P2	PPH1A9-10
PPC1Def5	Rep2Def5	PPC1P3	PPH1A11
PPC1Def6	Rep2Def6	PPC1P4	PPH1A12
PPC1Def7	Rep2Def7	PPC1P4Cor	PPH1A11
PPC1Def8	Rep2Def8	PPC1P4Schol	
PPC1Def9	Rep2Def9	PPC1Ax4	PPH1A17

	Rep2Ax6	PPC1P17	
PPC1Ax5	Rep2Ax7	PPC1P17Cor	
PPC1Ax6	PPH1A14	PPC1P18	
	Rep2Ax10	PPC1P19	PPH1A22
PPC1Ax7	Rep2Ax3	PPC1P20	PPH1A40
PPC1Ax8	Rep2Ax4	PPC1P20Cor	PPH1A41
PPC1Ax9	Rep2Ax5	PPC1P21	PPH2A1-2
PPC1Ax10	Rep2Ax2	PPC2Post	PPH1A75
	Rep2Ax9	PPC2Def1	PPH1A53
PPC1Ax11	Rep2Ax1		PPH2A1-2,4
PPC1P5	PPH1A14	PPC2Def2	PPH1A51-52
	Rep2P1	PPC2Def3	PPH2A20
PPC1P5Schol	PPH1A16	PPC2Def4	PPH1A26-27
PPC1P6	PPH1A18	PPC2Def5	PPH2A16-18
	Rep2P2	PPC2Def6	PPH2A10-11
PPC1P6Schol	PPH1A19-21	PPC2Def7	PPH1A26-27
PPC1P7	PPH1A19-21	PPC2Def8	PPH2A24-31
	Rep2P3	PPC2Def9	PPH2A33
PPC1P7Schol	Rep2Ax8	PPC2Ax1	PPH1A52
	Rep2Ax10		PPH2A18
PPC1Lem1		PPC2Ax2	PPH1A53
PPC1Lem1Cor	PPH1A15	PPC2Ax3	
PPC1Lem2		PPC2Ax4	PPH2A54
PPC1Lem2Cor		PPC2Ax5	
PPC1P8	Rep2P4	PPC2Ax6	PPH1A53,65,68-70
PPC1P9	PPH1A18	PPC2Ax7	PPH1A53,65,68-70
PPC1P9Schol	PPH1A23	PPC2Ax8	
PPC1P10		PPC2Ax9	PPH1A26
PPC1P11			PPH2A34
PPC1P12	PPH1A21	PPC2Ax10	PPH2A21-22
PPC1P12Cor1		PPC2Ax11	PPH2A22
PPC1P12Cor2	PPH1A15	PPC2Ax12	PPH2A54
PPC1P12Cor3	PPH1A23	PPC2Ax13	
PPC1P12Cor4	PPH1A24	PPC2Ax14	PPH2A33-34
PPC1P13	PPH1A29	PPC2Ax15	
PPC1P14	PPH1A30,43	PPC2Ax16	PPH2A34
PPC1P14Schol	PPH1A33	PPC2Ax17	
PPC1P15	PPH1A31	PPC2Ax18	
PPC1P15Schol	PPH1A29-37	PPC2Ax19	
PPC1P16	PPH1A23	PPC2Ax20	

PPC2Ax21	PPH2A33	PPC2P21	PPH2A40,43
PPC2Lem1	PPH2A16	PPC2P22	PPH2A40,44
PPC2Lem2	PPH2A5-6	PPH2P22Cor1	
PPC2P1	PPH2A4	PPH2P22Cor2	
PPC2P2	PPH2A4	PPH2P22Cor3	
PPC2P2Cor	PPH2A10-12	PPC2P23	
PPC2P2Schol		PPC2P24	PPH2A46
PPC2P3	PPH2A16-18	PPC2P25	PPH2A47
PPC2P4	PPH2A19	PPC2P26	
PPC2P4Cor	PPH2A19	PPC2P26Cor	
PPC2P5	PPH2A20	PPC2P27	PPH2A48
PPC2P5Schol		PPC2P27Cor	
PPC2P6	PPH2A21-22	PPC2P27Schol	
PPC2P6Schol	PPH2A23-27	PPC2P28	PPH2A49
PPC2P7	PPH2A18	PPC2P29	PPH2A50
PPC2P8	PPH2A29	PPC2P30	PPH2A51
PPC2P8Schol		PPC2P31	PPH2A52
PPC2P8Cor	PPH2A33	PPC2P31Schol	
PPC2P9	PPH2A33	PPC2P32	PPH2A56-57,59
PPC2P9Lem	PPH2A33	PPC2P33	PPHA49,56-57
PPC2P10	PPH2A33	PPC2P34	PPH2A60
PPC2P11	PPH2A34	PPC2P35	PPH2A59
PPC2P11Schol	PPH2A36	PPC2P36	PPH2A56-58
PPC2P12	PPH2A36	PPC2P37	PPH2A61
PPC2P13	PPH2A36	PPC2P37Schol	PPH2A54-56,62
PPC2P13Schol		PPC3Pref	PPH3A42-47
PPC2P14	PPH2A37	PPC3Post	PPH3A47
PPC2P14Cor	PPH2A38	PPC3Def1	PPH3A66
PPC2P15	PPH2A39	PPC3Def2	PPH3A65-66
PPC2P15Schol		PPC3Def3	PPH3A56
PPC2P15Cor	PPH2A39	PPC3Def4	PPH3A49
PPC2P16	PPH2A39	PPC3Ax1	PPH3A49
PPC2P17	PPH2A39	PPC3Ax2	PPH3A50
	PPH3A56-59	PPC3Ax3	PPH3A50
PPC2P18	PPH2A40	PPC3Ax4	PPH3A51
PPC2P19	PPH2A40-41	PPC3P1	PPH3A48
PPC2P19Cor	PPH2A40	PPC3P2	PPH3A49
PPC2P20	PPH2A40,42		
PPC2P21	PPH2A40,43		
PPC2P22	PPH2A40,44		

Appendix 2

INTRODUCTION TO MEYER'S DISSERTATION

Steven Barbone
and
Lee Rice

Lodewijk Meyer's dissertation, which follows these brief introductory remarks, deserves more careful study than contemporary scholars have given it. It is our hope that its presentation here, with notes and comments, might help to bring it to the attention of others.[1] For our part, we do not pretend to offer anything but the most cursory introduction and some reflections on Meyer's possible influence on Spinoza.

The dissertation clearly is based on the Cartesian model of a mechanistic universe. In such a universe, all motion is explained (or caused) by other motions, and matter is pushed by other moving matter. In the Cartesian universe, there is only 'impulsion' but never 'attraction', and so action at a distance cannot possibly occur. Meyer accepts this consequence of Descartes's plenum, and he defends it in A14.[2] Another consequence of the plenum which Meyer seems to approve is the simultaneous motion of particles (see A17). In an indefinitely extended universe in which there cannot be any vacuum or void, any motion other than that of a sphere's turning on its axis must necessarily trigger, if we can use this term (despite its suggestion of a first or initial mover), the simultaneous movement of at least one other particle.[3] It also implies that if there is any movement, then the quantity of motion must remain constant[4] and that once any particle

---

1. As mentioned in the general introduction, the work was first published in the *Chronicon Spinozanum* 2 (1922), 183–195. A subsequent Latin version (with emendations) and a translation in French, but without notes or commentary, were prepared by Reneé Bouveresse and Dominique Descotes and were included in Renée Bouveresse, *Spinoza et Leibniz: L'idée d'un animisme universel* (Paris: Vrin, 1992), 295–304 (French) and 305–312 (Latin).
2. On the plenum, see PPH2A16–21; PPH3A49.
3. See PPH2A33. Descartes uses the example of a rod in the *Dioptics* to show that simultaneous motion is possible: when one end of the rod is moved, the other end simultaneously moves.
4. See A2Ax4.

begins its circular motion, it must continue forever in that motion no matter how extended that circle might be. To solve this problem, Meyer posits 'limiting points' (A18) to these circular movements. These limiting points seem to function as maximum or minimum quantities of motion that a given particle has. Motion, then, is an affection, which can be exhausted or augmented, and it makes sense to speak of a thing's having more or less motion. Rest likewise seems to be such an affection so that a certain particle may have more or less rest. The point becomes clear in Art. 31 where Meyer speaks of two parts of matter that are at rest but yet move toward each other with equal motion. Motion and rest, two distinct affections, are transferred from particle to particle, and this preserves the constant quantity of motion and rest in the universe without necessitating that any particle now in motion continue forever in motion.

It is not, however, Meyer's explanations of motion and rest that we find especially interesting. More interesting are his purpose and conclusion. Meyer seeks to discover the "essences of things" [A1]. What Meyer is attempting to explain is how, in this plenum universe, there exists this body or that body, or in other words, how one may differentiate natural bodies. He finds that there are three first principles of natural things, which are matter, motion, and rest [A41]. It is to these three principles, then, that one must look to understand a thing's essence. We have no interest here in determining how, if at all, Meyer's physics might have influenced Spinoza's philosophy, yet we cannot refrain from noting that Meyer's dissertation contains what could be the seeds of Spinoza's theory of physical individuation as found in his "Physical Treatise," that is, E2P13. Meyer states ". . . a natural body will be nothing other than a part of matter endowed with a certain combination of motion and rest" [A40]. Could this be the root of Spinoza's own definition of an individual as a collection of bodies that preserve an unvarying relation of motion-and-rest among themselves?[5] It is, after all, the preservation of a certain pattern of motion-and-rest among an individual's parts which defines an individual as a particular individual, that is, this pattern is the individual's essence.[6]

We see other glimpses of Spinoza's physical theory of individuals in

5. See E2P13Def; Lem5; Lem6; Lem7; Lem7Schol.
6. See Hans Jonas, "Spinoza and the Theory of Organism," *Journal of the History of Philosophy* 3 (1965), 43–57 [reprinted in M. Grene, ed. *Spinoza: A Collection of Critical Essays* (Garden City: Anchor Press, 1973), 259–278]; see esp. (1973), 267. See also Alexandre Matheron, *Individu et communauté chez Spinoza* (Paris: Editions de Minuit, 1969), esp. 11–43 for a discussion on Spinozistic individuation.

Meyer's sparse use of the word 'virtue' (*virtus*), which is often coupled with 'force' (*vis*). It appears that the quantity of motion (or of rest) a particle has is a function of its virtue,[7] so that the more virtue the particle has, the more it is able to continue its particular movement. Spinoza later is to write, "By *virtue* and *power* I mean the same thing,"[8] and we know that he also equated power with *conatus* and with essence.[9] It may not be a mistake to pursue the connection between the concept of virtue in Meyer's dissertation and the role of *conatus* in Spinoza's later philosophy. For Spinoza, an individual's *conatus* is that power by which it continues to exist as that individual, and the more the individual is successful at existing as that individual (i.e., the more powerful is the individual's *conatus*) the more virtuous that individual is.[10] Meyer's use of the term in Paradoxes 9 and 10 and Spinoza's echoing of this notion in E4P20 support this claim.

Meyer's dissertation stands as an interesting stepping stone from Descartes's physical theory to Spinoza's. Even though we here cannot argue conclusively concerning the amount of influence Meyer's work had on Spinoza, we have noted some possibilities. We remark also that one may take this work as further evidence that Spinoza, at least through his friends, was committed to a physical model to explain the essences of things. In any case, the work of one of Spinoza's circle of friends is an invaluable resource for our better understanding of Spinoza and of his philosophy.

Inaugural Philosophical Dissertation on
Matter, and Its Affections: Motion and Rest.

Lodewijk Meyer.

1. In our opinion, the true and legitimate method for tracking down the essences of things, as distinct from their modes, is as follows: we should review one by one whatever attributes the thing may possess, discarding them until we arrive at one such that, when it is posited, the thing is posited, and when it is withdrawn, the thing is withdrawn; something that is the foundation and basis of all the other attributes.[11] If we therefore adopt this procedure in the case of matter, of all the features usually ascribed to it

---

7. *Virtus* is translated as 'virtue' (A7–8), 'power' (A16), and as 'potency' (A19).
8. See E4Def8.
9. See E3P7.
10. E4P20Dem.
11. See PPC2Ax2 and E2Def2 for Spinoza's definition of 'essence'.

by the generality of philosophers, we shall find that only extension in length, breadth, and depth satisfies this requirement. Hence we may rightly take matter to be 'a thing extended in every dimension'.[12]

2. Although everyone may well be thoroughly convinced that such a thing exists in Nature, we aim to provide a demonstration that will satisfy those who refuse to admit anything that is not proved by unshakable and undeniable reasoning. And because every formally correct proof must be based on what is already granted, we have to make the following presuppositions, as is the practice in metaphysics:

I.

1. Besides ourselves—namely, things that think and understand— there is a most perfect Being, or God.

2. Whatever we clearly and distinctly perceive is true.[13]

II. The following axioms must be granted:

1. If something happens with no action on the part of a second thing, this latter cannot be said to be its cause.

2. There is nothing in the effect that is not in the cause.[14]

3. To nothing there belongs no affection.[15]

4 In Nature as a whole nothing perishes or comes into being.

5. No cause acts beyond its competence.

III. It is postulated:

1. Whatever is, besides God, must have a cause.[16]

2. We clearly and distinctly perceive the extended thing.

3. Since our intellect (by Postulate 2) clearly and distinctly perceives extension as external to itself, there must (by Postulate 1) necessarily be a cause of this perception.[17] This must be either our intellect itself, or God, or some other thing existing besides these. But it cannot be the intellect

---

12. See PPC2Def1.
13. See PPC1P14; PPH1A30, 43.
14. See PPC1Ax9.
15. See PPC2Ax1.
16. Cf. PPC1Ax7.
17. This proof of the existence of the external world is similar in some respects to that given by Descartes in Med5, but it is not used by Spinoza in the PPC.

(Axiom 1), because in this occurrence the intellect is passive, not active; more frequently it is all accomplished not merely without the assistance of the intellect, but in spite of it. And neither can God be said to be the cause of anything different from himself apart from the extended thing. Indeed, if God were to bring it about that our mind should be affected in the manner already described, he must undoubtedly be deemed a deceiver, which is in flat contradiction with his perfection (Supposition 1).[18] So the only other possibility is that it proceeds from the extended thing, which therefore exists.

4. Because extension (Section 1) constitutes the essence of matter and makes it different in reality from other things, it must be something real and positive, for that is how matter is. Therefore, wherever there is extension, there matter is also present.[19] And since (Axiom 3) to nothing there belong no affections, there cannot possibly be extension in nothing, or space in which there is no thing at all, that is, a vacuum, as is assumed by philosophers.[20] Nowhere in matter will there be intervals or gaps, and every part of it will always be surrounded and enclosed by other parts contiguous to it.[21]

5. Now, of all the characteristics to be observed in matter, the first thing that can be conceived to befall it when it is considered in this way is that some of its parts change their contact with their surroundings, whereas others retain this contact. For from this fact alone can readily be deduced all the varying and different forms of matter which, because they are perceived as clearly and distinctly as matter itself, must likewise not be denied to matter.[22]

6. When a part of matter changes contact with other parts adjacent to it, this cannot come about unless the latter parts, too, change contact at least with respect to the former part. It is therefore evident (Postulate 1) that there must be a cause why the former part changes contact with all its surroundings, whereas the latter parts change contact only in that part facing toward the former part, while retaining contact with the other parts. Now in the first place it is obvious that, in the case of the latter parts, the

---

18. See Med3, where Descartes also moves from an ontological to a moral sense of 'perfection'. Spinoza summarizes the argument in the Prolegomenon to PPC1.
19. See PPC2P2 and P2Cor.
20. A similar proof is given by Spinoza in PPC2P3.
21. See PPC2P8 for Spinoza's more expansive treatment of this claim.
22. Is this a hint of what might later become a theory for distinguishing individuals in Spinoza? See E2P13; F. Ablondi and S. Barbone, "Individual Identity in Descartes and Spinoza," *Studia Spinozana* 10 (1996), 69–91 (esp. pp. 77–80).

partial change of contact is caused by the change of contact in the former part; for if the former part did not change its contact, neither would the latter parts do so but rather would retain their contact.[23] That the former part changes contact with adjacent parts all around is not caused by the latter parts, for they retain contact. And that the latter parts retain contact with all other parts except the former part is not caused by the former part, for it changes contact with all its surroundings. Therefore there must be a particular cause why in the former part there is a change of contact with all its surroundings, whereas in the latter parts there is a retaining of contact in all directions but this, a cause that is capable of producing the change of contact in the former part and the retaining of contact in the latter parts.

7. This change and retention of contact, being two modes of matter really existent in Nature and not merely the products of our mind, ought properly and philosophically to be designated as motion and rest, and motion should be defined as change of contact in matter, rest as retention of contact.[24] But because we should be diverging too far from common linguistic usage—although a philosopher ought not to be at all concerned with this—and because, more importantly, the properties of matter and rest will thus be more easily explained, it will be better if we comprehend under the terms 'motion' and 'rest' not only change and retention of contact but also the force [*vim*] or virtue [*virtutem*] by which these are produced.

8. Nor do we think it necessary to explicate and to elaborate the nature, considered in itself and absolutely, of the proximate cause of motion and rest when these are regarded from a general point of view. We believe that it is sufficient for our purpose if, in addition to change and retention of contact that originate from this cause, we concern ourselves only with the virtue [*virtutis*], which it imparts to matter.

9. So because all variety in matter depends on motion and rest (Section 5) and is real, they too must be something real; and because (Axiom 4) nothing

23. See PPC2P7.

24. The argument thread running from this point in A7–A11 makes it clear that the notion of rest is being conceived not as an absence of motion, but rather as a state of equilibrium. This concept gives rise in Spinoza to what Bennett calls a 'field metaphysics' (see our introduction). Meyer contrasts it more sharply to the Aristotelian physics than do Descartes and Spinoza. In Aristotle, motion is an activity, rest the absence of that activity. In the new physics of Galileo and Descartes, motion and rests are states rather than activities, which gives rise to the principle of kinematic relativity in classical physics, and later to that of dynamic relativity in Einstein's general theory.

perishes or comes anew into being, it follows that the same quantity of motion and rest has always existed in matter and will forever remain.[25]

10. If in every part of matter there were an equal quantity of motion and rest, matter would necessarily be uniform in all directions, and would exist in a mode that is always the same. But because difference and variety are to be observed in matter (as has been shown in Section 5), one of its parts must possess more motion or rest than another.

11. And because there is to be found in matter not only diversity but also variation (by the same Section), it is evident that there is in a single part more motion and rest at one time than at another, and consequently (Section 9), because the quantity of motion and rest remains constant, a portion of motion and rest must be transferred from one part of matter to another. So whatever is set in motion or receives rest, receives its motion or rest from something else.

12. So if a part of matter transfers all its motion to another part, which was at rest, with the result that the part in motion comes to rest and the other part, which was at rest, is set in motion, that which is now at rest has received all the rest it has received from the one it has set in motion, and conversely the one that is now in motion has received all the motion it has received from the other, to which it has imparted its own rest. For because the one that is now in motion and was previously at rest has lost its rest, and the other that is now at rest and was previously in motion has lost its motion, and because the quantity of motion and rest in matter remains always the same (Section 9), it necessarily follows that all the rest that has been lost by the one that was previously at rest and is now in motion has been transferred to the one that set it in motion, and all the motion lost by the one that was previously in motion and is now at rest has been received by the part that was at rest, if we consider the other parts of matter as persisting in the same state, as we here suppose. The reasoning is exactly the same in the case where the motion and rest is not completely transferred, but only partly. This makes it obvious that the part that sets another in motion bestows on it—or on several, if it sets more than one in motion—as much motion as it itself loses and receives as much rest as is lost in turn by the part or parts that were at rest.

---

25. Contrast this argument for the conservation of energy ('motion' and 'rest') to that given by Spinoza, who follows Descartes in deriving it from the divine nature itself as the general cause of motion and rest. See PPC2P13 and the lemmas following E2P13.

13. Again, when a part of matter is in motion, because there cannot be a vacuum, the part behind it will also move; alternatively, if the latter remains at rest, some other matter will intervene between the part of matter in motion and the part at rest. And because these parts in their turn are set in motion, by the same reasoning the parts behind them will also be set in motion; and because these again are set in motion, the same sequence of events will be repeated until we come to the part that was originally set in motion. Hence it is evident that every case of motion involves a circularity of some kind.[26]

14. Furthermore, because in such a circular movement the part immediately to the rear—or else the part that intervenes between the part originally set in motion and the part at rest—has received its motion (Section 2) from another part, and that in turn from another, until we come to a halt at the first part set in motion, it is therefore evident that it is this part that is the cause of all these motions, and certainly not the part at rest, which was left behind. Hence it follows that no body at rest can cause another body to move toward itself; and thus, strictly speaking, there is nothing called Attraction; all motion is the result of impulsion.[27] This same point can also be easily demonstrated as follows. If a part of matter at rest were to set in motion toward itself another part that is at rest, the latter would lose its rest and receive motion that, because this must necessarily be transferred to it (Section 2) from another part, cannot be transferred from the part at rest (Axiom 2), because this part lacks motion. Therefore it is not set in motion by this part.

15. Furthermore, because (Section 13) motion of any kind involves circularity, no part can move unless the part immediately in front of it moves, nor again this one unless the part immediately in front of it moves, and so on. Hence it is clear that no motion can be produced at a distance, and therefore neither any transference of rest, because motion and rest are always interconnected.

16. When a part of matter in motion sets in motion another part that was at

26. The 'circle of moving bodies' concept in Descartes is developed by Spinoza in PPC2P8Cor.
27. This leads to the principle of dynamic relativity which Leibniz was to defend against Newton in the Leibniz-Clarke Correspondence. Although Descartes, Spinoza, and Leibniz all adopted the principle, none was actually able to provide the necessary physical basis for it until Mach showed how relativity could be extended to centrifugal motion in the nineteenth century. Einstein's general theory is a logical extension of Mach's principle.

rest, it must possess a quantity of motion greater than the other's quantity of rest. It cannot have an equal quantity, and certainly not a smaller quantity. Because the quantity of motion and rest is determined by the force and power [*virtute*] with which the part in motion changes its contact and the part at rest retains its contact, it is obvious that if the part in motion has the same force for changing contact as the part at rest has for retaining contact, the latter cannot be set in motion by the former; and therefore if the former is to set the latter in motion, it must necessarily possess more motion than the latter has rest.

17. Moreover, in the case of circular motion, the part on which motion is first impressed cannot move unless the part immediately in front of it moves simultaneously, nor this part again unless the part immediately in front of it moves, and so on until a full circle is completed, as demonstrated in Section 15; and the first to move is the cause of all the motion of the parts in front of it. Now (Section 16) a part of matter in motion cannot set in motion a part of matter at rest unless the former possesses more of motion than the latter of rest. It therefore follows that there must be more of motion in the part that is first to move than there is of rest in all the other parts.[28]

18. So if a part in motion possesses in itself more of motion than all the parts constituting the circle possess of rest, when the circle is completed, it will exert force upon the part in its rear, and if it can set this in motion, there will be a new circular movement for the same reason, and after that another again, until it has exhausted all its motion. And the more motion it possesses, the more circular movements it will produce, and the more circular movements it produces, the more contacts it will abandon.[29] The first and last of these contacts are called the limiting points of the movement, the former being the point *a quo*, and the latter the point *ad quem*. The distance between the points is called the line of movement, and the matter in which these circular movements take place and in which the line of movement is conceived to be (i.e., the matter through which there is motion) is called the medium.

---

28. The reader may well ask how might there be both simultaneous movement of all the parts and a first movement by one part. This aspect of Cartesian physics—that matter at rest requires an external 'thrust' to set it in motion—was recognized and criticized by Spinoza; see Ep81 (esp. note 393, p. 352).

29. Meyer seems to be claiming here that, on completion of circular motion, a body will set itself again in motion: an idea foreign to both Descartes and Spinoza. In fact, here the body appears to deliver a kick to its own backside. [Tr.]

19. Because, as has just been demonstrated, the more motion a part possesses, the more it will abandon contact with other parts, and because it is evident that the more it abandons contact with other parts, the longer will be the line of motion, it also follows that the more motion a part possesses, the longer the line it will describe. And because this continuous describing of a line is nothing other than the forward movement of the part in motion, it is evident that the more motion it possesses, the more potency [*virtutis*] it has for forward movement or continuation.

20. If a part of matter, in continuing to move, meets with another part that has as much, or even more, of rest than the former has of motion, the former, as has been demonstrated in Section 16, will not be able to transfer to the latter any amount of its motion. Therefore, because (Section 9) the quantity of motion in matter remains always the same, it will retain its motion. And because the part with which it has collided prevents it from proceeding onward, it will necessarily return in the direction from which it came. This returning is called reflection.[30]

21. The same thing will occur if it collides on its path with a part that is not at rest but is moving with equal or greater motion. Because the colliding part possesses motion that is either equal to or less than that possessed by the part with which it has collided, it will also be possessed (Section 19) of less or equal force for continuing on its way. Therefore, since (Postulate 5) no cause acts beyond its competence, it will not be able to drive the other back, but will itself be reflected.[31]

22. A part of matter in motion (Section 15) will always collide with another, and this latter, if it possesses more or an equal number of degrees of rest or of contrary motion, will repel the former (as demonstrated in Section 21); or if it possesses fewer degrees, will not do so. It is therefore obvious that the determination of the line of motion of the colliding part depends on the parts of matter with which it collides in its motion. For if it is not reflected, it will proceed in a straight line; but if it is reflected, it will

---

30. See PPC2P28. In the following axioms (A21–A35), Meyer presents a general account of reflection, but his treatment is much more general and sketchy than that given by Spinoza (PPC2P21–P32) and Descartes. Meyer's dissertation would be categorized, using the seventeenth century typology, as in general rather than special metaphysics: it deals with motion only generally. Special metaphysics derives the specific rules, in this case the Cartesian laws of impact. Meyer's treatment in what follows indicates that, unlike Spinoza, he had not come to see the difficulties in the Cartesian laws, nor therefore to seek to resolve them with new physical principles.

31. See PPC2P27.

either describe the same straight line or else two straight lines meeting at the point of the reflection and thus making an angle.

23. When a part that is not reflected continues to move in a straight line, not only, as demonstrated in Section 12, does it impart its motion to the parts at rest constituting the medium through which it is moving, but they in turn transfer rest to it. This transference is called 'resistance of the medium', and this applies not only to a medium whose parts are completely at rest, but also to one whose parts are moving in the same or contrary direction, but with less motion; for to that extent they participate in rest.

24. Such resistance is to be found in every medium, and there can be no medium that is entirely without it. For such would not be a medium, because within it there could be no change of contact and therefore no motion, the one (Section 18) being requisite for the other. For if one posits a medium that has no resistance, its parts must have as much motion as the part that is supposed to be in motion and must be moving in the same direction as the moving part. But if this were the case, the part that is supposed to be moving will not change its contact. Therefore, in such a medium there will be no motion.

25. From the deductions we have already made, all variety in the transference of motion and rest can very easily be derived and demonstrated, thus:

26. If a part of matter moves through a medium that is everywhere endowed with equal resistance, and the parts of this part possess so much rest that in no way can they be moved by the parts of the medium with which it collides, it will steadily abate its motion, while proportion is maintained between its degrees of motion and the resistance of the medium. The more numerous the degrees of this motion, the less will be the resistance and the longer the line of movement; and the fewer the degrees of this motion, the more will be the resistance and the shorter the line of movement.[32]

27. If the same part, before it has abated all its motion, collides on its path with another part that is exactly like it with respect to the quantity of rest of its parts and possesses as much of rest as the first has of motion at the time of the collision, it will necessarily be reflected with no loss of degrees of motion. And this will be even more the case if there was more of rest in the part at rest than of motion in the part in motion.

---

32. Meyer envisages the possibility that a body may be so fragile as to disintegrate, a point not taken up by Descartes or Spinoza in their treatment of the laws of impact. But in order to avoid ambiguity, both here and later in Section 31, Meyer should have made some distinction between the *pars materiae* (Spinoza's *corpus*) and the parts of the medium itself. [Tr.]

28. And if both these parts, the one in motion and the one at rest, are perfectly flat where they collide with each other, the part in motion will be reflected at the same angle of incidence at which it collided, namely, either a right angle or an acute angle, but never an obtuse angle. And the same thing will occur if the part in motion is perfectly round and the part at rest perfectly flat, or round, or even concave, provided that the circle of the hollow of the part at rest is greater than the circle of the rounded part of the part in motion.

29. If the same part in motion has more of motion than the part at rest has of rest, it will continue its movement and will drive forward the part at rest, imparting to it so much of its motion and receiving from the other so much of its rest that thereafter they will both together move in the direction taken by the part in motion.[33]

30. If the same part in motion collides with another like itself, as previously, which is not at rest but moving in the same direction and on the same line as the former, the former will necessarily possess more of motion than the latter (otherwise the former could never overtake the latter), and the former will transfer to the latter half the amount of motion by which it exceeds the latter at the point of collision, and will receive from the latter half the amount of rest by which the latter exceeds the former; and thereafter they will continue to move along together.[34]

31. Furthermore, in the case of two parts of matter whose parts are so much at rest that not only are they unable to be moved by parts of the medium but also by one another,[35] if they meet each other from opposite directions and in the same line of movement and possess equal motion at the point of collision, they will both be reflected, returning in the direction from which they came, with no transference of motion.

32. But if they have unequal amounts of motion, the part that has more motion will repel and drive back that which has less motion, imparting to it half the excess of its own motion and receiving from the other half the excess of the other's rest. Thereafter they will both proceed to move in the direction taken by the faster moving part, with equal quantities of motion.[36]

33. It is possible to consider two parts of matter not only as moving toward each other and colliding, but as traveling through the same medium or

33. See PPC2P30.
34. See PPC2P27.
35. See my note to Section 26 earlier regarding the parts of the medium. [Tr.]
36. See PPC2P27.

different mediums, and to compare their movements with the movement of another body (say, the heavens, or other bodies that imitate the movement of the heavens) or—and this would be clearer—with time.

34. Thus, if through the same medium, or two different mediums that are nevertheless endowed everywhere with the same resistance, two parts of matter not on a collision course move with such a proportionality between their quantity of motion, magnitude, constitution, and medium resistance that in the same or equal times they describe equal lines of movement, these parts will be said to be moving equally quickly or equally slowly. But if they do not move with such a proportionality, but in such a way that in the same or equal times they produce unequal lines of movement, the part that describes the longer line will be said to move more quickly, and the part that describes the shorter line will be said to move more slowly. The motion of the former, with respect to or in relation to the motion of the other, will be called 'quickness', and, conversely, the motion of the latter with respect to the motion of the former will be called 'slowness'.

35. I might have added proofs of all these propositions, if I did not think them obvious to anyone who merely gives careful consideration to things that have gone before and attends to them diligently, and if our Dissertation were not in danger of becoming excessively lengthy.

36. These three—matter, motion, and rest—which we have hitherto been discussing, we hold to be the true first principles in Nature. For they do not derive from one another, nor from other things, and all things derive from them. They are three in number: the two contraries, motion and rest, and their common substratum, matter.[37] These satisfy the conditions that philosophers seek in first principles.

37. Furthermore, each of them is something real, namely, the substance matter and its two modes, motion and rest, the latter of which, as is clear from what has been said previously, must be taken into consideration quite as much as the former in the explanation of natural things. It is therefore very surprising that, whereas among physicists one finds such an extensive and lengthy treatment of the nature and kinds of motion, they have preserved so deep a silence concerning rest. And this is also the case with Aristotle, even though in his definition of Nature he puts motion and rest on an equal footing.

38. I can imagine no reason for this silence other than that they have

---

37. I am taking *subjectum* as substrate, whereas the French translator renders it as "sujet." [Tr.]

regarded rest as the negation or absence of motion. Even if the contrary had not already been abundantly proved, this opinion could easily be refuted by the following argument. If rest were nothing other than the negation or absence of motion, a body at rest could be moved by the smallest degree of motion, there being no force of resistance in mere negation.[38] But daily experience bears abundant witness that bodies at rest commonly offer more or less resistance to the motion of other bodies, and that one body is more ready than another to accept motion from a colliding body. Therefore it must be admitted that there is something real that is the cause of this resistance, something to which we give the name rest.[39]

39. The Peripatetics, following the example of their leader, divide motion into Quantitative Motion, which again is either Diminution or Increase, Qualitative Motion, which is Alteration, and Motion relative to place, which is called Local Motion or Movement. But because local motion is no different from that which we have already defined, and without it there cannot be diminution or increase or alteration, we think that local motion should be classified as the genus, diminution, and increase and alteration as the species.

40. Not only do we affirm matter, motion, and rest to be the first principles of natural things, but we furthermore do not acknowledge any other affections of a natural body than the motion and rest of matter, or those affections that derive from them. Because, as has been said, the first principles of natural things are only matter, motion, and rest, a natural body will be nothing other than a part of matter endowed with a certain combination of motion and rest.[40] And because (Axiom 2) there is nothing in the effect that was not in the cause, there will be no affection in a natural body whose origin is not to be regarded as deriving from these.

41. This conclusion is also to be inferred from the definitions of all those affections that philosophers customarily ascribe to a natural body. Continuousness (*continuitas*) is the rest, regarded only by itself, of the parts of a body; Division (*divisio*) is the motion of those same parts; Textural Looseness (*raritas*) is such a disposition of the rest or motion of the parts of a

---

38. Again the notion of rest is explained in terms of resistance, and an equilibrium of forces operating as vector components in a field.

39. Cf. PPC2P29; PPH2A50.

40. So the so-called secondary properties are not genuine physical properties of the object, but rather reactions in the sensorium. See PPC2P1. Again, we see what could be the beginnings of what a Spinozistic account of individuation; see E2P13Lem7Schol.

body that there are wide gaps between the parts, filled by other matter. If there are no such gaps, or small gaps, there is Density (*densitas*). Finitude is the negation of any further combination of motion and rest in a body. Figure is a quality or mode of this negation. Place is the limit of surrounding body, related to adjacent bodies and regarded as unmoving. Time is the duration of a body as compared with the movement of the heavens, and measured by it.

42. Therefore, because all these affections pertain either to rest, like Continuousness, or to motion, like Division, or to both, like Textural Looseness and Density, or else they are negations, like Finitude and Figure, or beings of reason, like Place and Time, it is evident that no affections of a natural body are real that do not derive from motion and rest, and are not affections of matter, and that these three alone are to be regarded as the first principles of natural things.

Paradoxes.[41]

1. The logic that is so widely propagated by the Peripatetics is vain and useless, because without its help mathematicians have accomplished more and met with greater success in the sciences than philosophers who use their logic in other parts of philosophy.

2. There are only two categories of being, Thing and Mode.

3 'Man is a rational animal' is not a perfect definition.[42]

4. Physics and Ethics can and should be taught through demonstrative proof.

5. There is no substantial form.

6. Even if no sun existed, this sublunary world would still be illuminated.

7. There is no physical soul either in the body or outside the body.[43]

---

41. The paradoxes listed are not connected to the physical principles that precede them in the dissertation, which again suggests that the dissertation should be construed as 'general metaphysics' rather than philosophy of nature properly. Perhaps Meyer includes them here to indicate their status as problems requiring separate and independent resolution.

42. Cf. CM1/1.

43. The Latin reads, "Anima Physice nec est in corpore, nec extra Corpus." The French translator renders *physice* as "physiquement parlant": I suggest rather that it is a transliteration of the Greek adjective. [Tr.]

8. Sensation occurs not through nerve fibers, but through the spirits.[44]

9. The basic principle of Ethics is that everyone should seek his own advantage.[45]

10. Virtue [*Virtus*] is the constant will of the soul to seek its own advantage when this is grasped by true understanding; vice, when this is based on mere opinion.[46]

11. Metaphysics is concerned only with beings of reason.

12. The squaring of a circle is impossible.

---

44. The French translator has, "mais par l'esprit": I suggest rather that the Latin *spiritus* here refers to animal spirits. [Tr.]
45. Cf. E4P20.
46. Virtue in Spinoza's *Ethics* turns out to nothing other than the power that people have to seek and to achieve their own advantage; this power, of course, is enhanced by true understanding. See Steven Barbone, "Virtue and Sociality in Spinoza," *Iyyun* 42 (1993), 383–395.

Bibliography

Latin and Dutch Editions

[NL] *De Nagelate Schriften van B.d.S. Als Zedekunst, Staatkunde, Verbetering van't Verstant.* Amsterdam, publisher not cited, 1677.

[OP] *B. de S. Opera Posthuma, quorum series post Praefationem exhibetur.* Amsterdam, publisher not cited, 1677.

Opera quae supersunt omnia. 4 vols. Leipzig: Bernhardt Tauchnitz, 1844. Carolus Bruder, ed.

Opera quotquot reperta sunt. 4 vols. Hague: Martinus Nijhoff, 1914. J. Van Vloten and J. P. N. Land, eds.

Opera, im Auftrag der Heidelberger Akademie der Wissenschaften, ed. Carl Gebhardt. 5 vols. Heidelberg: Carl Winter Universitätsverlag, 1925.

Translations and Editions of PPC and CM

Appuhn, Charles, Tr. *Oeuvres,* Tome I. Paris: Garnier-Flammarion, 1964. [KV, TIE, PPC, CM, with notes.]

Britan, H.H., Tr. *The Principles of Descartes' Philosophy.* La Salle: Open Court, 1905.

Buchenau, A., Tr. *Descartes' Prinzipien der Philosophie.* Berlin: Felix Meiner Verlag, 1978.

Curley, Edwin, Tr. *The Collected Works of Spinoza.* Vol. 1. Princeton (NJ): Princeton University Press, 1985.

Domínguez, Atilano, Tr. *Tratado de la reforma del entendimiento; Principios de filosofía de Descartes;* Pensamientos metafísicos. Madrid: Alianza Editorial, 1988.

Elwes, R.H.M., Tr. *Chief Works.* 2 vols. New York: Dover, 1951.

[Pléiade] *Oeuvres complètes de Spinoza.* Translated and edited by R. Caillois, M. Francès, and R. Misrahi. Paris: Gallimard, 1954.

Scribano, Emanuela, Tr. *Principi della filosofia di Cartesio. Pensieri metafisici.* Roma-Bari: Editori Laterza, 1990.

Secondary Literature

Ablondi, F., and Barbone, S. (1996). "Individual Identity in Descartes and Spinoza." *Studia Spinozana* 10, 69–92.

Allen, H. J. (1976). "Spinoza's Naturalism and our Contemporary Cartesians." In J. B. Wilbur (Ed.), *Spinoza's Metaphysics* (pp. 132–154). Assen: Van Gorcum.

Ariew, R., and Grene, M. (1995). "Ideas, in and before Descartes." *Journal of the History of Ideas* 56, 87–106.

Bachelard, G. (1933). "Physique et métaphysique." In Societas Spinozana (Ed.), *Septimana Spinozana* (pp. 74–84). The Hague: M. Nijhoff.

Barbone, S. (1992). "Virtue and Sociality in Spinoza." *Iyyun* 42, 383–395.

———. (1995a). "Infinity in Descartes." *Philosophical Inquiry* 17, 23–38.

———. (1995b). "Inneity in Descartes' Regulae." *Tijdschrift voor filosofie* 57, 297–307.

Belin, Marie-H. (1988). "*Les principes de la philosophie de Descartes*: Remarques sur la duplicité d'une écriture." *Archives de Philosophie* 51, 99–106.

Bennett, J. (1980). "Spinoza's Vacuum Argument." *Midwest Studies in Philosophy* 5, 391–400.

———. (1984). *A Study of Spinoza's Ethics*. Indianapolis/Cambridge: Hackett.

———. (1996). "Spinoza's Metaphysics." In D. Garrett (Ed.), *The Cambridge Companion to Spinoza* (pp. 61–88). Cambridge University Press: Cambridge.

Beyssade, Jean-M. (1979). *La philosophie première de Descartes*. Paris: Presses Universitaires de France.

———. (1992a). "On the Idea of God: Incomprehensibility or Incompatibilities?" In S. Voss (Ed.), *Essays on the Philosophy and Science of René Descartes* (pp. 85–95). Cambridge: Oxford University Press.

———. (1992b). "The Cogito: Privileged Truth or Exemplary Truth?" In S. Voss (Ed.), *Essays on the Philosophy and Science of René Descartes* (pp. 31–39). Cambridge: Oxford University Press.

Bilbol-Hesperies, A. (1990). *Le principe de vie chez Descartes*. Paris: Vrin.

Bouillier, F. (1868). *Histoire de la philosophie cartésienne* (3rd ed.). Paris: Delagrave.

Bouveresse, Renée. (1992). *Spinoza et Leibniz: L'idée d'un animisme universel*. Paris: Vrin.

Breton, S. (1983). "Optique, théologie, philosophie." *Bijdragen* 44, 366–380.

Brunschvicq, L. (1894). *Spinoza*. Paris: Alcan.

———. (1904). "La révolution cartésienne et la notion spinoziste de la substance." *Revue de Métaphysique et de Morale*, 12, 755–798.

———. (1933). "Physique et métaphysique." In Societas Spinozana (Ed.), *Septimana Spinozana* (pp. 43–54). The Hague: M. Nijhoff.

———. (1951). *Spinoza et ses contemporains* (4th ed.). Paris: Presses Universitaires de France.

162   *The Principles of Cartesian Philosophy*

Buchdahl, G. (1969). *Metaphysics and the Philosophy of Science.* Cambridge (MA): MIT Press.

Burgersdijck, Franco. (1653). *Institutionum metaphysicarum libri duo* (Ed. Adriaan Heereboord). London.

_____. (1668). *Institutionum logicarum synopsis, sive rudimenta logica.* Cambridge: J. Field.

Chronicon Spinozanum. 5 vols. The Hague: Spinoza Society, 1921–1927.

Clay, J. (1933). "Physik und Metaphysik." In Societas Spinozana (Ed.), *Septimana Spinozana* (pp. 55–73). The Hague: M. Nijhoff.

Cohen, I.B. (1964). "*Quantum in se est*: Newton's Concept of Inertia in Relation to Descartes and Lucretius." *Notes and Records of the Royal Society of London* 19, 131–155.

Collins, J. (1971). *American Philosophical Quarterly Monograph Series: 5. Descartes's Philosophy of Nature.* Oxford: Basil Blackwell.

Cottingham, J.G. (1988). "The Intellect, the Will, and the Passions: Spinoza's Critique of Descartes." *Journal of the History of Philosophy* 26, 239–257.

Cremaschi, S. (1981). "Concepts of Force in Spinoza's Psychology." In *Theoria cum Praxi* (pp. 138–144). Hannover: Studia Leibniziana.

Cristofolini, P. (1992). "La mente dell'atomo." *Studia Spinozana* 8, 27–35.

Curley, E.M. (1975). "Descartes, Spinoza, and the Ethics of Belief." In M. Mandelbaum and E. Freeman (Eds.), *Spinoza; Essays in Interpretation* (pp. 159–190). LaSalle: Open Court.

_____. (1977). "Spinoza as an Expositor of Descartes." In S. Hessing (Ed.), *Speculum Spinozanum: 1677–1977* (pp. 133–142). London: Routledge & Kegan Paul.

_____. (1978). *Descartes against the Skeptics.* Cambridge: Harvard University Press.

D'Espagnat, D. (1988). "Spinoza et la physique contemporaine." In R. Bouveresse (Ed.), *Spinoza: Science et Religion* (pp. 209–214). Paris: Vrin.

Dijksterhuis, E. J. (1950). *Descartes et le cartésianisme hollandais.* Paris: Presses Universitaires de France.

Dijn, Herman de. (1994). "Philosophie als Scientia naturalis." In V. Caysa and Klaus-D. Eichler (Eds.), *Praxis-Vernunft-Gemeinschaft. Festschrift für Helmut Seidel* (pp. 116–133). Hannover: Beltz-Athenäum.

_____. *Spinoza: The Way of Wisdom.* West Lafayette (IN): Purdue University Press, 1996.

Doney, W. (1971). "Spinoza on Philosophical Skepticism." *Monist* 55, 617–635. [Reprinted in M. Mandelbaum and E. Freeman (Eds.), *Spinoza; Essays in Interpretation* (pp. 139–158). LaSalle: Open Court.]

Duchesneau, F. (1978). "Modèle cartésien et modèle spinoziste de l'être vivant." *Cahiers Spinoza 2*, 241–286.

Dunin-Borkowski, S. von. (1933). "Die Physik Spinozas." In Societas Spinozana (Ed.), *Septimana Spinozana* (pp. 85–101). The Hague: M. Nijhoff.

Edgar, W.J. (1976). "Continuity and the Individuation of Modes in Spinoza's Physics." In J.B. Wilbur (Ed.), *Spinoza's Metaphysics* (pp. 85–105). Assen: Van Gorcum.

Fernández García, Eugenio. (1988). "*Potentia* et *potestas* dans les premiers écrits de Spinoza." *Studia Spinozana* 4, 195–223.

Freudenthal, J. (1899). *Spinoza und die Scholastik.* Leipzig: Verlag von Veit.

———. (1927). *Spinoza: Leben und Lehre.* Heidelberg: Carl Winter.

Gagnebin, S. (1971). "La révolution cartésienne." In *A la recherche d'un ordre naturel* (pp. 277–292). Neuchatel: Baconnière.

Gamarra, D. (1993). "Descartes y Spinoza: sobre la verdad y la idea." *Acta Philosophica* 2, 317–328.

Garber, D., and Cohen, L. (1982). "A Point of Order: Analysis, Synthesis, and Descartes's *Principles.*" *Archiv für Geschichte der Philosophie* 64, 136–147.

Gewirth, A. (1967). "Clearness and Distinctness in Descartes." In W. Doney (Ed.), *Descartes* (pp. 250–277). Garden City: Doubleday.

Gil, D. (1993). "Le 'vrai' vrai spinoziste de Brunschvicq à Bachelard." In O. Bloch (Ed.), *Spinoza au XXe Siècle* (pp. 41–70). Paris: Presses Universitaires de France.

Gilson, E. (1923). "Spinoza interprète de Descartes." *Chronicon Spinozanum* 3, 68–87.

Giornale critico delle filosofia italiana 56 (1977), nos. 3–4. [A tercentennial number devoted to Spinoza.]

Grene, M., and Nails, D. (Eds.). (1986). *Spinoza and the Sciences.* Dordrecht: Reidel.

Grosholz, D. (1994). "Descartes and the Individuation of Physical Objects." In K.F. Barber and J.J.E. Gracia (Eds.), *Individuation and Identity in Early Modern Philosophy* (pp. 41–58). Albany: SUNY Press.

Gueroult, M. (1960). "Le Cogito et l'ordre des axiomes métaphysiques dans les *Principia Philosophiae Cartesianae* de Spinoza." *Archives de Philosophie* 23, 171–185.

———. (1968a). *Descartes selon l'ordre des raisons.* Paris: Presses Universitaires de France.

———. (1968b). *Spinoza, dieu (Ethique I).* Paris: Editions Aubier-Montaigne.

———. (1970). *Etudes sur Descartes, Spinoza, Malebranche et Leibniz.* Paris: Presses Universitaires de France. [Reprint, Hildesheim: Georg Olms Verlag, 1970.]

Hall, M.B. (1966). *Robert Boyle on Natural Philosophy.* Bloomington (IN): Indiana University Press.

Hammacher, K. (1994). "Kosmologie, Ethik und Affektenlehre bei Spinoza." In V. Caysa and Klaus-D. Eichler (Eds.), *Praxis Vernunft-Gemeinschaft. Festschrift für Helmut Seidel* (pp. 307–330). Hannover: Beltz-Athenäum.

Hassing, R.F. (1980). "The Use and Non-Use of Physics in Spinoza's *Ethics.*" *Southwestern Journal of Philosophy* 11, 41–70.

Heereboord, Adriaan. (1650). *Disputationes ex philosophia selectae.* Leiden.

———. (1680). *Meletemata philosophica.* Amsterdam.

Henry, M. (1992). "The Soul According to Descartes." In S. Voss (Ed.), *Essays on the Philosophy and Science of René Descartes* (pp. 40–51). Cambridge: Oxford University Press.

Hessing, S., ed. (1977). *Speculum Spinozanum.* London: Routledge and Kegan Paul.

Hoenen, P.H.J., SJ. (1967). "Descartes's Mechanicism." In W. Doney (Ed.), *Descartes* (pp. 353–368). Garden City: Doubleday.

Hoeven, P. van der. (1980). *De cartesiaanse fysica.* Leiden: Brill.

Hubbeling, H.G. (1980). "Spinoza comme précurseur du reconstructivisme logique dans son livre sur Descartes." *Studia Leibnitiana* 12, 88–95.

Iriarte, J. (1938). "La filosofía 'geométrica' en Descartes, Spinoza y Leibniz." *Gregorianum* 19, 481–497.

Jonas, Hans. (1965). "Spinoza and the Theory of Organism." *Journal of the History of Philosophy* 3, 43–57. [Reprinted (1973) in M. Grene (Ed.), *Spinoza: A Collection of Critical Essays* (pp. 259–278). Garden City: Anchor Press.

Kamiya, M. (1983). *Théorie cartésienne du temps.* Paris: Vrin.

Klever, W.N.A. (1988). "Moles in Motu: Principles of Spinoza's Physics." *Studia Spinozana* 4, 165–194.

———. (1990). "Anti-falsificationism: Spinoza's Theory of Experience and Experiments." In E. Curley and P.-F. Moreau (Eds.), *Spinoza: New Issues and Directions* (pp. 124–135). Leiden: Brill.

———. (1992). "Ethique spinoziste comme physique de l'homme." In A. Domínguez (Ed.), *La Etica de Spinoza: Fundamentos y significado* (pp. 29–36). Castilla-La Mancha: Ediciones de la Universidad.

———. (1993a). "Annotations sur Gueroult." In O. Bloch (Ed.), *Spinoza au XXe Siècle* (pp. 89–104). Paris: Presses Universitaires de France.

———. (1993b). "Qui était l'Homunculus?" *Bulletin de l'association des amis de Spinoza* 29, 24–27.

———. (1995). "The Motion of the Projectile—Elucidation of Spinoza's Physics." *Studia Spinozana* 9, 335–340.

Bibliography 165

____. (1996). "Spinoza's Life and Works." In D. Garrett (Ed.), *The Cambridge Companion to Spinoza* (pp. 13–60). Cambridge: Cambridge University Press.

____. (1997) *Mannen rond Spinoza (1650–1700)*. Hilversum: Verloren.

Koyré, Alexandre. (1957). *From the Closed World to the Infinite Universe.* Baltimore: Johns Hopkins Press.

____. (1971a). "Les philosophes et la machine." In *Etudes d'histoire de la pensée philosophique* (2nd ed., pp. 305–340). Paris: Gallimard.

____. (1971b). "Remarques sur les paradoxes de Zénon." In *Etudes d'histoire de la pensée philosophique* (2nd ed., pp. 9–36). Paris: Gallimard.

____. (1971c). "Le vide et l'espace infini au xviie siècle." In *Etudes d'histoire de la pensée philosophique* (2nd ed., pp. 37–92). Paris: Gallimard.

____. (1978). "Bonaventura Cavalieri et la géométrie des continus." In *Etudes d'histoire de la pensée scientifique* (pp. 297–324). Paris: Presses Universitaires de France.

Lachièze-Rey, P. (1950). *Les origines cartésiennes du dieu de Spinoza* (2nd ed.). Paris: Vrin.

Lachterman, D.R. (1977). "The Physics of Spinoza's *Ethics.*" *Southwestern Journal of Philosophy* 8, 71–111. [Reprinted in R.W. Shahan and J.I. Biro (Eds.), *Spinoza: New Perspectives* (pp. 71–112). Norman: University of Oklahoma Press.]

Lantin, R. (1994). "Individualism, Physicalism, and Spinoza on Minds and Bodies." *Manuscrito* (São Paulo), 17, 35–64.

Lécrivain, A. (1977). "Spinoza et la physique cartésienne." *Cahiers Spinoza* 1, 235–266.

____. (1978). "Spinoza et la physique cartésienne (suite): la Partie II des *Principia.*" *Cahiers Spinoza* 2, 93–206.

LeFèvre, R. (1959). *Initiation Philosophique. La métaphysique de Descartes.* Paris: Presses Universitaires de France.

Lennon, T.M. (1994). "The Problem of Individuation Among the Cartesians." In K.F. Barber and J.J.E. Gracia (Eds.), *Individuation and Identity in Early Modern Philosophy* (pp. 13–40). Albany: SUNY Press.

Leopold, J.H. (1902). *Ad Spinozae opera posthuma.* The Hague: Martinus Hijhoff.

Lewis, C.E. (1984). "Baruch Spinoza, A Critic of Robert Boyle: On Matter." *Dialogue* (PST) 27, 11–22.

Lewkowitz, J. (1902). *Spinozas Cogitata Metaphysica und ihr Verhaltnis zu Descartes und die Scholastik.* Breslau.

Loeb, L.E. (1981). *From Descartes to Hume: Continental Metaphysics and the Development of Modern Philosophy.* Ithaca: Cornell University Press.

Mason, R.V. (1993). "Ignoring the Demon? Spinoza's Way with the Doubt." *Journal of the History of Philosophy* 31, 545–563.

Matheron, A. (1969). *Individu et communauté chez Spinoza.* Paris: Editions de Minuit.

———. (1991). "Physique et ontologie chez Spinoza: l'énigmatique réponse à Tschirnhaus." *Cahiers Spinoza* 6, 83–110.

Maull, Nancy. (1986). "Spinoza in the Century of Science." In M. Grene and D. Nails (Eds.), *Spinoza and the Sciences* (pp. 3–13). Dordrecht: Reidel.

McKeon, Richard. (1928). *The Philosophy of Spinoza.* New York: Longmans, Green and Co.

McLaughlin, P. (1993). "Descartes on Mind-Body Interaction and the Conservation of Motion." *Philosophical Review* 102, 155–182.

Meinsma, K.O. (1983). *Spinoza et son cercle.* Translated by S. Roosenburg and J.-P. Osier with appendices and notes by Henry Méchoulan and Pierre-François Moreau. Paris: Vrin.

Messeri, M. (1984). "Il corpo singolo nella teoria fisica della materia di Spinoza ed in quella di Descartes." *Annali della scuola normale superiore di Pisa* 14, 771–795.

Meyer, Lodewijk (1660). *De materia ejusque affectionibus, motu et quiete.* Amsterdam: Francisci Hackii.

———. (1988). *La philosophie interprète de l'Ecriture sainte.* Tr. with introduction and notes by Jacqueline Lagrée and Pierre-François Moreau. Paris: Intertextes Editeur.

Moreau, Pierre-François. (1994a). "Epicure et Spinoza: la physique." *Archives de Philosophie* 57, 459–470.

———. (1994b). *Spinoza: l'expérience et l'éternité.* Paris: Presses Universitaires de France.

Newman, L. (1994). "Descartes on Unknown Faculties and Our Knowledge of the External World." *Philosophical Review* 103, 489–531.

Parrochia, D. (1984). "Optique, mécanique et calcul des chances chez Huygens et Spinoza." *Dialectica* 38, 319–345.

———. (1985). "Physique pendulaire et modèles de l'ordre dans l'*Ethique* de Spinoza." *Cahiers Spinoza* 5, 71–92.

———. (1989). "Les modèles scientifiques de la pensée de Spinoza." In Groupe de recherches spinozistes (Ed.), *Travaux et documents 2: Méthode et métaphysique* (pp. 47–66). Paris: Presses de l'Université de Paris-Sorbonne.

Pereboom, D. (1994). "Stoic Psychotherapy in Descartes and Spinoza." *Faith and Philosophy* 11 592–625.

Prato, I. (1989). "Il problema dell'energia." *Ethica, Notiziario trimestrale dell'Associazione per l'Aedes Spinozana d'Italia,* 1(3).

Ramirez, E.R. (1981). "Spinoza, en torno al movimiento." *Revista de filosofía* (Costa Rica), 19, 45–48.

Ramond, C. (1988). " 'Degrés de réalité' et 'Degrés de perfection' dans les *Principes de la philosophie de Descartes*." *Studia Spinozana* 4, 121–146.

_____. (1994). "Sur un verbe manquant: Espace qualifié et espace quantifié dans la philosophie de Spinoza." *Revue Epokhe* 4, 31–43.

_____. (1995). *Quantité et qualité dans la philosophie de Spinoza.* Paris: Presses Universitaires de France.

Revue Internationale de Philosophie 31 (1977), nos. 119–120. [Devoted to Spinoza.]

Revue philosophique de la France et de l'Etranger 167 (1977). [Devoted to Spinoza.]

Rice, L.C. (1975). "Spinoza on Individuation." In M. Mandelbaum and E. Freeman (Eds.), *Spinoza; Essays in Interpretation* (pp. 195–214). LaSalle: Open Court.

_____. (1977). "Emotion, Appetition, and Conatus in Spinoza." *Revue Internationale de Philosophie* 31, 101–116.

_____. (1991). "Tanquam Naturae Humanae Exemplar: Spinoza on Human Nature." *The Modern Schoolman* 68, 291–303.

_____. (1992). "La causalité adéquate chez Spinoza." *Philosophiques* 19, 45–60.

_____. (1994). " Le nominalisme de Spinoza." *Canadian Journal of Philosophy* 24, 19–32.

_____. (1996a). "Spinoza's Relativistic Aesthetics." *Tijdschrift voor Filosofie* 58, 476–489.

_____. (1996b) "Spinoza's Infinite Extension." *History of European Ideas* 22, 33–43.

Rivaud, A. (1924–25). "La physique de Spinoza." *Chronicon Spinozanum* 4, 24–57.

_____. (1933). "Quelques remarques sur la notion d'essence dans les doctrines de Descartes et de Spinoza." In Societas Spinozana (Ed.), *Septimana Spinozana* (pp. 208–225). The Hague: M. Nijhoff.

Rod, W. (1982). *Descartes: Die Genese des cartesianischen Rationalismus* (2nd ed.). Berlin: Walter Verlag.

Rodis-Lewis, Geneviève (1992). "From Metaphysics to Physics." In S. Voss (Ed.), *Essays on the Philosophy and Science of René Descartes* (pp. 242–258). Cambridge: Oxford University Press.

Rousset, B. (1991). "Le réalisme spinoziste de la durée." In *L'Espace et le Temps* (pp. 176–180). Paris: Vrin.

———. (1994). "Spinoza, lecteur des *Objections* de Gassendi à Descartes." *Archives de Philosophie* 57, 485–502.

———. (1996). *Spinoza, lecteur des Objections faites aux Méditations de Descartes et ses Réponses*. Paris: Kimé.

Rupert, A., and Hall, M.B. (1964). "Philosophy and Natural Philosophy: Boyle and Spinoza." In F. Braudel (Ed.), *Mélanges Alexandre Koyré II: L'aventure de l'esprit* (pp. 241–256). Paris: Hermann.

Schmidt-Biggeman, W. (1992). "Spinoza dans le cartésianisme." In Groupe de Recherches Spinozistes (Ed.), *L'Ecriture sainte au temps de Spinoza et dans le système spinoziste* (pp. 71–90). Paris: Presses de l'Université de Paris-Sorbonne.

Seris, Jean-P. (1992). "Language and Machine in the Philosophy of Descartes." In S. Voss (Ed.), *Essays on the Philosophy and Science of René Descartes* (pp. 177–193). Cambridge: Oxford University Press.

Shirley, E.S. (1993). "A Refutation of the Dream Argument." *Southwestern Journal of Philosophy* 9, 1–22.

Siebrand, Heine. (1986). "Spinoza and the Rise of Modern Science in the Netherlands." In M. Grene and D. Nails (Eds.), *Spinoza and the Sciences* (pp. 61–91). Dordrecht: Reidel.

Steinberg, D. (1993). "Spinoza, Method, and Doubt." *History of Philosophy Quarterly* 10, 211–224.

Studia Spinozana 4 (1988). [Theme: "Spinoza's Early Writings."]

Szczeciniarz, Jean-Jacques. (1993). "Spinoza et Koyré." In O. Bloch (Ed.), *Spinoza au XXe Siècle* (pp. 159–176). Paris: Presses Universitaires de France.

Thijssen-Schoute, C. L. (1954). *Lodewijk Meyer en diens verhouding tot Descartes en Spinoza*. Leiden: Brill.

Tournadre, G. (1982). *L'Orientation de la science cartésienne*. Paris: Presses Universitaires de France.

Valk, Th. de. (1921). "Spinoza en Vondel." *De Beiaard* 6, 440–458.

Vokos, G. (1993). "Ferdinand Alquié, lecteur de Spinoza." In O. Bloch (Ed.), *Spinoza au XXe Siècle* (pp. 105–112). Paris: Presses Universitaires de France.

Voss, S. (Ed.). (1992). *Essays on the Philosophy and Science of René Descartes*. Cambridge: Oxford University Press.

Vuillemin, J. (1990). "Physique panthéiste et déterminisme: Spinoza et Huygens." *Studia Spinozana* 6, 231–250.

Wagner, S.I. (1992). "Mind-Body Interaction in Descartes." In S. Voss (Ed.), *Essays on the Philosophy and Science of René Descartes* (pp. 115–127). Cambridge: Oxford University Press.

Webb, M.O. (1989). "Natural Theology and the Concept of Perfection in Descartes, Spinoza, and Leibniz." *Religious Studies* 25, 459–475.

Wells, N.J. (1965). "Descartes and the Modal Distinction." *Modern Schoolman* 43, 1–22.

Wolfson, H.A. *The Philosophy of Spinoza.* 2 vols. Cambridge (MA): Harvard University Press, 1934.

Woolhouse, R.S. (1990). "Spinoza and Descartes and the Existence of Extended Substance." In A.J. Cover and M. Kulstad (Eds.), *Central Themes in Early Modern Philosophy* (pp. 23–48). Indianapolis/Cambridge: Hackett.

____. (1993). *The Concept of Substance in Seventeenth Century Metaphysics: Descartes, Leibniz, Spinoza.* London: Routledge and Kegan Paul.